D. H. LAWRENCE'S MANUSCRIPTS

Also by Michael Squires

LADY CHATTERLEY'S LOVER (*editor*), The Cambridge Edition
THE CHALLENGE OF D. H. LAWRENCE (*with Keith Cushman*)
THE CREATION OF *LADY CHATTERLEY'S LOVER*
D. H. LAWRENCE'S 'LADY': A New Look at *Lady Chatterley's Lover*
(*with Dennis Jackson*)
THE PASTORAL NOVEL: Studies in George Eliot, Thomas Hardy, and
D. H. Lawrence

D. H. Lawrence's Manuscripts

The Correspondence of Frieda Lawrence, Jake Zeitlin and Others

Edited by

MICHAEL SQUIRES

Professor of English
Virginia Polytechnic Institute and State University

St. Martin's Press   New York

First published in the United States of America in 1991

Printed in Hong Kong

ISBN 0–312–06109–9

Library of Congress Cataloging-in-Publication Data
D. H. Lawrence's manuscripts: the correspondence of Frieda Lawrence,
Jake Zeitlin, and others   /   edited by Michael Squires.
p.   cm.
Includes index.
ISBN 0–312–06109–9
1. Lawrence, D. H. (David Herbert),   1885–1930 — Correspondence.
2. Lawrence, D. H. (David Herbert),   1885–1930 — Manuscripts–
–Catalogs.   3. Lawrence, Frieda von Richthofen,   1879–1956–
–Correspondence.   4. Zeitlin, Jake, 1902–   — Correspondence.
5. Authors, English — 20th century — Correspondence.   6. Manuscripts,
English — Catalogs.   I. Squires, Michael.
PR6023.A93Z53   1991
823'.912 — dc20
[B]   91–6791
                                                              CIP

For Lynn and Andrew

Contents

List of Illustrations

Editorial Procedures

I have generally adopted the procedures followed in *The Letters of D. H. Lawrence*, published by Cambridge University Press (1979–):

1. Inadvertent misspellings or typing errors have been silently corrected. However, no regularization of spelling, punctuation or syntax has been attempted in the letters of Frieda Lawrence, Angelo Ravagli, Knud Merrild or Else Merrild, for whom English was a second language.
2. Cancelled words have been recorded in the notes to the letters, to the right of the square bracket (e.g. family]   father).
3. The ampersand is recorded as "and".
4. Abbreviated proper names are, on their first occurrence in a letter, expanded in square brackets.
5. Words underlined are italicized. Titles of major works are italicized, but titles of short stories, essays, and poems are put in quotation marks.
6. When a complete letter is in a foreign language, the original text is followed by a translation.
7. The sender's address appears on a single line, the date on the next line, ranged right. Where the date is omitted, a conjectural date is supplied in square brackets. The complimentary close and signature (if signed) also appear on a single line, ranged right. If the letter is a typed carbon copy, as are most of Jake Zeitlin's, the author's initials have been supplied in square brackets.
8. Letters written jointly by Frieda Lawrence and Angelo Ravagli are presented whole. Ravagli's marginalia are printed as postscripts, and identified: [*Angelo Ravagli begins*].
9. New paragraphs are always indented.
10. For ease of reference all letters are numbered sequentially. Following the number are the name of the writer, the name of the recipient, and the date (in square brackets if conjectural). Letters not printed whole are labelled 'abridged' in parentheses; omissions are marked by ellipses in the text. The headnote indicates if abridged, identifies the source of the text of each letter (e.g. MS UCLA), and uses the following abbreviations:

MS	manuscript
TS	typescript
TSCC	typescript carbon copy
UCLA	University of California at Los Angeles

HRC	Harry Ransom Humanities Research Center, University of Texas at Austin
UCBerkeley	University of California at Berkeley
Roberts	Professor Warren Roberts
New Mexico	University of New Mexico, Albuquerque
Stanford	Stanford University

11. Editorial links appear in italics.
12. In form, the three appendixes have been lightly regularized.

Acknowledgements

I owe the greatest debt to Jake Zeitlin, who not only saved his letters to and from Frieda Lawrence but also agreed to a series of interviews – on 14 March 1985, 10 May 1986, and 2 November 1986. Much of what I learned about Lawrence's manuscripts I learned from Jake, whose keen memory never faltered. He died on 30 August 1987 while the book was in progress.

Several others kindly agreed to be interviewed: Josephine Ver Brugge Zeitlin on 14 March 1985; Matthew Huxley on 17 January 1987; Warren Roberts on 16 July 1987; Lawrence Clark Powell on 25 July 1987; Ward Ritchie on 19 July 1988; Amalia de Schulthess on 9 July 1989; Jenny Wells Vincent on 16 July 1989; and Rosalind Wells on 16 September 1989. I deeply appreciate their cooperation, their candour, and their prompt responses to my numerous written queries.

James Davis, Rare Books Librarian at UCLA, first told me about the correspondence of Frieda Lawrence and Jake Zeitlin and proved unfailingly helpful; my wife, Lynn K. Talbot, contributed immeasurably to my work on the book; and James C. Cowan wrote an exemplary report on the manuscript.

I also wish to thank the following individuals for their particular contributions: Leigh Allison, Bart Auerbach, Al Bearce, Tom Brumback, Hilbert H. Campbell, Becky Cox, Ken Craven, Keith Cushman, Peter Donahue, Michael Fainter, Cynthia Farar, Kathlene Ferris, Simonetta de Filippis, Pat Fox, Elizabeth Hahn, Charles Haney, Tyrus Harmsen, Cathy Henderson, Margaret Kimball, Anita Malebranche, Sarah Polirer, Gerald Pollinger, Sarah Roberts-West, Lynn and Ruth Rogers, Valery Rose, Keith Sagar, Tamera Shepherd, Paul Sorrentino, John N. Swift, Sara Timby, William B. Todd, Lindeth Vasey, and Betsy Webb.

The editor and publishers wish to thank the following individuals and institutions for granting permission to publish letters, photographs and excerpts from interviews: Thomas E. Alford, Los Angeles Public Library; Chilton Anderson; Arizona Board of Regents, Center for Creative Photography, for photograph of T. E. Hanley © 1981; Edmund R. Brill; John Carswell; Deborah Benson Covington; Anne C. Edmonds, Mount Holyoke College Library; Harry Ransom Humanities Research Center, the University of Texas at Austin; Harvard University Archives; A. Fredric Leopold; Department of Special Collections, Occidental College Library; Gerald J. Pollinger; Lawrence Clark Powell; Hazel Ransom; F. Warren Roberts; Anthony B. Rota; Amalia de Schulthess; Department of

Special Collections, the Stanford University Libraries; The Bancroft Library, University of California, Berkeley; Department of Special Collections, University Research Library, University of California, Los Angeles; Special Collections, General Library, University of New Mexico; Jenny Wells Vincent; Keene Watkins; Rosalind Wells; Herbert F. West, Jr; Yale University Committee on Literary Property; Jake Zeitlin; and Josephine Ver Brugge Zeitlin.

Every effort has been made to trace all the copyright holders, but if any have been inadvertently overlooked, the publishers will be pleased to make the necessary arrangement at the first opportunity.

Introduction

This volume offers a wholly new account of D. H. Lawrence's manuscripts after his death. Collecting more than 300 letters and documents, all of them previously unpublished, the book traces the fate of D. H. Lawrence's manuscripts from their arrival at Jake Zeitlin's bookshop in 1937 to the sale of the three versions of *Lady Chatterley's Lover* to the University of Texas in 1964. Because all the manuscripts were so nearly purchased together in 1937, only then to be sold individually to collectors or given away as gifts, the letters have the tension of a dramatic performance. As they unfold, they capture the vagaries of Lawrence's reputation in the decades after his death, freshly reveal how the manuscripts provided his wife Frieda with financial support, exhibit the art of negotiation, and, by articulating the varied responses that the manuscripts evoked, provide a valuable coda to Lawrence's life. This Introduction aims to put the letters in a historical context and to characterize the persons who figure most importantly in the volume; it draws largely on personal interviews with those most fully acquainted with Lawrence's manuscripts – Jake Zeitlin, Lawrence Clark Powell, Warren Roberts, and Amalia de Schulthess.

After D. H. Lawrence died in 1930, a great treasure of manuscripts remained. Their fate followed the same pattern that Lawrence's life had taken. Just as he began his life in England, then travelled widely before coming to rest in nearby Italy and France, so too were his manuscripts initially kept together in Taos, New Mexico, then scattered widely before most of them came to their permanent home at the University of Texas at Austin, not far away. The story of these manuscripts has all the fascination of biography – conflict, absorbing detail, and a sense of completion.

The story begins during Lawrence's lifetime. In his last year Lawrence recognized that his manuscripts, sought after by collectors, would help provide financial security for Frieda (1879–1956), who in fact outlived her husband by twenty-six years. The manuscript of *Sons and Lovers*, which Lawrence had presented to Frieda as a gift, had allowed her to buy Lobo (later Kiowa) Ranch near Taos from the rich American socialite, Mabel Dodge Luhan. To the Florentine bookseller Giuseppe ("Pino") Orioli, who had received an inquiry from a New York dealer, Lawrence wrote on 25 October 1929: "I don't want to sell the MSS. of Lady C. – and I don't much want to sell the proofs. . . . Find out what the man would give for the proofs." Although Lawrence disliked the burden of possessions, he recognized the value of his manuscripts. To Dorothy Brett, a close friend who looked after the Kiowa Ranch in his

1

absence, Lawrence wrote on 23 June 1929 about his manuscripts, which lay in a cupboard at the ranch:

> You know I keep them as a sort of nest egg. One day I shall need them, so I depend on them for my reserve. For this reason I don't sell them. I've only sold one manuscript in my life and that is the complete version of *Sun* which Harry Crosby printed unexpurgated in Paris. . . . Beyond that nothing. . . . You will see that I need to keep track of my manuscripts, sold or unsold. . . .[1]

To an unidentified recipient Frieda Lawrence wrote from the Villa Beau Soleil (MS HRC) in Bandol, France, where the Lawrences lived in late 1929: "It would also be interesting to know how much you paid for those 2 manuscripts [*Women in Love* and *Psychoanalysis and the Unconscious*] – you see till lately we never thought of the manuscripts as valuable and often Lawrence burnt them, but I tried to rescue them, as I thought they looked nice." And Lawrence wrote to his sister Ada Clarke on 1 September 1929, "if I died the MSS. and pictures would have to be sold to secure something of an income for Frieda".[2]

After Lawrence died, the dealer A. S. W. Rosenbach approached Frieda about selling the manuscripts. "On the spur of the moment I said 25000 Pounds", she recalled (Letter 48). Horrified, Norman Douglas warned Frieda against inflating the value of her husband's work: "I am afraid", he advised on 29 March 1930 (MS UCLA), "you are infected with *Tazzelwormimania* if you think you can ever get £25,000 for his manuscripts. You won't get £2500." Douglas predicted "very little demand, except on the part of 5–6 collectors".

Yet Edward Titus promptly offered to buy. On 18 April 1930 he wrote to Frieda:

> Now, regarding manuscripts, which you say Rosenbach is willing to buy . . . if you will let me know what there is . . . and . . . the offer that Rosenbach is likely to make you for these same manuscripts, I myself may be able to offer you, and pay you, as much as he.[3]

The bidding had begun. Frieda informed him on 25 April 1930, "There are, thank goodness, lots of Mss", and on 28 April Titus added: "I would be particularly interested, of course, in 'Lady Chatterley's Lover.'" She held him off: "My asking Rosenbach for 25,000 £ may not be *practical* business, but it's *big*, imaginative business and I know in my bones what Lorenzo's things are worth", she wrote on 30 April 1930. But because Lawrence died without a will, his estate was left in dispute. Frieda, contesting the claim of Lawrence's brother and sister, eventually won rights to Lawrence's published and unpublished literary work. She was "entitled" to the manuscripts, wrote her attorney C. D. Medley on 11 December 1931 (TS HRC).

This litigation behind her, Frieda returned to the Kiowa Ranch, 17 miles from Taos, in the spring of 1933 – this time to stay – and brought with her an Italian army captain, Angelo Ravagli (1891–1976), who in these letters is called "Angelino", then much later "Angie". Frieda had been fond of him ever since he was the Lawrences' landlord in Spotorno, Italy, in the winter of 1925–6. Of peasant origin and impoverished childhood, he was, writes Robert Lucas, "grateful to the army for giving him a position and bolstering his self-respect".[4] For a while Frieda was able to live on the royalties she earned – especially from Edward Titus's 1929 Paris edition of *Lady Chatterley's Lover*, which had been twice reprinted – but these soon dwindled.

While Frieda worked on her autobiography *Not I But the Wind...*, published in 1934, Angelo, granted a three-year leave from the Italian Bersaglieri Corps, worked at the 160-acre ranch, repairing and building. They strove for a Lawrentian simplicity. Cows, horses, pigs, and lambs all demanded attention. In an unpublished letter to Laurence Pollinger, dated 14 May 1933 (MS HRC), Dorothy Brett wrote: "Frieda is very happy on the Ranch. ... It is a tremendous consolation to her and a great joy." As early as 17 July 1922 Lawrence had written to his American agent Robert Mountsier, "Frieda says she is determined to have a little farm in America."[5] Having virtually started over, Frieda was almost 54, Angelo 12 years younger. At the Harry Ransom Humanities Research Center is his note that, "Today, May 30, 1933 we started to build the New House in Kiowa Ranch – San Cristobal, New Mexico." The ranch was called *Kiowa* because the Kiowa Indians used to camp nearby.

But the winters were harsh, and journeys to more temperate climates such as southern California were expensive. At the ranch a room for Lawrence's pictures, which had arrived from Italy in 1936, was needed (Letter 18); so were other improvements. And in 1937 Frieda purchased Los Pinos, a charming place down in the Taos valley, four miles from town, where the winters were milder: "in winter, the ranch is too cold and high and snowy" (Letter 171). But the house needed a bathroom (Letter 178). Moreover, Frieda was of necessity providing Angelo with a monthly cheque: $120 a month in 1938.[6] "You know I feel what is mine is yours", she wrote to him on 21 December 1937. Even though the Depression, which lingered on, had shrunk all markets, Frieda and Angelo decided to begin selling Lawrence's manuscripts. They needed money. The question was, to whom might they turn for assistance?

They were fortunate. They located a struggling but enterprising young bookseller named Jacob Israel Zeitlin (1902–1987), known to everyone as "Jake".

As I remember, it was early in 1936 that Galka Scheyer, a colorful, red-haired woman living out here in Los Angeles,[7] brought Frieda Lawrence to my shop. Galka represented a group of European painters called the Blue Four [*Die Blau Vier*]; she was their agent. Galka, Frieda and Angelino, and I went out and had lunch, and Galka said that they wanted to sell the manuscripts, and that I had been recommended, and would I be interested? And I said, "Does a cat like cream?" We met a couple of times, and then we started corresponding.

Jake and Frieda liked each other at once. Jake wrote to Nathan van Patten, library director at Stanford University, on 1 April 1936: "I have just met Frieda Lawrence and . . . have found her everything you would expect . . ." (Letter 3). To a book-collecting attorney, Frank J. Hogan, he wrote on 3 April: "She is grand and we have had some great talks" (Letter 4).

Interviewed in 1986, Jake recalls: "My first impression of Frieda was that she was a very vigorous woman, someone with lots of vitality, whose presence you were aware of. She was straightforward and uninhibited, with no pretense about her. If she was offended by something you said or did, she told you right away. But she had a lot of kindness in her too, and trusted everybody. She seemed naive. Like a child, she could be very exuberant about colorful things like a scarf or a bright dress."

Jake remembers Angelo as being a charming man, devoted to Frieda and looking after her. "He was a handsome, outgoing guy – very neat and clean. I could see where Frieda was taken with him. She seemed to dominate in lots of ways – and he deferred to her – but she depended on him in all practical matters. He was a very practical man. He had no sentimental attachment to these manuscripts, but he was very much concerned that she get the most out of them. Frieda and Angelino were always having differences and quarrels of one kind or another. But he was very good to her. I think he chased other women, but aside from that, I think he was devoted to her. Their squabbling was just a part of their kind of life."

Frieda agreed to give Jake some of Lawrence's manuscripts to sell. On 1 April 1936 they signed an agreement (Letter 2). "Boy, am I excited!" Jake exclaimed in Letter 5. Initially Frieda gave him just the manuscript of *The Rainbow*. As Jake explained in Letter 4, "her eldest sister, Else, is married to a Jewish professor [Edgar Jaffe] at Heidelberg and their life has become unbearable. Frieda wants to raise enough money to bring them to this country." Later Jake received a big trunk full of Lawrence's manuscripts. Astonished, he wrote: "Somehow there is no other way one can quite feel so near to this man . . . as to read his words in his own handwriting. . . . It is like reading a freshly opened letter."[8] Later he explained: "As I remember, the trunk of manuscripts was delivered to me by Knud Merrild. Frieda had great respect for Merrild and great trust in him."

Jake Zeitlin had taken a curious, unexpected route to the business of selling books and manuscripts. Born 4 November 1902 in Racine, Wisconsin, Jake had moved with his family to Kennedale, Texas, in 1904. "My parents had a pastoral dream", he recalls. "They wanted a farm. But they got the worst one in the state. They had come into town with an old flat-bed wagon and a team of horses. Well, farming was not for them." They moved to Fort Worth, at that time a small town, and opened a bakery-supply business called the Acme Vinegar Company. "We took over a business and just kept the name."

Unhappy but ready for adventure, Jake left home. "It was a matter of impulse. As I remember, there were no precipitating circumstances. I got up one morning before daylight, went out to the railroad yards, and got on a freight train." It was 1916; Jake was fourteen years old. "It was in the autumn, because I know I worked for one farmer harvesting corn. They cut the stalks with a scythe and let them lie on the ground until they got dry. And then I would come along and, with heavy cotton gloves, tear the ears off and throw them into a wagon as it went up and down the rows. Hoboing around Texas and Oklahoma, I worked on a lot of farms and ranches." Three years passed. Having returned home, Jake became a travelling salesman for the family's bakery-supply business. "That's what really gave me my training in the book business."

> I was always fond of books, and one summer [in 1919] a man came to work as my helper on a truck I was driving. He and his friend [Jerry Nedwick] had been picked up by the cops in the railroad yards; they had been hoboing. And my father bailed them out and put them to work. The man that went to work for me was named Ben Abramson. Later he went to Chicago and started the Argus Bookshop, one of the biggest and best-known bookshops ever in Chicago. It's an interesting thing: I never saw him again. But I have a file of correspondence *that* thick from him.

In a letter of 1 July 1935 (MS UCLA), Ben Abramson acknowledged that he had "directed your [Jake's] steps toward bookselling". In Letter 102 Jake wrote to Abramson, "I still look upon you as my original mentor and inspiration in all things bookish", and in Letter 176 recalled their "long sunny talks ... on the truck in Texas". These talks, he says, "sort of enchanted me, seduced me into the idea of being a bookseller". Finally, in 1925, Jake left Fort Worth, moving slowly toward a distinguished career.

> I couldn't see any future in the [bakery-supply] business. So when I was twenty-two years old, I married a girl in Texas [Edith Motheral]

who was a very beautiful, very impulsive young woman, and sent her on to California.[9] I started walking, and hitchhiked a good part of the way. It took me about a month. And when I came to Los Angeles, my first job was as a busboy in a cafeteria, but I got fired from that. Then I got a job as a gardener's helper on one of Mr. E. L. Doheny's trucks. Ten years later I was having tea at Mrs. [Estelle] Doheny's house, together with Dr. Rosenbach. My first bookselling job, late in 1925, was at Holmes's Book Company downtown. After three weeks, I was fired for incompetence. Later, when I opened up a shop of my own down the street, old Holmes used to say that he had given me my start in the book business. Then I went to work in Bullock's department store, stayed about a year and four months, and because I developed some signs of TB, I had to go into a sanatorium for about three months. When I came out, nobody would give me a job, so I started carrying a satchel full of books and going to call on the people who had bought books from me when I was in the book department at Bullock's. I picked up a few customers, borrowed a little money, and in 1927 started a bookshop.

Jake set up shop at 567 South Hope Street. "It was the doorway of a bookshop, and it was a number I invented." Within a year he had moved to slightly larger quarters at 705½ Sixth Street. "Along came the Depression, and I got boxed in by that. In order to extricate myself from those problems, I went into a corporation, but when the voting stockholders started fighting with each other, I had to liquidate that and start over again. I had very little money." In 1934 Jake moved to 614 West Sixth Street. It was to the Sixth Street shop that Galka Scheyer brought Frieda and Angelo in 1937.

Jake decided that the best way to win recognition for Lawrence's manuscripts was first to exhibit them – at Stanford University and at the Los Angeles Public Library – and then to issue a descriptive catalogue. "Frieda liked the idea. I think she felt that she needed money. They weren't in poverty – they must have had some money. And they lived very frugally – they liked the idea of being frugal. But they were also very generous." At Stanford the exhibition, which took place 21 September to 31 October 1936, seemed to Jake "overwhelming" (Letter 45). It included 144 items – manuscripts, typescripts, proofs, paintings, and photographs.

An acquaintance of Frieda's named Harry K. Wells (1911–76), who was young and energetic and intelligent, hoped that Harvard University would purchase the whole lot so that he could have access to them in his projected biography of Lawrence (Letter 82). To that end he and his wife Jenny (b. 1913) visited Frieda in New Mexico. On 10 October 1936 Frieda wrote to her California friend Una Jeffers:

> I had a charming young couple Harry K Wells here, he just lives and breathes Lawrence, is collecting all Lawrence's letters for Harvard and is writing and knows more about our lives than I do –   (Letter 40)

In 1935 the Wellses, natives of the American Midwest, had begun a Lawrence pilgrimage, bicycling through England, meeting Frieda's sister Else Jaffe in Heidelberg, spending the winter of 1935–6 in Cornwall, and, as they went, purchasing hundreds of Lawrence's letters. A year earlier, at Harvard, Wells had written an honour's thesis on Lawrence as a poet of organism. Invited by Frieda to visit the Ranch, the couple arrived in August 1936 by train, and stayed ten days in the original house that Lawrence had occupied.

In November 1936, Wells, now a graduate student, arranged for Frieda to come to Harvard to lecture (on 11 December) and for Jake to ship the Lawrence manuscripts for display in Harvard's Treasure Room (Letters 24–5). For two months Frieda and Angelo stayed with the Wellses in Concord, Massachusetts. Interviewed in 1989, Jenny Wells Vincent remembers that

> We had wonderful times with Frieda and Angelino. I remember her writing us to ask if she would need any formal attire at Harvard, and we wrote her that there was only one dinner that might require formal dress. So she busied herself to create an evening gown out of gold lamé, trimmed with brown velvet. With it she wore a beautiful turquoise necklace, and on her feet, sneakers! The dinner that night took place in the house that was once Amy Lowell's. I remember Angelino fretting about the American custom of the men retiring to one room, to smoke and chat, and the ladies to another. He quickly joined the ladies.
>
> They were a lot of fun to have in our home. Angelino made bread and spent a lot of his time copying our reproduction of a Van Gogh portrait of a peasant. What he painted was very good, but he produced an Italian peasant rather than a French one. Angelino and Frieda had a very "open" relationship, which was new to me. There was a great deal of freedom between them. He was a very sociable person and loved to be with people. In the summer he used to go to all the dances; Frieda was happy she didn't have to go with him. She used to say, "Angie, I hope you can find another nice woman this summer that you can take to all the dances, because I'm certainly not going." They seemed to be able to enjoy each other's company without being possessive. Their relationship was an inspiration to me!

But during their visit to Massachusetts, Wells apparently persuaded

Frieda that she should withdraw the manuscripts from Jake (Letter 64), who remembers that

> Harry Wells was always trying to get hold of these manuscripts, and he got the notion lodged in Frieda's head that I was unreliable. All of a sudden she wrote me and said she wanted the manuscripts back [Letter 66]. I was puzzled and hurt. Later she and Angelino came back to Los Angeles, and she said, "Harry Wells told me things about you which made me mistrust you. But I was mistaken." She was very apologetic.

Frieda brought the manuscripts back to Jake. Harvard's tentative bid of $10 000, chary even by Depression standards, was rejected; and the "special price of $25,000" (Letter 80), to which Jake and Frieda agreed, would have placed "too great a drain" on Harvard's resources (Letter 83). On 22 May 1937 Wells finally returned the manuscripts to Jake with the comment, "TOO BAD" (Letter 93).

To prepare the descriptive catalogue of Lawrence's manuscripts Jake soon invited Dr. Lawrence Clark Powell (b. 1906), who later became University Librarian at UCLA, Dean of its Library School, and still later a novelist and memoirist.[10] Interviewed in 1987, Larry Powell remembers that "Jake opened his first shop about 1927. I was small and slight, but full of zeal, and as a student at Occidental College I used to go to town to buy books, and I found his shop. I grew up with Ward Ritchie, the printer, who was doing printing for Jake. And we just drew into it." At the University of Dijon, Powell had completed a dissertation on Robinson Jeffers in 1932. When he returned from France in 1933,

> Jake hired me not because I had a doctorate in literature but because I could type and he needed a typist. I was his secretary. Because I wanted time to write, I worked halftime for Jake for a dollar a day, thirty dollars a month. Fay and I married in 1934, and we lived on it! You have no idea: milk was a nickel a quart, bread a nickel a loaf, meat – we ground beefheart, made hamburger out of it, at five cents a pound. Sure, you could live on little.

From 1934 to 1936 Powell worked in Jake's shop – as typist, window dresser, wrapper, and delivery boy. "They were wonderful graduate years. Jake was a very wise man. But he was tough: he didn't pay me enough (often he didn't *have* the money) and he was demanding."

Then, explains Jake, "a librarian at the Los Angeles Public Library named Albert Read said to Powell, 'You're no good on that side of the desk. You ought to be on my side of the desk. You ought to be a librarian.' So Powell left my employ. Friends lent him money enough to go up to Berkeley and get a library degree." Subsequently Powell earned his MLS. When he returned to Los Angeles in 1937, he discovered that there were no library jobs to be found.

> Everything was at a standstill. And Jake said, "I've got manuscripts here from Frieda Lawrence; they're in the bank vault. I want someone to catalog them. I'll pay you a hundred dollars." I was living then out in Westwood, near UCLA. My uncle, a civil engineer, had retired early, was well-to-do, and had a big house in Westwood. He was going to be away for the summer, and he let my wife Fay and me, and our two kids, have the house. By that time I had my own Lawrence collection – not collector's books but reading texts. You see, I was planning to write a book on Lawrence, and Jake knew that I was steeped in Lawrence. In 1932, after I had got my doctorate, I lived on the beach near Nice, and I visited Lawrence's grave at Vence. So Jake thought, "Here's just the guy to do the catalog."

Their agreement is recorded in Letters 95–6. As Jake wrote on 2 June 1937, "The manuscripts have arrived and are now in our vault, where Dr. Lawrence Clark Powell is at work on them" (Letter 99). Because Frieda did not want the manuscripts removed from the bank, Powell worked in the vault of the Security National Bank located at Sixth and Grand, one block from Jake's shop at the corner of Sixth and Hope. As Powell recalls,

> I did the catalog in a month, from June 1 to June 30, working under pressure, in the unheated bank vault with a temperature of about 60 degrees. It was a tomb, really. I took my notes right from the manuscripts. Jake didn't want a full-scale bibliographical description; he wanted a sales catalog – he wanted to sell the manuscripts! At night, back in Westwood, I did the so-called literary notes, the excerpts from the literature. Jake had said, "Make it readable, for God's sake. I want something readable." Then I saw it through the press; Jake left all that to me. Nobody had any money. We had good will, we had ambition, we had youth, but no money. So Jake got Elmer Belt to pay for it.[11] His office was across the street from Jake's shop. He was a leading urologist and a great book collector – very successful, very wealthy. He was interested in Jake and in me, not in Lawrence.

On 13 November 1937 Jake Zeitlin registered *The Manuscripts of D. H. Lawrence: A Descriptive Catalogue*, compiled by Lawrence Clark Powell, with the copyright office in Washington, DC. Frieda thought the catalogue "beautiful" (Letter 171). It was warmly reviewed by

Edward L. Tinker in the *New York Times Book Review* (27 February 1938). Handsomely printed by Ward Ritchie in a run of 750 copies, and featuring an orange-and-blue phoenix on the title page, it described the 124 Lawrence manuscripts and typescripts in Jake's possession and included excerpts from the published criticism. Appendix B provides the bibliographical descriptions in condensed form. As a supplement, Jake issued a price list for dealers, which Powell helped prepare; and these (and other) prices have been inserted into the entries of Appendix B.

The 6 November 1937 entry in Larry Powell's unpublished journal reads:

> The Lawrence cat[alog] is published. I dressed the mss. exhibit at the Library [the manuscripts were exhibited at the Los Angeles Public Library, 1–20 November 1937], also a case full of Lawrence books and MF's [M. F. K. Fisher's] walnut carved phoenix. At the opening we had Aldous Huxley. Turned away several hundred people. Seated 400. I presided. The evening went smoothly. Aldous gave a very fine, sensitive, beautiful talk about Lawrence; and of the inadequacy of words to describe the intensity of his qualities. Afterwards we gathered at Ritchie's for a beer party. I worked like a dog in staging this show and getting the cat[alog] ready.

Ward Ritchie, having studied printing with Schmied in Paris, had founded the Ward Ritchie Press in 1932 and had often done printing for local bookshops. Interviewed in 1988, Ritchie recalls that

> When Frieda offered Jake the manuscripts of D. H. Lawrence, he naturally decided that I would print the catalog. It was special to me because it was a more substantial catalog than most. With a small staff, I was no longer doing the actual printing: I did the design and layouts, and managed the Press. Because of my great interest in Lawrence, I wanted to make the catalog as nice as possible, and it probably took us two months to print. After the opening of the manuscript exhibition, everyone gathered at my house on Griffith Park Boulevard; that was our usual way of celebrating. My studio had an old Washington handpress, a grand piano, a huge fireplace, a grandfather clock – it was decorated beautifully – and so people liked to come there.

The *Catalogue* served Jake as the chief means of communicating with buyers. According to Jake's records, 72 copies were sent out – to professional buyers such as Jacob Blanck, Ben Abramson, Philip Duschnes, Bertram Rota, Ernest Maggs, A. S. W. Rosenbach, Ed Hanley, and others; copies also went to Jake's customers and Frieda's friends. In vain Jake hoped that the manuscripts would be purchased by a university library. "Lawrence's memory would be so much better served if they could be kept together", he wrote to Frieda in 1936 (Letter 45). And to Wells he wrote, "What a marvelous thing it would be to have such a collection all in one place!" (Letter 53). It would provide "excellent source material for students of contemporary literature" (Letter 140).

In the summer of 1937 Jake had visited Frieda at the Kiowa Ranch near Taos. "I should like to come out there for a few days", he wrote her on 8 June (Letter 101). Driving east by way of Fort Worth, Texas, he stayed at the ranch for about two days in July (Letter 107). "There were several cabins on the ranch", he recalls. "The Huxleys were in one; I was in another. Not really primitive, just the necessary accommodations. They had wooden floors. I met the Huxleys at breakfast, and I remember that Frieda and Angelo cooked up a big omelette of tender pumpkin blossoms." Eager to keep Lawrence's reputation alive, Frieda was warm and generous. In conversation she and Jake apparently decided to ask $30 000 for the complete collection of manuscripts (Letter 108).

The Huxleys – Aldous, Maria, and their son Matthew – were also staying on the ranch that summer. In a letter of 3 June 1937, Aldous Huxley (1894–1963) described their new surroundings to his brother Julian:

> We have a log cabin – to which a bathroom is in process of being added – on Frieda Lawrence's ranch in the mountains here. A very extraordinary place – more than 8000 feet up in a clearing in the woods, which are composed of pine, aspen, birch and oak-scrub. Below in the plain – which lies at about 7000 feet – is the sage-brush desert, pale whitey-green and tawny, with the canyon of the Rio Grande running through the midst and blue mountains beyond. The sky is full of enormous dramas of cloud and sunshine – with periodical thunderstorms of incredible violence. Boiling hot sunshine alternates with cold shade and icy nights. There were whirlwinds of dust in the desert below us and, after rain, the roads are impassable. Nearest town (20 miles off) is Taos. . . .
>
> Frieda is well, cheerful and a great deal calmer than she used to be. Later middle age is suiting her. The Capitano turns out to be a very decent sort of middle-class Italian – rather naif, at the same time intelligent and active. As far as one can judge he doesn't exploit Frieda: on the contrary, manages her affairs very efficiently.[12]

In a letter of 13 October 1937, Maria Huxley (1898–1955) remembered that their little house, next to Frieda's, "stood under large trees and was surrounded by green grass and there were animals and there was quietness and there was peace and above all that there was Frieda whom we had always been very fond of". [13] Matthew Huxley, interviewed in 1987, said, "To me it was a wonderful time. We stayed there at least two months, and I got to know Frieda quite well. She was a marvelously outgoing, warm, loving woman. And Angelino was a seriously competent man, as far as I thought, and very fond of Frieda – and very protective of her, defending her against the outside world."

On the second day of Jake's visit, Frieda and Angelo organized an excursion to the Santo Domingo Rain Dance. As Jake recalls:

The Huxleys and Angelino and Brett – we all met in Santa Fe, and we picked up Witter Bynner, a well-mannered Harvard man who was living in Santa Fe, then went to the Santo Domingo Rain Dance. Frieda went in one car, and Angelino went in another car with me and a young woman whom he pestered – hands all over her: he tried to seduce her.

We all sat in a row on the ground, with our backs up against the wall of one of the adobes, and the rain dance was performed in front of us. There were quite a number of dancers, somewhere around twenty, and a big crowd of tourists. It lasted all afternoon. They kept on, and by God, it did rain – it rained like hell. When the rain dance ended, we drove as fast as we could to get back to Santa Fe because we were afraid that we might get caught in a flash flood.

Larry Powell, who visited the Kiowa Ranch later, recorded in his unpublished journal (16 August 1940) that "Frieda and Angelino have improved the place in the last 10 years that they have lived here. Built a new house. We are staying in the old one that sheltered Lawrence. . . . The great pine tree still stands there in front. Last night the pack rats bounced on the roof 'like hippopotamuses.' The old white horse Azul[14] is still here. And two others. A new cow has replaced dead Susan."

Back in Los Angeles Jake had begun to sell the manuscripts – for example, the manuscript of *Paul Morel* to T. E. Hanley for $1500, six unpublished poems to Albert Bender of San Francisco, and a group of short stories that Bertram Rota bought for the English collector George Lazarus (Letter 116). Frieda was pleased. When she and Angelo came to Los Angeles to escape the cold winters, they would often visit Jake and his third wife Josephine Ver Brugge. Divorced from his second wife Gina in 1938 – "you were'nt the man for her", says Frieda (Letter 164) – Jake had married Josephine in October 1939, and she, specializing in scientific periodicals, became his business partner. Interviewed in 1985, Josephine recalls:

When I came to California in 1937, and asked Jake for a job, the thing that was most impressive about him was that I had just finished reading *Not I, But the Wind* . . ., and I thought, 'This man *knows* Frieda Lawrence.' Frieda herself was always completely straightforward and honest, without pretense, and I always had the feeling that she was a peasant. That was partly the effect of her liaison with Angelino, because he was rather a peasant, I thought. She was a very large woman at this time in her life – but hearty, spirited, and full of great vigor. Her naturalness and her self-assurance I found very persuasive. She had a gusto for life and people, and the activity of people. And when we went to their house, Angelino would cook this very simple food. He made no pretense of being an intellectual. He just went about his life from day to day, as if, 'Isn't this a strange fortune that's caught me up, that I associate with these people!' What did they talk about? All I remember is just the daily life – how you travel and where you went and who you'd seen and what you'd done. When they would come, we would see them two or three times. I don't think I saw them more than five or six times in all.

Jake adds that when Frieda and Angelo came to Los Angeles, they would rent an apartment (early in 1936, for example, they stayed at 1601 North Stanley Avenue in Hollywood):

And they would entertain, always inviting friends, and they cooked mostly spaghetti and food like that. And always lots of wine. He did all the cooking; he was very devoted to her. But it didn't stop him from chasing after other women.[15] The Huxley's? They liked Angelino and seemed to always welcome him. I don't think they disapproved of him; they thought he was kind of a dog, but only because he chased after women. But I never heard them criticize.

While in Los Angeles, Frieda and Angelo also saw Knud Merrild (1894–1954), a calm, handsome painter, and his wife Else. "Knud was a lovely person, a Dane who made his living by doing very fine interior painting – marbling and interesting wood textures; he did his own abstract paintings and collages on the side." He and Kai Götzsche (1886–?), a fellow painter, had lived with the Lawrences at the Del Monte Ranch in the winter of 1922–3, and he had written a book about the experience called *A Poet and Two Painters* published in 1938. Through Merrild – and through Jake – the Powells also became close friends of Frieda and Angelo in the late 1930s. Merrild and Götzsche were painting a mural for Harry and Olivia Johnson – for the den of their Brentwood home. Powell recalls that

Through Merrild we met often at the Johnsons' house. Frieda and Angie were still wintering in L.A., and they would come to dinner with us, and we would go to dinner with them and with Aldous. We traded back and forth. Frieda was very fond of me and very fond of Fay. She gave out a great deal of human warmth. She'd laugh! Oh, God, she had this belly-laugh, a wonderful, exuberant, expansive laugh. She was so warm, so happy about things. She was a very generous woman, very abundant. I didn't sense her as a sexual person; I was probably too much younger. I just liked her vitality and I got a lot from it.

Powell's response to Angelo Ravagli was more guarded:

Angie was a manly guy, forthright, *Italian*. He was expansive in a different way. Unlike Frieda, Angie was always talking with his hands. He was volatile, genial, a very companionable guy. But I spotted him. He was a wolf, really – a satyr. He screwed anything he could. Frieda tolerated it because he was a very sturdy mainstay and companion and handyman. His class? He was working class. Peasant class. He wasn't intellectual. God, no. He worked with his hands – carpenter, painter, potter, plumber. He was strong and rugged. Not big, but square – stocky. He did *all* the things Frieda needed. On the ranch, of course, his help was indispensable. Just the right kind of guy for Frieda.

But although he provided security, Frieda was always the focus of conversation:

When they were together, Frieda really carried the ball. She carried it over everybody, really. She was outspoken and vital, and entertaining and humorous. Everything amused her. Angie was not subdued, but she was obviously the leader. He was unobtrusive yet by no means a nonentity. He would remark on things – puncture balloons if necessary. He wasn't a dummy; I think he was smart. He was an extraordinary man, really. Lawrence accepted him – Lawrence apparently *responded* to him.

On 21 January 1939, a Saturday evening, Ward Ritchie was visiting with Frieda at Fletcher Martin's house when suddenly she made him a surprising proposal. He recorded the event in his unpublished journal:

The Martins called and asked me to come over for dinner. Fletcher said that Witter Bynner, his boyfriend Bob Hunt (whom I had known in high school), the Knud Merrilds, and Frieda Lawrence were there. I immediately drove over and climbed up the fifty steps to their lair. Soon I was talking with Frieda. She told me that she had two early versions of *Lady Chatterley* which had never been published and suggested that I might be interested. . . . They had been kept in a small yellow chest that Lawrence had decorated. Every time she had looked at the chest, knowing what was kept there, she shuddered. . . . She mentioned that she had never received any royalties from the book, except from France.

"They excited me very much", he recalled fifty years later. "And then Frieda said, 'Wouldn't you like to publish them?' At that time I was in a fine-press tradition, and she thought it would be nice to have a beautiful limited edition of them. Later on, however, we started thinking (this was before *Lady Chatterley* was allowed here) that we were just a small press with four or five people, and to get involved in all the legal problems that such a job might entail . . . we just couldn't afford it."

As the years passed, Lawrence's manuscripts were gradually sold or, in a few cases, given away.[16] Says Jake: "I remember once Frieda said, 'Well, I gave one of these manuscripts to a young man who came up to the ranch and told me he was so fond of Lawrence that he'd love to have a manuscript, and I just gave it to him.'"[17] In Letter 212 Jake remarked to Frieda, "you are as always, too generous." In his book Merrild wrote that Frieda "would gladly give almost anything away, until she had nothing" (p. 193). "Without Angelo", Jake observes, "she would have been flimflammed out of everything."

From annotations found in Jake's personal copy of the *Catalogue*, Appendix B identifies some of the buyers or recipients of the manuscripts. Bertram Rota (1903–1966), a London bookseller, was one. Says Jake: "He was a very special man, one of the few people in England who specialized in modern English literature, when nobody else would pay any attention to it. And finally his day came when Harry Ransom [at the University of Texas] started to collect, and he had it."

The major purchaser, without question, was a wealthy collector named Thomas Edward Hanley (1894–1969). "His father had been one of the founders of the oil industry, and Ed's money came from gas wells, which kept pouring out gas. He also had a brick factory, and he was known as the Brick King." Ed Hanley made his home in an old wooden house in Bradford, Pennsylvania, in his later years marrying an Egyptian belly dancer named Tullah Innes.[18] Larry Powell, who met him in 1934, remembers him as big, sombre, somewhat phlegmatic. Hanley had excellent taste, though, and an exceptional instinct for value, forming a great collection of paintings and drawings as well as books and manuscripts. Jake recalls that

Hanley would come out and spend between three and four months in Los Angeles. When he first arrived he'd say, "Show me what you've got that's interesting." And he would put aside a substantial lot and say, "Just hold them." And then, on the basis of my expectancy of his buying these, I would have to be patient and listen to him every day when he came in and repeated the same conversation – mostly about other book dealers and his collection of books and art. He was the world's most God-awful bore.

He would take a small, cheap room at the Hollywood Roosevelt Hotel next to the elevator machinery, which made a hell of a lot of noise, and stay there during his entire visit. He said he'd rather spend the money on books. And no matter where you went to dinner, all he wanted was a hamburger or a steak and a glass of milk. He was a great follower of the circus, too. And I remember going out to the circus with him once; he knew all the razor-backs and the clowns and the acrobats. Unmarried for many years, he was always squiring around these beautiful showgirl types.

But his one quirk was that he never paid cash for what he bought. "He always paid so much a month, drawing interest in the meantime." As Jake told Frieda in Letter 118, "It is his usual custom to pay in installments." He was still doing so in 1954, when Frieda wrote that Hanley "pays us so much a month" (Letter 261). From among Lawrence's manuscripts, Hanley made shrewd choices. Early, he chose the corrected and expurgated typescript of *Lady Chatterley's Lover* as well as *The Fox* and "Introduction to These Paintings", paying $1900 for the group (Letter 179). Later, when the University of Texas at Austin began collecting Lawrence, the Hanley collection was the University's central acquisition.

After a wounding skirmish with his creditors, Jake returned to Frieda the manuscripts that remained unsold; his four-page handwritten list is dated 3 March 1942. Back in 1938 Jake had been threatened with the possibility of bankruptcy: "I didn't know how to buy, so that I always paid too much for what I bought. And I always used very good printers, to get out good-looking catalogs and calendars, and although they created a good image for me, they were disproportionately expensive." Worried that Lawrence's manuscripts might be seized if his business were forced into receivership, he arranged in 1941 to have them put into a bank vault and named Knud Merrild as trustee (Letter 224). Says Jake: "I remember going to the [Security National] bank and getting the manuscripts from the vault and putting them on a handtruck and turning them over to him. I was afraid that if somebody decided to sue me, they might seize the manuscripts and then sell them. I wanted to make sure that in the course of my problems these manuscripts didn't become involved. I think that was when they were returned to Frieda in

New Mexico." In appreciation Frieda gave Merrild the manuscripts of *Apocalypse* (Letter 237), which went to his wife Else after he died. They were valued at $225 by the Wellses and at $400 in the Powell catalogue.

Jake did not see Frieda and Angelo again until 1954 when the Ravaglis (they had married on 31 October 1950) asked him to appraise the remainder of their Lawrence collection. On 24 September 1954 Frieda wrote to Richard Aldington, "Jake Zeitlin is coming from Los Angeles to appraise the Mss and so on, that are left."[19] "Frieda and Angelino were then living down near Taos, in a house [Los Pinos] that she called the lower ranch. She had given the land across the road to [Dorothy] Brett, and Brett was living there. Frieda said, 'The University of Texas wants a third party to do an appraisal of the manuscripts.' Harry Ransom had said to her, 'Set a price.' So they asked me to come out." According to Letter 255, Jake arrived at the Santa Fe airport on 9 October. "I remember most of all the golden cottonwoods and the clear air, and a long visit with Brett, who was very sweet and very deaf, and who showed me a lot of her paintings. I went over all the manuscripts – working right there in the house – and drew up a list with details, the number of pages, and so on. I wasn't there very long, not more than three days in all." He was paid $300 (Letter 261). Dated 10 October 1954, Jake's appraisal, which appears as Appendix C, documents what remained for sale. For years Ed Hanley continued to buy Lawrence materials directly from Frieda, usually paying whatever appraised values Jake had, either in 1937 or in 1954, assigned.

For some years Lawrence's reputation had been growing, and his manuscripts were increasingly in demand. Warren Roberts (b. 1916) has explained how he learned in 1954, while still a graduate student at the University of Texas, that Frieda had, even then, held on to some of Lawrence's manuscripts at Los Pinos.[20] Excited, he and Harry Ransom (1908–76), the man who had presciently persuaded the Texas Board of Regents to declare books a capital improvement, "immediately thought about the possibility of establishing a D. H. Lawrence collection at Texas" ("Memoir", p. 24). Ransom, then Dean of Arts and Sciences, shortly became Provost (1957), President (1960), then Chancellor (1961–71). On 12 October 1954 Frieda told her American agent Alan C. Collins that "The University of Texas, the richest in the world[,] is making a Lawrence centre in Austin ... and are buying everything they can connected with Lawrence" (Letter 256). Frieda and Angelo agreed to stop in Austin on their way to Port Isabel, in southern Texas, where in 1948 they had bought a house for the winter months near excellent fishing waters and a perfect beach. In early November the Ravaglis reached Austin, with their collection of manuscripts and rare books, and attended a literary celebration at the University. "They gave us a great reception in Austin", Frieda wrote to John Middleton Murry at the end of 1954.[21] But hopes of purchase collapsed. Interviewed in 1987, Warren Roberts remembers that before the Ravaglis left,

> Angie wanted some kind of a paper from Ransom [agreeing to buy the manuscripts], and Ransom wouldn't give it to him, so Angie got angry. He wanted something specific from Ransom, and actually I think he had a right to expect it. Ransom just wanted to tell him that we were going to buy the manuscripts, without saying when he would pay or anything else.

In turn, Ransom "took Angie's reaction as a personal affront" ("Memoir", p. 27), and the negotiations ended. As Frieda ruefully commented to Roberts on 30 November 1954, "Angelino got worked up and wrote more harshly than he ever meant to. . . . You see Angelino wants to be businesslike and American!" (Letter 261). Larry Powell also remembers that Ransom "didn't like paper work. He wanted his word to be it. Everything he and I did was by word of mouth." Yet, Roberts wrote later, "Frieda generously insisted that the manuscripts and books remain in Austin until the spring [of 1955]", for the benefit of students working on Lawrence. "Fortunately, the University eventually obtained most of the items through a variety of other sources" ("Memoir", p. 27), especially through Hanley.

From Frieda the University of Texas learned about Hanley. Warren Roberts recalls that Hanley "had been buying Lawrence manuscripts from her for several years, paying by monthly installment". Letter 269 provides confirmation, for Frieda wrote on 7 July 1956 that Larry Powell wanted to buy the manuscript of *The Rainbow* for UCLA, "but Hanley does too". (He paid $3500 for it.) Like Jake, Warren Roberts believed that Hanley "had an uncanny instinct for buying the right manuscript or book, a distinction rare even among collectors. . . . The acquisition of Hanley's collection brought the largest single archive of Lawrence papers to the Humanities Research Center" ("Memoir", p. 31), wrote Roberts, who for fifteen years (1961–76) directed the Center. "Dr. Ransom had arranged its purchase with the help of Jim Drake [of James F. Drake & Co.] . . . a well-known antiquarian bookseller in New York" ("Memoir", p. 31). As Roberts recalls, Hanley's collection came to the HRC in a curious way:

> The insurance people came out and found that in this old, wooden Victorian house Hanley had stuck about five million dollars' worth of French impressionist paintings and two or three million dollars' worth of books and manuscripts. And they threatened to cut off his insurance unless he got rid of one or the other. He chose to get rid of

the books and manuscripts rather than the paintings. So we got that collection, with all the Lawrence, and later we bought a second collection from him.[22] The negotiations for the first one were done by Jim Drake and Ransom, and they bought that when I was in Italy, and it was unpacked just after I got back [in the summer of 1958], and then I went up and got the second collection. We had an exhibit [at the HRC] in November, 1958.

Well supplied with money and eager to build its manuscript holdings, Texas soon added Frieda's papers to its Lawrence collection. Angelo's telegram announcing Frieda's death on 11 August 1956 (Letter 270) arrived just as Roberts and his wife Pat were departing on a two-year Fulbright Fellowship to the University of Pisa, so that "it was impossible for me to go to Taos for the funeral or to do anything useful about acquiring the Lawrence memorabilia Angie might still have. Later I learned that Angie had quickly sold the remaining Lawrence manuscripts to private collectors and institutions. However, many of these ended up in the Hanley library and thus came to the University after all" ("Memoir", p. 35). When Roberts went to Taos in 1958, he learned, however, that Frieda's personal papers had not yet been sold, so he arranged in 1959 for the University to buy them from Angelo for $5000. "These papers of Frieda's proved much more valuable for research than the comparatively minor Lawrence typescripts which Angie kept after Frieda's death" ("Memoir", p. 36).

While these transactions went forward, other manuscripts of Lawrence fared differently. As detailed in Letters 272–98, Jake had learned that Else Merrild, formerly living in Los Angeles but now having returned to her native Denmark, wanted to sell the manuscripts of Lawrence's late work *Apocalypse*, composed in 1929. Her husband Knud Merrild and his Danish friend Götzsche had once wintered with the Lawrences in the mountains above Taos. "I cannot emphasize enough how glad, gay and jolly we were, feeling pioneerish", Merrild wrote about their time together; he found Frieda "really very wonderful" and Lawrence "a man of strong personality and character, almost overpowering and absolutely fearless".[23] After Merrild wedded Else and came to Los Angeles, Frieda and Angelo often saw them. Los Angeles had become a sort of meeting ground. Says Jake:

Merrild was a very decent, straightforward man – a very likable Dane. He wasn't assertive; his wife Else was much more assertive than he was. Else was handsome and impressive – the match of Frieda, with that same stalwart forthrightness. When Viking published Merrild's book [in 1938], I gave a party at my shop – about 1938 or 1939 – and had an exhibition of his drawings, including a portrait that he had done of Lawrence. He had a very personal style of painting. Frieda and Angelino and the Huxleys and Dudley Nichols, the Hollywood writer, came to the party. That was when I was in the carriage house on Carondelet Street [1938–48], and we had a wonderful turnout. After most of the crowd left, we played games and were very lively. It was a very beautiful party – one of the most satisfying that I've ever had. The exhibition brought some little notice to him: like dropping a rock in a pool.

Merrild had been much involved with Lawrence's manuscripts, having helped Frieda protect them during Jake's financial troubles. In later years Merrild and Else had returned to Denmark, where he died on New Year's Eve 1954. "After Merrild died, Else seemed to have collapsed from the inside", recalls Jake. "From time to time she would come out for the winter and have an apartment not very far from here. There was still that same outward look, that self-assurance that she and Frieda both had, that Nordic *Heldenfrau* quality. But something seemed to have evaporated and gone out of her."

By 1960 Else Merrild, having visited with Jake in Los Angeles, was ready to sell the two manuscript versions of *Apocalypse*.[24] Naturally she wanted "to get the best price" (Letter 282). In an amusing exchange of letters, Else proved herself a skilled negotiator. She refused first $3000, then $4000, then $5000; then asked $8000; but decided finally that she would take $6000 "for them both" (Letter 289). To that figure Jake naturally added a profit – $1000 for himself and $500 for Lew Feldman, the respected dealer who arranged for both manuscripts to be purchased in 1961 by the University of Texas for $7500.

The three holograph manuscripts of *Lady Chatterley's Lover* had never been given to Jake to sell. After Lawrence's death, they had remained in the care of Pino Orioli, the Florentine bookseller who had helped Lawrence to publish the novel's third version in 1928. Angelo's purpose in going to Italy a decade later – he left on 5 December 1937 – was not only to see his wife and children, whom he had left behind in Spotorno, but to retrieve the *Lady Chatterley* manuscripts from Orioli, who had earlier refused to surrender them to Marianne von Eckhardt, Frieda's niece and informal agent, telling her that "it was too much responsibility to hand them over to a third party" and falsely claiming that "one of them . . . belonged to him" (Letter 126). In late 1937 Stefano Manara, an attorney in Florence who was also Angelo's stepfather-in-law, surprised Orioli with a power of attorney; recognizing that opposition was useless, Orioli "put on a good face and handed over the precious manuscripts" (Letter 159), which Manara then delivered to Angelo's house, where they were soon retrieved.

For years the manuscripts remained with Frieda, sheltered for a time in Witter Bynner's safe at Santa Fe. No doubt they were her favourites, each exquisitely written by Lawrence, scarcely corrected, immensely valuable, a fascinating revelation of the novelist's mind, and an incisive commentary on their last years together. She kept them back as long as possible. On 12 April 1952, Frieda wrote to Larry Powell: "I dont really want to sell the Mss" (Letter 248). On 5 January 1953, she wrote (MS HRC): "they are my 'pièce de résistance' and I want a lot for them". To Warren Roberts she wrote later: "You know we have nothing left but the 3 Lady Cs and I enjoy looking at them and reading them in the raw as it were." Roberts remembers that Frieda kept the three *Lady Chatterley* manuscripts in a cardboard box under her bed.

Finally even they were sold. Jake offers his explanation:

While I was in Taos in [October] 1954 to do the appraisal, we were having dinner at a restaurant called the Red Robin. One night, in came this woman by the name of Amalia de Schulthess. She was an extraordinarily beautiful woman, one of the most beautiful women of her time. And she was married to a Swiss named Hans de Schulthess who was from a wealthy, aristocratic, uppercrust banking family. He liked doing spectacular things and had a lot of notions of macho. She was an artist – a very fine sculptress. They were both rather flamboyant. Hans was the nephew of Dr. Martin Bodmer, a customer of mine who, in his day, was the greatest book collector in the world. And Hans had an interest in books and art. So the de Schulthesses came to my bookshop, and we got to be friends.

Jake had told them about Frieda. Interviewed in 1989, Amalia de Schulthess vividly remembers her first meeting with Frieda Lawrence, which occurred during her initial trip to Taos, then a flourishing art colony. Although she had brought with her a letter of introduction from Jake, she did not need to use it. One summer's day in 1953 she and the friend she was travelling with were driving up the bumpy, rutted road toward the Kiowa Ranch, at the onset of a thunderstorm, when

suddenly there came a car from the other side. Neither of us could pass. So I got out and said, "Oh, I'm so sorry." In the back of the car sat Frieda Lawrence!

"Oh," she said, "don't you worry – don't you move. We will move." By the time they had moved their car, we had exchanged quite a few words, and she said, "Why don't you come by?"

"I would like that very much," I replied. I didn't mention the letter of introduction. A couple of days later I called and said, "I'm the woman who met you head-on on the road. If you like, I would love to come and say hello to you. I am a friend of Jake Zeitlin, and he said we should meet."

I don't remember Frieda's looks so well – more the impact of her personality. Yes, her hair was blond and cut short, not glamorous at all. It was her presence that I felt. When she entered a room, the atmosphere changed, became charged, electric. She was very powerful and intensely female. (Age did not change that.)

With time, we visited back and forth, and she got to know my husband, Hans, who was very much interested in D. H. Lawrence and his writings. My husband was tall and good looking; they liked each other right away. Frieda *liked* good-looking young men. She liked the adulation, being something of a star, being so attractive to young men who wanted to know about her – about her life, and about Lawrence. But to my knowledge there was nothing more than that: just a coterie of young men adoring her.

Which we can't say for the little Italian. Unfortunately, her husband noticed me sizably, which I didn't encourage. It was more of a humorous situation than anything else, and in time I became reasonably fond of him. Until Frieda died, we all saw each other often and exchanged some letters. And of course she would talk to me openly, and as I was quite young and inexperienced then, it was all rather fascinating.

Amalia regarded Angelo as a typical small-time Italian Don Juan, "rather gauche and something of a peasant". His amorous exploits around Taos disturbed Frieda. To herself Amalia thought:

"Oh, how humiliating! Really! There he is with somebody who is such an interesting creature." It took a certain amount of insensitivity, which he had lots of. If he had been a little more savvy, a little more a "man of the world" who knew how to behave, it would have been less aggravating. I think Frieda indulged him in a way, although there is no doubt in my mind that she was fond of him. And in his way he was very fond of her too.

When Hans and Amalia signed Frieda's guest book on 12 July 1954, they gave their address as 1141 Tower Road in Beverly Hills. They had met more than a decade earlier at a junior college in Trogen, Switzerland. Recalls Amalia:

I told Hans that I would never marry him if we stayed in Switzerland. Our families did not approve of our intentions to get married, his especially. I proposed going to America and getting married there – quite a healthy distance from Switzerland. I had always wanted to go to America. I had read Wild West novels – by Zane Grey, for instance – and I imagined the spaces of the American West especially as being big and wonderful.

She and Hans emigrated in 1941, married, and in 1943 settled on the West Coast and ultimately in Los Angeles.

After the de Schulthesses and the Ravaglis became good friends, visiting back and forth, and exchanging letters, Jake remembers that

> when Frieda showed Amalia the *Lady Chatterley's Lover* manuscripts, why, there was nothing in the world she wanted so much as those manuscripts. So Hans, her husband, down here in Los Angeles, came to Frieda and said, "I want to buy those manuscripts."[25] And he agreed to pay her $10,000 – at that time a lot of money. And then he said to Amalia, "I will give you those manuscripts."

Amalia speculates that Frieda and Angelo finally sold the manuscripts because they needed the money but also because Frieda was particularly fond of the person who wanted to buy them. Probably Jake helped to set the price, for he described them in 1956 (Appendix C, No. 85). The three manuscripts were then put in a vault in a Hollywood bank.

For years Amalia had lived partly abroad, especially in Florence, where she pursued her work as a sculptor. Then tragedy struck: while travelling through Europe in the summer of 1962, Hans was killed. Although now divorced, the couple had remained very close friends. In Amalia's words,

> He came by to visit me and our younger daughter Celeste, who was in summer school in Florence. My older daughter Catherine was with me then. Hans and Celeste took off for Vienna, where they were going to meet his family for a get-together. He was driving a Maserati. A few days later they crashed on a country road in Austria, trying to pass somebody at high speed. They didn't make the curve. Celeste was thrown out of the car, but he wasn't. He was gravely hurt and taken to a hospital in Vienna, where he never regained consciousness. The doctors said, "If he survives, he will be a vegetable." After ten days he died – on August 28th, 1962. When we opened the bank safe some months later, there were the three *Lady Chatterleys*. I just broke down . . . I just broke down. I was very fond of the three manuscripts, very attached to them emotionally, because my husband had liked them so much. We had shared them!

Because of extraordinary complications in settling Hans's estate, including litigation (Letter 313), Amalia, although the principal heir, could not maintain the scale of living to which she had been accustomed.

> I had a beautiful house – the actor Fred MacMurry's barn, which I helped redesign and which was airy and spacious. After being struck

by a drunk driver while I crossed a street at night, and ending up in the Santa Monica Hospital for four months, I had plenty of time to reflect. I said, "What is more important – my work? or spending every cent on keeping this house? What I really want to do is to put all my energy and means into my work." I realized that to remain in my house was simply not feasible. So I sold my house and my car – and much else – while I was still in the hospital. Once back home I also sold a good part of my library – to Jake. It was then that I began thinking of the *Lady Chatterley* manuscripts. I realized what treasures the manuscripts really were, Lawrence's handwriting so delicate, nearly feminine, with so few corrections. I felt they should not remain in private hands but should be held in a place where students of Lawrence could go and examine them. This is how Jake got hold of them again.

Jake had not seen the *Lady Chatterley* manuscripts for years, but he knew their value. Probably unaware of Amalia's altered circumstances, he recalls that one day in early 1963:

Amalia called me up and said, "Look here, I never look at these manuscripts. Why don't you come out and see me." So I went out and visited her in Brentwood, out near Santa Monica. And she said, "If I could get a good price for them, I'd sell them." She was a very shrewd Swiss woman. So I looked them over in Amalia's house, and I said, "If you'll give me some time, I think I can sell them for you and get you a good price."

Jake of course knew that Harry Ransom at the University of Texas, a man of enormous vision and greater ambition, had begun to form a collection of modern literature; Jake had also discovered that Ransom's unacknowledged agent was Lew Feldman, a New York dealer in rare books and manuscripts.

When Harry Ransom became Chancellor of the University [in 1961], he sent out a letter to a number of booksellers, outlining his plan to build a great collection of books and manuscripts at the University of Texas. It sounded so grand, so elaborate, that none of us believed it. And the only guy who went to see him and who took him seriously was Lew Feldman, who said to him, "Look, I will finance these things until you get the money." The University of Texas owned a lot of oil land – still does. The provision was that the income from this land was to go only for permanent improvements. And it took Harry Ransom some time to get the Regents of the University of Texas to pass a resolution declaring that books were permanent improvements in the university. And with that, Harry Ransom was able to start buying – and actually fulfill his dream. And before he was through, he'd spent a minimum of forty million dollars.

Now, I had a hell of a time. I would tell Harry Ransom what I had [in the way of collections], and a few days later, I'd get a call from Lew Feldman, even though Ransom had pledged me not to mention things to Feldman or anybody else. Feldman would worm out what Ransom was considering, and Feldman would say, "We will take those." And so he bought from me many collections which I had [earlier] offered the University of Texas.

Lew David Feldman (1906–76) had originally trained to be a rabbi but had run away and joined the Marine Corps; he briefly operated a book-rental agency in Washington, DC. Warren Roberts, who knew him well, recalls, though, that "Feldman didn't really get [his business] going until the sixties", when he inherited money "from a brother who had fattened beef in Denver". Expansive, friendly, brash, "Feldman could do anything. He was aggressive, and he had money." Jake had met him much earlier:

He had originally started his book business in Jamaica, Long Island, where I met him. He called his business the House of El Dieff [his initials]. And then he moved to New York City. He never had an open shop – he had an apartment and a storeroom, but he only saw people by appointment. He was a tall, very impressive looking man, and he'd been a Marine Corps sergeant. And he had a way of imposing himself, of getting people to do what he wanted them to do. He had an excellent memory. If he ran across a description of anything, he remembered that completely. I met him in the thirties when he came to call on me in my shop and to see what collections I had for sale. In the thirties and forties and fifties, we had various transactions. He would buy collections. As the agent for Harry Ransom at the University of Texas, he had a great deal of influence over Ransom and would buy things that Ransom would then feel obliged to take. He was very aggressive, and he really raised the whole market, especially in modern literary first editions and manuscripts. He outbid everyone else at auction, because he knew he could sell them, so that he put a new level to the market. He wanted the reputation. Yes, we were competitors – and occasionally cooperated. But I guess I resented his ability to take things which I had not been able to sell to Ransom, and then go back and sell them to him. And I could never understand his particular magic. But he did it. He was very intuitive. He knew when and how to make his presentations. No doubt about it, he was one of the most successful dealers of our century.

Because Feldman was close to the buyers at Texas, he learned which Lawrence materials were for sale:

> And so, in this way, he heard from Harry Ransom that I was representing Amalia de Schulthess. And we met somewhere in New York, and he said, "Why don't we work together on this. We can buy the manuscripts together, and we'll share in whatever we make from them. You know that the door's open to me, and Ransom would give anything for those manuscripts." So finally I started negotiations with her on behalf of Lew Feldman.

On 15 March 1965 he reported to Feldman that "it was no easy matter to persuade Mrs. de Schulthess" to part with the manuscripts, she being "not altogether inclined to sell" (Letter 321).

> Eventually I bought them from her for $30,000.[26] I then sent the manuscripts to Lew, and he then paid me my half of $45,000, which is what he said he sold them for.[27]

As detailed in Letters 299–324, the *Lady Chatterley* sale was finally consummated in 1965. By that time Jake had gradually specialized in the history of science, seldom handling the Lawrence manuscripts that came on the market.

When I last saw Jake in 1986, he was a splendidly resourceful man, generous in his help, wise in spirit, eager to be precise and accurate in his recollections, humble in the face of enormous wealth and a great reputation. He seemed very remarkable. So do his letters, many of them written more than half a century ago when he was a struggling entrepreneur of extraordinary warmth and intelligence, just the kind of man Frieda would be inclined to like. Her own letters – to him and others – are direct, guileless, informative, often tangy, always absorbing.

The letters and documents that follow – well over three hundred – examine the strange fate of Lawrence's manuscripts. Their dispersal has ended happily, for most of them are now owned by the University of Texas, where they are available for study by scholars from all over the world. Apart from the compelling stories they tell, the letters are important because they record the transmission of a major writer's manuscripts amid the play of market forces, freshly illuminate the personalities of Frieda and Angelo and their life together, gauge the fall and then rise of Lawrence's literary reputation, and reveal the extent to which these manuscripts supported Frieda and Angelo for twenty years, affording Frieda both the time to write and the energy to shore up Lawrence's eroded reputation. Shortly before her death in 1956, Frieda wrote to her sister Else: "This was a very good year financially. ... I never thought that I would be on such a green branch! I know Lorenzo would not begrudge it me!"[28]

Notes

1. Quoted in Sean Hignett, *Brett, From Bloomsbury to New Mexico: A Biography* (New York: Franklin Watts, 1985) p. 204.
2. *The Collected Letters of D. H. Lawrence*, ed. Harry T. Moore (New York: Viking, 1962) p. 1191.
3. *Frieda Lawrence and Her Circle: Letters from, to and about Frieda Lawrence*, ed. Harry T. Moore and Dale B. Montague (London: Macmillan, 1981) p. 7. The two quotations that follow are from pp. 9 and 10.
4. *Frieda Lawrence: The Story of Frieda von Richthofen and D. H. Lawrence* (New York: Viking, 1973) p. 263.
5. *The Letters of D. H. Lawrence*, vol. IV, ed. Warren Roberts, James T. Boulton, and Elizabeth Mansfield (Cambridge: Cambridge University Press, 1987) p. 277.
6. Unpub. letter (MS HRC), Frieda Lawrence to Angelo Ravagli, 3 December 1938.
7. Emmy ("Galka") Scheyer (1889–1945) had emigrated from Germany in 1924.
8. Jake Zeitlin, "Introductory Note", *The Manuscripts of D. H. Lawrence: A Descriptive Catalogue*, compiled by Lawrence Clark Powell with a foreword by Aldous Huxley (Los Angeles: Public Library, 1937) p. v. See Appendix B, hereafter referred to as the Powell catalogue.
9. They were divorced in 1930. Jake married his second wife, Jean ("Gina") Weyl, in 1931.
10. The first volume of Powell's autobiography recounts this period of his life. See his *Fortune and Friendship* (New York: Bowker, 1968).
11. Among Jake's papers is a note that reads "750 – 75 cents / 750 copies $350. / 25% cost JZ. / 50% cost Mrs. Dakin." Presumably Belt provided the difference. A close friend of Jake's, Susanna Bryant Dakin (1905–66) lived in Pasadena; she was a wealthy patron of literature who died in a plane crash in Mexico.
12. *The Letters of Aldous Huxley*, ed. Grover Smith (London: Chatto & Windus, 1969) pp. 421–2.
13. Letter to Roy Fenton, in ibid., p. 425.
14. Azul had been Frieda's horse since 1924, when she and Lawrence first moved to the Kiowa Ranch.
15. Confirmation can be found in Letter 71 (1 April 1937), in which Angelo wrote to Jake: "The girls was very beautiful, but insignificant for me beacause I found them very could – ".
16. For example, Frieda asked Jake to send her the manuscript of "New Mexico": "I want to give it to Christine Hughes" (Letter 163). Frieda wrote to Witter Bynner, "Did I tell you I left you one of Lorenzo's Mss. in my will?" (undated letter in *Frieda Lawrence: The Memoirs and Correspondence*, ed. E. W. Tedlock Jr (New York: Knopf, 1964) p. 320). To Richard Aldington she wrote on 29 November 1949, "I want very much to give you a Lorenzo Mss!" (*Frieda Lawrence and Her Circle*, p. 96).
17. The manuscript was "A Little Moonshine with Lemon" (*Catalogue*, No. 75), according to Jake's notation: "Gift by Frieda to young man

(unknown)''. In a communication written 5 November 1987, Larry Powell recalls that Willard Hougland may also have been the recipient of Frieda's generosity: ''Hougland appeared in my office at UCLA in the 1950s and *gave* us one or more of the mss – one being Powell #1B.''

18. Her book about their marriage is titled *The Art of Love & the Love of Art* (Blue Earth, MN: Piper, 1975).

19. *Frieda Lawrence and Her Circle*, p. 113.

20. See ''D. H. Lawrence at Texas: a Memoir'', *University of Texas Library Chronicle*, n.s., no. 34 (1986) pp. 23–37. Hereafter cited as ''Memoir'' in the text.

21. *Frieda Lawrence: The Memoirs and Correspondence*, p. 383.

22. Only two Lawrence manuscripts were in the second collection: a black notebook of 161 pages (*Catalogue*, No. 118) and two manuscript versions of ''Art and Morality'' (No. 116).

23. Knud Merrild, *A Poet and Two Painters* (1938), reissued as *With D. H. Lawrence in New Mexico: A Memoir of D. H. Lawrence* (London: Routledge & Kegan Paul, 1964) pp. 64, 83, 85.

24. Earlier the typescript of *Apocalypse* had been purchased by T. E. Hanley for $450.

25. Letter 254, dated 1 October 1954, confirms Hans de Schulthess's intent to purchase.

26. Along with a rare copy of the novel (one of two) printed on blue paper by the Tipografia Giuntina in Florence.

27. The Humanities Research Center paid $50 000 for the three manuscripts of *Lady Chatterley's Lover* (private communication, 16 August 1987). Letter 316 also indicates that $50 000 was the anticipated selling price.

28. *Frieda Lawrence: The Memoirs and Correspondence*, p. 402.

The Letters

1. Angelo Ravagli to Jake Zeitlin, [1934]

Text: TS UCLA

Kiowa Ranch, San Cristobel, New Mexico

Jake Zeitlin: Books
705½ West Sixth Street
Los Angeles, California

Dear Sir;-

We are pleased to announce our satisfactory arrangements with the Viking Press, by which we can sell *Not I, But the Wind* . . . to book dealers at six dollars per copy, to be delivered C.O.D.[1] This price is the same as that offered by the Viking Press and with the added advantage of selling before October, 1934. Those buying from the Press must withold their sales until that time.

Hoping that this announcement will prove bennificial to you, I am
Sincerely,   Angelino Ravagli.

Note
1. An edition published in 1934 by the Rydal Press, Santa Fe, NM.

2. Frieda Lawrence to Jake Zeitlin, 1 April 1936

Text: TS UCLA

Los Angeles, California
April 1, 1936

Mr Jake Zeitlin
c/o Jake Zeitlin, Inc.
614 West 6th Street
Los Angeles, California

Dear Mr Zeitlin:

I hereby authorize you to act as my sole agent in the sale of the original holograph manuscript of D. H. Lawrence's novel *The Rainbow*. I am its sole owner and have full authority to dispose of it. The price set is $7,500.00, on which your commission is 15%.

In case I offer for sale any other of D. H. Lawrence's manuscripts owned by me, I hereby authorize you to act as my exclusive agent in their disposal.

Both of these authorizations are to extend until January 1, 1937.

Very truly yours,   Frieda Lawrence

Agreed: Jake Zeitlin

3. Jake Zeitlin to Nathan van Patten, 1 April 1936
Text: TSCC UCLA

April 1, 1936

Mr Nathan Van Patten, Director
Stanford University Libraries
Stanford University, California

Dear Mr Van Patten:[1]

I have just met Frieda Lawrence and of course have found her everything you would expect as a most stimulating and interesting person.

She tells me that the coming 11th of September would be the 50th birthday of Lawrence,[2] and that she would like very much to see some form of Memorial Exhibition held at that time. As you may remember, Bumpus of London held a magnificent Lawrence exhibition in the spring of 1933. It drew a great deal of attention and comment and those who saw it remember it as a most impressive affair.

Mrs Lawrence has all of that material in her bank in London and would be glad to make it available for an exhibition, if Stanford University would be interested in holding it. Because of the facilities that you as a librarian of an educational institution would have, I think that it would be easier for you to arrange for the transportation and bringing in of this material than any private individual. In conjunction with such an exhibition I think it would be a very fine thing to issue a volume of tribute to Lawrence with contributions from outstanding literary men of today. Mr Lawrence Clark Powell here with me would be very glad to handle the gathering and editing of material for such a volume if Stanford University Press would care to publish it.

I think that this could be made a grand event for all of us and of course I would cooperate in every way. Please let me know as soon as possible what you think about the idea. Of course I know that you yourself would be immensely enthusiastic, but no doubt you will have to consult others at the University.

I shall await your reply and will let Mrs Lawrence know what you say as soon as I hear from you.

With cordial regards,   [JZ]

P.S.   Mrs Lawrence tells me that the three original manuscripts of *Lady Chatterley's Lover* are in Florence. She would like to bring the definitive one over here, but of course feels that it would not be wise to do so through any ordinary channel. Would Stanford University as an institution have any extra privileges permitting the bringing in of such a thing without examination? I know of course what your own interest would be and it may be that the manuscript would be offered for sale once it gets into the country.

Sincerely,   [JZ]

Notes
1. Nathan van Patten (1887–1956), director of libraries at Stanford University, 1927–47. Lawrence Clark Powell remembered him as "shy and reserved and indifferent to small talk" ("Nathan van Patten", *Libri*, 7 (1956) pp. 88–90).
2. It would have been Lawrence's 51st birthday.

4. Jake Zeitlin to Frank J. Hogan, 3 April 1936
Text: TSCC UCLA

April 3, 1936

Mr Frank J. Hogan
Colorado Building
Washington, D.C.

Dear Mr Hogan:[1]

I have just met Frieda Lawrence. She is grand and we have had some great talks. How you would enjoy her healthy frankness and quick understanding! I had expected to meet just the wife of a great man who died, but I found her to be a considerable person on her own account. And she talks beautifully of Lawrence and Katherine Mansfield and the others. Tonight we go to the Japanese quarter for dinner and then to see a wrestling match.

Frieda has made me her sole agent for the sale of D. H. Lawrence's manuscripts. They have never been available before and no complete manuscript of any of his novels has ever been sold. All of them are in the Westminster Bank in London, except *Lady Chatterley's Lover* which is in Florence because it cannot be brought safely to England.

The most important of Lawrence's (and my favorite) is *The Rainbow*. It is the book in which Lawrence found himself and commenced the fight for a franker relationship between men and women. I am sending you herewith a detailed account of the origin of this book, prepared by Larry Powell, which will tell you what *The Rainbow* meant in Lawrence's life and in literature.

Yesterday afternoon I talked for over two hours with Hugh Walpole about Lawrence and *The Rainbow*. I wish I had taken notes for it became an interview on the novelists of Walpole's time as he knew them. While Walpole is of another tradition, he greatly admires the work of such writers as Aldous Huxley and Virginia Woolf, and he is very fair. He said, "When I was a few years younger I believed that the first quarter of our century had produced two literary geniuses – Lawrence and Forster. Forster has not lived up to that standard. So I must say Lawrence is the one undoubted genius of our age."

I wish you could get this great manuscript of *The Rainbow*. Before seeing anyone else or publicizing the fact that I have it for sale, I am writing you. I know you believe in Lawrence and admire his work. You have a great novel collection; this would crown it.

Summer before last Bumpus of London held a memorial exhibition of Lawrence's manuscripts and first editions. It was the greatest event of its kind for many years. Larry Powell was there, as was Hugh Walpole, and both went several times.

The reason Frieda is for the first time selling some of her manuscripts is that her eldest sister, Else, is married to a Jewish professor at Heidelberg and their life has become unbearable. Frieda wants to raise enough money to bring them to this country. Lawrence and Else were the closest of friends, and it is interesting to note that *The Rainbow* is dedicated simply "To Else". It would be most touching if the sale of *The Rainbow* manuscript were the means of bringing Else and her family to a new life in this free country.

Won't you please let me know that you are interested so that I may get more exact details as to the manuscript and its price? Nothing has ever excited me as much, and I should take great pride in negotiating it for you.

Jean and Lucille[2] both send their love and yearn for your return.

Faithfully,	[JZ]

Notes

1. Frank J. Hogan (1877–1944) was a rare-book collector, an authority on Shakespeare, president of the American Bar Association (1939), and the attorney who successfully defended Los Angeles oilman E. L. Doheny against charges of bribing Secretary of the Interior Fall in the Teapot Dome scandal.
2. Jean worked in the office of E. L. Doheny's attorney; Lucille Miller was librarian to Mrs E. L. Doheny. Along with Jake, they often had lunch with Frank Hogan at the California Club.

5. Jake Zeitlin to Virginia Warren, 3 April 1936

Text: TSCC UCLA

April 3, 1936.

Miss Virginia Warren
c/o Frank J. Hogan
Colorado Building,
Washington, D.C.

Dear Virginia:

I am writing your boss today about the manuscript of D. H. Lawrence's novel *The Rainbow*. Knowing your own enthusiasm for Lawrence I want you to be sure to read the letter and the description. Boy, am I excited!

I wish you were here to meet Frieda Lawrence. She is such a grand, frank, wholesome woman. She has the manuscript of *Lady Chatterley's Lover* as well, but it is in Florence, and I believe there would be great difficulty in bringing it in.

Please do what you can to see that your boss does not put this to one side in the rush of work. I don't want anyone else to get it.

Best regards,   [JZ]

6. Nathan van Patten to Frieda Lawrence, 6 April 1936

Text: TSCC Stanford

April 6, 1936.

Mrs. Frieda Lawrence
Los Angeles, California.

My dear Mrs. Lawrence:

The Stanford University Libraries would like very much to hold an exhibition in memory of your distinguished husband, D. H. Lawrence.

You will understand, of course, in holding such an exhibition it is our purpose: (1) to commemorate the life and work of one of the outstanding personages of our time and (2) promote the cultural interests of our students. Under the circumstances all arrangements will be made directly with you. I shall be happy to cooperate in every possible way.

I assume that there will be no expense to us in connection with this exhibition other than that involved in its protection while in our possession.

Sincerely yours,   Nathan van Patten, Director.

7. Nathan van Patten to Jake Zeitlin, 6 April 1936
Text: TS UCLA

The Stanford University Libraries
April 6, 1936.

Mr. Jake Zeitlin
614 West Sixth Street
Los Angeles, California.

My dear Mr. Zeitlin:
Thank you for your letter of April 1, 1936 suggesting that we hold a D. H. Lawrence memorial exhibition.
This interests us.
I have written to Mrs. Lawrence today concerning the project.

Sincerely yours,   Nathan van Patten, Director.

8. Jake Zeitlin to Nathan van Patten, 9 April 1936
Text: TSCC UCLA

April 9, 1936.

Mr. Nathan van Patten,
Stanford University,
Palo Alto, California.

Dear Mr. van Patten:
Mrs. Lawrence has shown me your letter to her regarding the Lawrence exhibition. She and I will confer regarding this matter today, and I shall then write you.
In connection with all the manuscripts of Lawrence, I shall be glad to cooperate with you in every way to make the exhibition a success.
It was at my special urging that Mrs. Lawrence agreed to let me offer you the opportunity of having this exhibition.

Sincerely,   [JZ]

9. Nathan van Patten to Jake Zeitlin, 10 April 1936

Text: TS UCLA

The Stanford University Libraries
April 10, 1936.

Mr. Jake Zeitlin
614 West Sixth Street
Los Angeles, California.

Dear Mr. Zeitlin:

Thank you for your letter of April 9, 1936.

If arrangements for the Lawrence exhibit are not completed before the end of the month you may look forward to seeing me in Los Angeles.

I am planning to go to the California Library Association meeting in San Diego, April 29th–May 2nd inclusive.

Sincerely yours,   Nathan van Patten, Director.

10. Jake Zeitlin to Nathan van Patten, 11 April 1936

Text: TSCC UCLA

April 11, 1936.

Mr. Nathan van Patten,
Stanford University Libraries,
Palo Alto, California.

Dear Mr. van Patten:

I think it would be very good to be able to talk things over personally in regard to the Lawrence exhibition, and Mrs. Lawrence would gladly stay over until about the 28th, if she were sure you were coming down.

If, in the meantime, it were possible to start off the documents in transit to you, I think it would be a great help.

Mr. Frank Hogan, whom you will remember meeting for luncheon at the California Club, will be here in May or June, and has expressed great interest in seeing the documents while out here.

Can you tell me any details that are especially required in having this shipment sent directly to you? Mrs. Lawrence plans to instruct her agent in London to get the material from the vault of the Westminster Bank, wrap them in a number of separate packages, and forward direct to you, with the declaration made out to the effect that the material is for educational and exhibition purposes.

She is willing to pay all costs in transit, and insurance until delivery to you.

You might let me know if this is satisfactory, and we can then start things on the way.

Sincerely,   [JZ]

11. Jake Zeitlin to Frieda Lawrence, 14 April 1936
Text: TSCC UCLA

April 14, 1936.

Mrs. Frieda Lawrence,
1601 N. Stanley,
Hollywood, California.

Dear Mrs. Lawrence:

I am enclosing copies of letters I wrote to Mr. van Patten on April 1st and April 11th. These will supply you with the necessary material for writing your agent.

In instructing him, I should suggest that you have him get in touch with some book dealer in London, such as Mr. Ernest Maggs, with whom I have had business connections for a long time. Mr. Maggs or Mr. Percy Muir of Elkins Matthews, could advise him as to the best method of shipment.

By all means, instruct him to send them by a boat coming directly to the Pacific Coast rather than one going to New York.

I think that with the advice and assistance of these people, there can be no possibility of a hitch.

As regards insurance, have him cable us a notice of shipment the day it is sent, and we will cover them through our insurance agency here for you.

If any other information is needed, I shall be glad to supply it.

Sincerely,   [JZ]

12. Frieda Lawrence to Nathan van Patten, 15 April 1936
Text: MS Stanford

1601 No Stanley Ave, Hollywood, Cal
15. April 36

Dear Mr van Patten,

I am very pleased that you want to make an exhibition of Lawrence's Mss –

Mr Zeitlin tells me you will be here on the 25th – Please ring me up when you come, then we can talk about the "how" and "when" and all the rest –

I want to go back to New Mexico on the 28th –

I am also having an exhibition of Lawrence's pictures here that might interest you –

Sincerely yours   Frieda Lawrence

13. Nathan van Patten to Jake Zeitlin, 16 April 1936

Text (abridged): TS UCLA

The Stanford University Libraries
April 16, 1936.

Mr. Jake Zeitlin
614 West Sixth Street
Los Angeles, California.

Dear Mr. Zeitlin:

If nothing interferes, you may count upon seeing me on the morning of April 29th.

It will be quite all right to have the Lawrence manuscripts shipped to us. These should be addressed as follows:

The Director of Libraries
Stanford University, Calif.

Assuming that we have the exhibition in September, it will probably be necessary for us to place the material in storage for two or three months with one of the local banks. . . .

Sincerely yours,   Nathan van Patten, Director.

14. Nathan van Patten to Frieda Lawrence, 23 April 1936

Text: TSCC Stanford

April 23, 1936.

Mrs. Frieda Lawrence
1601 North Stanley Avenue
Hollywood, California.

My dear Mrs. Lawrence:

I regret very much my inability to come South on the 25th.

It is my present intention to be in Los Angeles on April 28th and I hope it will be possible for you to see me then.

Sincerely yours,   Nathan van Patten, Director.

15. Jake Zeitlin to Nathan van Patten, 6 May 1936
Text: TSCC UCLA

May 6, 1936.

Mr. Nathan Van Patten, Director,
Stanford University Libraries,
Palo Alto, California.

Dear Mr. Van Patten:

I enjoyed your visit down here very much, and I hope that the brief meeting with Mrs. Lawrence was sufficient compensation to you for your trip.[1] I hope that the inclusion of the added guest in our party did not inconvenience you.

It will probably be a few weeks before we hear from London. If you will let me know as soon as you have word, I shall be very grateful, and if I should have any communication first, I shall get in touch with you.

It is very likely that I shall be travelling North within the next two weeks. I shall let you know when I am coming, and shall hope that you can spare me some time.

With cordial regards,   [JZ]

Note
1. The meeting was a luncheon held at the Biltmore on Tuesday, 29 April.

16. Frieda Lawrence to Jake Zeitlin, 13 May 1936
Text: MS UCLA

13. May 36

Dear Jake Zeitlin,

Here we are planting and washing and scrubbing, it's a treat –

I am telling you that a nice young Harvard student[1] soaked in Lawrence is collecting all L[awrence]'s letters for Harvard –

Also send me the address of the pirate publisher of Lady C[2] – will see if I can get round him –

The minute I dive into L's things I will send you something to print –

We had good times together did'nt we?

We are very busy –

We think of you all with affection –

Yours   Frieda L –

[*Angelo Ravagli begins*:]

My regards to you and to Gina

Angelino

Notes
1. Harry K. Wells.
2. Ben Abramson (1898–1955) was apparently responsible for a reset edition of *Lady Chatterley's Lover*. See edition 4.1 ("silver phoenix on spine") as described in Jay A. Gertzman's *A Descriptive Bibliography of "Lady Chatterley's Lover", with Essays Toward a Publishing History of the Novel* (Westport, Conn.: Greenwood, 1989) p. 44.

17. Jake Zeitlin to Frieda Lawrence, 18 May 1936
Text: TSCC UCLA

May 18, 1936

Mrs. Frieda Lawrence,
Kiowa Ranch, San Cristobal,
New Mexico.

Dear Frieda and Angelo,

We were delighted to hear from you and to know that you got back safely. We had good times that will make history for me. Mickey McGeary[1] and I were sentimentalizing about that classic evening. We shall never have a chance to beat each other up again with so much good feeling during and afterwards.

Could you tell me the name and address of the young Harvard student who is collecting Lawrence's letters? I might be able to do some business with him.

We have been getting our copies of *Lady C* from the Argus Book Shop, 333 S. Dearborn St., Chicago, Illinois. Please be careful not to give my name as the source of your information.

I was just on the point of writing you to ask if you hadn't found [time] to dig up the Lawrence play you spoke of for us to print, so I am glad to hear that we may look forward to seeing it soon.

You must be having a grand time at your ranch. Gina and I speak about you and Angelo there almost every day, and wish we could jump into the car and drive out and help with the work.

Next week we go to San Francisco for the Van Gogh show, and to do some business that I hope will be most profitable.

I suppose you have not had time to hear from Pollinger[2] about your manuscripts yet?

Gina sends her affectionate regards with mine to Angelo and you,

[JZ]

Notes
1. Mickey McGeary was secretary to the famous Hollywood director, Josef Von Sternberg.
2. Laurence Edward Pollinger (1898–1976), executor of the D. H. Lawrence estate.

18. Frieda Lawrence to Jake Zeitlin, [26? June 1936]
Text: MS UCLA

Kiowa Ranch
[RECEIVED JUN 29 1936][1]

Dear Jake Zeitlin,

I wanted to send you the play, then remembered that the *Viking's* will object – But I will ask them –

I dont think about anything except the lambs and pintos and pigs and radishes and alfalfa and Angelino is building a beautiful room for L[awrence]'s pictures, the ranch is looking fine – We are busy – Pollinger will be sending the Mss soon – [2]

I have just written to the Lady C man in Chicago, see what happens, *of course* I shant mention you –

The young Harvard man is Harry K Wells, he will be here in a day or two – [3]

I hope you enjoyed the Van Gogh and did some business – Una and Robin Jeffers[4] were here and we talked about Mr Powell, now they have gone –

Just a line to you and our kindest wishes to you both and the infants – Could'nt we just do with your help!

Yours sincerely   Frieda Lawrence

Hope you are flourishing!

Notes

1. Date stamped at end of letter.
2. Probably the 104 manuscripts exhibited by John and Edward Bumpus at their shop in London, April–May 1933.
3. Harry Kohlsaat Wells (1911–76) earned an A.B. from Harvard University in 1934; married Jeannette ("Jenny") Hill in the same year (they were divorced in 1947); spent a year and a half in Europe; then founded the San Cristobal Valley Ranch School in New Mexico. In the 25th Anniversary Report of the Harvard Class of 1933, Wells wrote: "In 1936 we returned to the States and entered upon a career of high school teaching which lasted until I went into the Army in 1943." In 1949 he earned a Ph.D. from Columbia University. He wrote *Process and Unreality: A Critique of Method in the Philosophy of A. N. Whitehead* (Columbia University Press, 1950) and other books.
4. Robinson Jeffers (1887–1962), American poet; Una Jeffers, his wife.

19. Frieda Lawrence to Nathan van Patten, 12 August 1936

Text: MS Stanford

Kiowa Ranch, San Christobal, New Mexico

12. Aug 36

Dear Mr van Patten,

Have you received the manuscripts? You ought to have them by now – They left London on the 11th of July and were insured for 5000 £s. Altogether I had to pay 29.£ 2 sh –

I am glad to have them in this country. I suppose there is no way of my getting these expenses refunded?

Did you get a letter from me to you that I sent to Mr Sellards?

But perhaps you are on a vacation.

I should be glad to hear from you soon that the manuscripts have arrived safely –

Sincerely yours   Frieda Lawrence

I am having a wonderful summer –

20. Nathan van Patten to Frieda Lawrence, 18 August 1936

Text: TSCC Stanford

August 18, 1936

Mrs. Frieda Lawrence
Kiowa Ranch
San Christobal
New Mexico

Dear Mrs. Lawrence:

The manuscripts were received some time ago but we did not open the case until yesterday. Enclosed is a copy of a letter which I have just sent to Davies, Turner & Co., Ltd. calling their attention to three minor discrepancies between the shipment and the list supplied to us.

We are looking forward to the exhibition with enthusiasm. I hope that you will be able to visit us at that time.

With kindest personal regards.

Sincerely yours,   Nathan van Patten, Director.

21. Angelo Ravagli to Jake Zeitlin, 19 August 1936
Text: MS UCLA

Kiowa Ranch, San Cristobal, N.M.
19 August, 1936

To Mr. Jake Zeitlin
614 West Sixth Street
Los Angeles, Calif.

Dear Jake,

Mrs Lawrence is a bit tired and busy all the time, so I want to write you to let you know what happens about the manuscript of D. H. Lawrence – They ought to have arrived in Stanford University long time ago, beacause they were mailed from London 21st of July.

We had not a word from Van Patten, nor from you; will you try to found out them and send a line to us as soon as possible? Thank you – What are you doing dear Jake in this time?

How are you, Gina and cildren? Every thing OK? I hope so – When is the time of your olyday? Dont you think it was interesting come to see us on the Ranch?

Now up here is all sample wonderfull, air, sun, vegetables, flours, corn, oats, cows, horses, cats, lambs, good milk, fresch water – ecet – ecet – My work is all ready finished, so I think I start again to paint somethink –

Hoping you are very well – both, and you are able to come, some time, before the winter – having ours best regards for you and Gina –

Sincerly   Angelo.

P.S. If I can see you before – I hope see you again this winter in Hollywood.

22. Frieda Lawrence to Jake Zeitlin, 31 August 1936
Text: MS UCLA

31. Aug 36

Dear Jake Zeitlin,

I had heard meanwhile from Mr van Patten – The Mss are there –

I am so glad you are doing [Knud] Merrild's "Bibsy" – It is good –, Also the Césanne – Use Lawrence's essay by all means – The Viking press may want to interfere but I think they have no right – They sold a 100 copies of the book of paintings without telling me or giving me anything – By great condescension they gave me one copy – So I am cross with them –

You sound very grand in your new "estate" –

Do come, it would be awfully nice – You ought to, also the Wellses are here and he wants to arrange an exhibition at Harvard – They are only staying till the 15th but are buying a place near. This is in a hurry to let you know, please tell Don Parker and best wishes to Mr Powell – Angelino has gone to Santa Fe with the new car – or he would send his greetings to you and Gina – We are quite grand also, have worked very hard – Have 2 cows, 5 horses, 1 black pig "Lalassie" 2 lambs, one calf, Lord and how they eat!

We still hope you may come – It's lovely now –

Ever yours   Frieda L –

23. Nathan van Patten to Jake Zeitlin, 1 September 1936
Text (abridged): TS UCLA

The Stanford University Libraries
September 1, 1936

Mr. Jake Zeitlin
614 West Sixth Street
Los Angeles, California

Dear Mr. Zeitlin:

Your letter of August twenty-fourth awaited my return from a trip north. In the meantime the Lawrence manuscripts arrived from London and I have notified Mrs. Lawrence to that effect. . . .

Sincerely yours   Nathan van Patten, Director.

24. Jake Zeitlin to Nathan van Patten, 8 September 1936
Text (abridged): TSCC UCLA

September 8, 1936

Mr. Nathan van Patten, Director,
Stanford University Libraries,
Palo Alto, California.

Dear Mr. van Patten:

I am glad to have word from you that the Lawrence manuscripts have arrived, and I am most eager to see what all is included. I shall try to be in Stanford about the 22nd in order that I may look them over and discuss your plans with you. Mrs. Lawrence writes me that she has a visitor from Harvard who is very anxious to arrange an exhibition of the manuscripts there. I also want to see what can be done here, and there are, of course, other places about the country that will want to show them. . . .

With cordial regards,   [JZ]

25. Harry K. Wells to Nathan van Patten, 8 September 1936
Text: MS Stanford

Kiowa Ranch, San Cristobal, New Mexico
9/8/36

Dear Mr. Van Patten,

Mrs. Lawrence has asked me to write you. I am a graduate student in Philosophy at Harvard and am doing my doctor's on D.H. Lawrence. We want to arrange to have an exhibition of the D.H.L. M.S.S. at Harvard and to that end would like to know how long you will have them at Stanford. Would it be possible for us to have them during the second semester of the current academic year? Please let me know. You can address me: *Harry K. Wells, 65 Langdon Street, Cambridge, Mass.*

Also Mrs. Lawrence would like to have a list of the M.S.S. which are now at Stanford – and I would appreciate one, too, if it is not too much trouble to you. Thanking you in advance and wishing you all success in the exhibition, I am, yours sincerely,

Harry K. Wells

26. Nathan van Patten to Frieda Lawrence, 12 September 1936
Text: TSCC Stanford

September 12, 1936.

Mrs. Frieda Lawrence
Kiowa Ranch
San Cristobal, New Mexico.

My dear Mrs. Lawrence:

At the request of Mr. Harry K. Wells, I am sending a copy of the list of D. H. Lawrence material shipped to us by Davies, Turner & Co., Limited, London, England.

This list is modified by the three slight discrepancies mentioned in my letter of August 18, 1936, sent to the shippers. You also have a copy of this letter.

We are planning to exhibit the Lawrence material between September 21 and October 31, 1936. I hope that you will find it possible to visit us during this period.

Sincerely yours,   Nathan van Patten, Director.

27. Frieda Lawrence to Nathan van Patten, [mid-September? 1936]

Text: MS Stanford

TAOS, NEW MEXICO

Dear Mr van Patten,

I hope you are pleased with all the odds and ends in the list you sent me. It will make such a lively exhibition – Thank you very much for the list.

I am tempted to come, but there is so much to do here and people coming and they are doing a play at Chicago (*David* I *think*) I shall want to go –

In January we will be in Hollywood. Will you please keep the Mss for me till then, or wait till you hear from me. There are several unpublished items, so we have to be careful.

Later on Harvard wants to make an exhibition.

Hoping to see you in California

sincerely yours   Frieda Lawrence

Wells is writing on Lawrence, he is an energetic, clever young man – I suppose you dont come my way, but if you do, come and see us –

Sincerely yours   Frieda Lawrence

28. Frieda Lawrence to Jake Zeitlin, [mid-September? 1936]

Text: MS UCLA

Dear Jake Zeitlin,

Mr van Patten will finish with the Stanford exhibition, on October 31. Harvard also wants the Mss. But I thought you might like to exhibit after the 31 of Oct. There are also several unpublished things – I would defy the Vikings if you want any. There are all sorts of odds and ends that will make the exhibition lively, paintings and drawings etc.

I wish you could come, it's wonderful, the hills mountains really turning the yellowest yellow you ever saw –

I have not heard from Merrild for some time, they were coming here –

We come to Hollywood again after Xmas.

They are going to do L[awrence]'s David I think in Chicago, that thrills me –

Love to you both from Angelino too

sincerely   Frieda L –

29. Nathan van Patten to Jake Zeitlin, 21 September 1936
Text: TS UCLA

The Stanford University Libraries
September 21, 1936.

Mr. Jake Zeitlin
614 West Sixth Street
Los Angeles, California.

Dear Mr. Zeitlin:

I am postponing my trip to Los Angeles until some time during the coming month. Please be sure to see me while you are up this way.

We will, of course, be happy to give Mr. Powell every assistance with his work on D. H. Lawrence.

I do not feel, however, that it would be proper for me to actually let him handle the manuscripts unless Mrs. Lawrence specifically requests me to do so.

With kindest personal regards, I am

Sincerely yours,   Nathan van Patten, Director.

30. Jake Zeitlin to Lawrence Clark Powell, 25 September 1936
Text: TSCC UCLA

September 25, 1936

Dr. Lawrence Clark Powell,
2726 Derby St.,
Berkeley, California.

Dear Larry,

Would you go over to Stanford and ask Mr. van Patten to let you look over the Lawrence material? I have written him to the effect that you are coming, and have sent him Mrs. Lawrence's letter authorizing us to have access to the material.

What I want you to do is to give me an estimate of how much it would be worth to you to prepare a descriptive catalogue which I could use in selling the material.

If your fee is not too high, I think I can get the proposition okayed. Please go over right away, and write me promptly, as we shall want to get started without delay.

Best regards,   [JZ]

31. Jake Zeitlin to Nathan van Patten, 25 September 1936

Text: TSCC UCLA

September 25, 1936

Mr. Nathan van Patten, Director,
Stanford University Libraries,
Stanford University,
Palo Alto, California.

Dear Mr. van Patten:

I am very sorry if I caused you to postpone your visit to Los Angeles. It has turned out that I had to stay here after all. Mr. A. J. Wall, Librarian of the New York Historical Society, is in town, and I have been spending a good deal of my time with him. It would have been pleasant for you two to have met, since I am sure you would have got along royally.

With regard to Mr. Powell's work on the D. H. Lawrence material, what I want to have him do is to prepare a descriptive and annotated catalogue which I intend to use in connection with its sale. Naturally, I expect all the work to be done on your premises – he will not have to take anything away with him.

As regards having access to the material, I am enclosing a letter of authority which Mrs. Lawrence has given me. In case you need any further authority, I shall be glad to supply it, however I think this letter will serve completely to protect you.

I am asking Mr. Powell to come over to see you for a preliminary inspection right away, and I shall appreciate any courtesies you may show him.

I shall look forward to your visit here in October, and hope that I can make it a really enjoyable sojourn.

Best regards,   [JZ]

32. Jake Zeitlin to Frieda Lawrence, 26 September 1936

Text: TSCC UCLA

September 26, 1936

Mrs. Frieda Lawrence,
Kiowa Ranch,
San Cristobal, New Mexico.

Dear Frieda,

How sad it makes us not to be able to visit you. We both want so much to come.

The documents will no doubt be on exhibition within the next few days. I have asked Mr. Powell to go over to Stanford and look them over with the end in view of having him prepare a complete descriptive catalogue. When the exhibition at Stanford is over, I am arranging with an institution here to exhibit the collection during the month of November. December, of course, is no month in which to exhibit anything.

Why not write your friend at Harvard that he can have it to show in January?

I am making extensive plans for offering some of the items to several good prospects as soon as I have the complete descriptive list. Since your contract with me is up at the end of this year, I wish you would write me a letter extending it to cover the year 1937, since I shall have such a short time to work on it during this year.

I am planning to make considerable outlay in order properly to sell some of the material and get the highest prices, and as soon as I have received your renewal, I shall proceed with my plans.

Gina and I send our best regards to Angie. He said something about being in Hollywood this winter. Just when do you think that will be?

With our most affectionate regards,   [JZ]

33. Lawrence Clark Powell to Jake Zeitlin, 28 September 1936

Text (abridged): TS UCLA

2726 Derby St, Berkeley
September 28, 1936

Dear Jake:

I have your letter regarding the possibility of my doing for you a sales catalog of the Lawrence material. I am interested. I had already written Van Patten and planned to run down for the show sometime in October. Now that you have greased the skids by a letter to V. P., I'll go this

Saturday and be able to see the stuff before it is put on display. V. P. tells me that they are issuing a brief handlist, based on the Bumpus one; not remembering the Bumpus list, I don't know what he plans, whether collation of mss. in addition to descriptive note (which it seems to me should be done in sales catalog) or just the latter.

Do you want it done fairly at length, going into each item, say, to the extent that I did the *Rainbow* description? If there is a lot of collating involved and examination of individual items rather carefully, it means that I would have to work there at the Stanford library – whereas, of course, the descriptive, literary, notes of origin and background, etc. of the mss. could be done here at home.

The point is, I don't have a lot of time free save Saturdays; and the round trip down the peninsula to Palo Alto, crossing the bay each way either by ferry here or one of the two lower toll bridges, would run into time and money.

Here's what I'll do: go down Saturday, look everything over, then report to you what seems to me the best way to catalog the stuff for sale. If I can get by with, say, one additional trip and do the bulk of the work here at home, I believe it would work out. . . .

affectionately, Larry

34. Nathan van Patten to Jake Zeitlin, 28 September 1936
Text: TS UCLA

The Stanford University Libraries
September 28, 1936.

Mr. Jake Zeitlin
614 West Sixth Street
Los Angeles, California.

Dear Mr. Zeitlin:

We will be happy, of course, to give Mr. Powell every assistance in the preparation of the catalog of Lawrence material.

I believe that he should arrange to do this work after the exhibition is concluded. You can readily understand how awkward it will be to remove items from the exhibit with any frequency.

Sincerely yours, Nathan van Patten, Director.

35. Nathan van Patten to Lawrence Clark Powell, 29 September 1936
Text: TSCC UCLA

September 29, 1936.

Mr. Lawrence Clark Powell
2726 Derby Street
Berkeley, California.

Dear Mr. Powell:

I wrote to Mr. Zeitlin yesterday saying that we would be happy to give you every facility for the cataloging of the Lawrence manuscripts. I pointed out to him however that it would be very inconvenient for us to have to remove piece after piece of manuscript from an exhibition while in progress. It would be better to plan to do this work after the close of the exhibition.

Saturdays the library offices close at noon and there would be no one here to open the cases. When we arranged the Lawrence exhibition I did not expect that this material was being brought into this country for sale. If I had even suspected this I would not have planned to show the manuscripts here.

When permission was given to me to hold this exhibition I was specifically instructed by the University to make my arrangements directly with Mrs. Lawrence and to prevent any commercial aspect to enter in the matter. It seems best to make these points clear.

We desire to be as helpful to Mr. Zeitlin as may be possible, but circumstances do not permit me to act upon my own responsibility in this connection.

Sincerely yours,   Nathan van Patten, Director.

c.c. to Mr. Jake Zeitlin.

36. Nathan van Patten to Frieda Lawrence, 2 October 1936
Text: TSCC Stanford

October 2, 1936.

Mrs. Frieda Lawrence
Taos, New Mexico.

My dear Mrs. Lawrence:

Thank you very much for your recent letter.

The Lawrence manuscripts are now on exhibition. We expect that this will be one of the most interesting exhibitions we have ever had here.

I am very sorry that you will not be able to visit us now. May we look forward to seeing you when you are in Los Angeles for the Winter?

Sincerely yours,   Nathan van Patten, Director.

37. Jake Zeitlin to Nathan van Patten, 5 October 1936

Text: TSCC UCLA

October 5, 1936

Mr. Nathan van Patten, Director,
Stanford University Libraries,
Stanford University,
Palo Alto, California.

Dear Mr. van Patten:

In view of the inconvenience of cataloging the material during the exhibition, I have decided to postpone making this until it closes.

I am sorry that you did not understand that Mrs. Lawrence's ultimate purpose was to sell some of the manuscripts. My own thought was that it would be quite a nice thing for you to have the first opportunity to exhibit the collection in this country. Harvard wanted the exhibit, and several local institutions would have been glad to have it.

In looking over the carbon of my letter to you of April 1st, I notice that in the post script I refer to the fact that there would be a possibility of the manuscripts being offered for sale. Please do not feel that I have wanted to take any commercial advantage of you in arranging this cooperation.

I shall definitely be going North between the 15th and 19th of this month. At that time I shall come to see you, and we shall have a good chance to talk over the matter.

With cordial regards,   [JZ]

38. Frieda Lawrence to Jake Zeitlin, 6 October 1936

Text: MS UCLA

6. Oct 36

Dear Jake Zeitlin,

Here is the extension – Dont mind if I want to keep some of my favourites.

Do you want more than 10 percent, that is what Pollinger wanted. I will ask Wells, if he has any Mss he wants to buy. He bought some very interesting D. H. L. to Bertrand Russell letters.[1]

Please thank Mr Parkes for the Argus list.[2]

Pornography and so on is by Faber and Faber.

But I have an idea that the book of Paintings is altogether pirated, there are too many about –

I want you to keep the Mss after the exhibition, that you arrange for me, till we come in January, then I can send them to Wells. It cost 29 £s to have them sent from England.

I am glad Mr Powell went to Stanford.

I think that's all. We have had snow already, but it's wonderful, next year you must come and enjoy it, you Gina, children and all –

Another book of L[awrence]'s Phoenix is coming.

I am writing again and like it. Angelino is painting the corral and the pub at his home.

They are going to do a play in Chicago. David very likely.

So I hope to see you before long, you sound very flourishing –

Kindest regards

Write again and say how Mr Powell liked the exhibition.

                    Yours sincerely and affectionately   Frieda

Please thank Mr Parkes.

No I did'nt send the extension, you type it and I sign – dont know how you want it worded –

Notes

1. In 1989 Jenny Wells Vincent recalled that she and her husband "took Bertrand Russell to lunch in London and arranged to buy his DHL correspondence. It was the summer of 1935. He said he needed the money, as he was about to be married again." According to Frieda Lawrence the Wellses paid $1000 for the letters (Letter 46).

2. The Argus Book Shop, Chicago, was operated by Ben Abramson. See Letter 16, n. 2.

39. Nathan van Patten to Jake Zeitlin, 8 October 1936
Text: TS UCLA

                    The Stanford University Libraries
                              October 8, 1936.

Mr. Jake Zeitlin
614 West 6th Street
Los Angeles, California.

My dear Mr. Zeitlin:

Thank you very much for your good letter of October 5, 1936.

I hope that you will not misunderstand my attitude in regard to the Lawrence manuscripts. I am anxious to do everything possible to further your interests and those of Mrs. Lawrence in connection with the sale of this material. At the same time I am under the obligation to keep our exhibits free from anything which might be construed as commercial.

I will look forward to seeing you here sometime between the 15th and 19th although you may see me in Los Angeles before then.

With all good wishes, I am

                    Sincerely yours,   Nathan van Patten, Director.

40. Frieda Lawrence to Una Jeffers, 10 October 1936

Text: MS UCBerkeley

10. Oct 36

Dear Una,

Thank you for your article – I have not seen Murry's introduction, so he "wants to come round."

I feel detached having made up my mind and more than my mind long ago – Now it bores me.

But Miriam's book was *moving*,[1] and I wrote to her, telling her, that after all she must be pleased and proud to have been so important to Lawrence's development – She must have been and I can only be grateful to her for his sake –

His home was just that passionate, limited life of the common people and her intellectual passion must have been a relief and outlet to him –

But I think his mother must have had a tremendous power of love and then when she was dying clung to him as a dying thing clings to life – I dont think his love was pathological, his mother was the "better horse", she must have been just very lovable and no complex about that –

Miriam does'nt amount to much humanly; in my opinion Miriam let Lawrence down. Had she given him one scrap of simple human warmth after the mother's death he might have loved her, but she just waited and did nothing – She lived only in her *head*, any thing physical was a sacrifice for her and then a man feels humiliated – Lawrence hated her for that, she had nothing of her own, no spontaneous life. Had he married her he would have been à la Aldous Huxley, purely intellectual and of course most people would have preferred that – He would have been a little local poet, a watered down Thomas Hardy –

After all it's human nature, every man, woman or child feels "I am the right thing". – I do the same and think, that I was the thing for Lawrence, anyhow he thought so too – – – There was so much fulfilment – or I could not feel so satisfied in my very bones and marrow –

We have had a beautiful summer – I had a charming young couple Harry K Wells here, he just lives and breathes Lawrence, is collecting all Lawrence's letters for Harvard and is writing and knows more about our lives than I do –

They bought a place not far away –

Also there is an exhibition of Lawrence's Mss at Stanford, if you can go, do –

We will come to Carmel, and will love to see you. Mrs Younghunter was thrilled by your house – We have had snow already, one day you must see the autumn here –

There has been such peace –
Angelino and I greet you from our yellow mountains –

All the best wishes to you   Frieda

Note

1. Jessie Chambers, the model for Miriam Leivers in Lawrence's novel *Sons and Lovers* (1913), had published *D. H. Lawrence: A Personal Record* (London: Cape, 1935) under the pseudonym E. T.

41. Jake Zeitlin to Frieda Lawrence, 12 October 1936
Text: TSCC UCLA

October 12, 1936

Mrs. Frieda Lawrence,
Kiowa Ranch,
San Cristobal, New Mexico.

Dear Frieda,

Enclosed is a copy of the renewal of our agreement. I am trying to include all the points which might be necessary to deal with. As regards commissions, selling rare manuscripts is much more costly a business than selling literary rights, and I really should have more than the agreed 15%. After all, I shall probably more than earn it in the increased prices I shall be able to get.

Within a few days I shall be going to Stanford. Mr. van Patten is not very much interested in letting us catalogue the manuscripts while they are on exhibition, so we shall have to wait until after it closes. You understand the spirit in which Mr. van Patten has been cooperating, so I need not comment further.

The first copy of the list that I make will be sent to you right away, so that you can show it to Mr. Wells. I shall also want to confer with you as to prices, since we shall naturally want to be in perfect agreement.

After I have been to Stanford I shall be better able to talk to you about future plans, but in the meantime I shall count on bringing them down here after the exhibition closes there and exhibiting them during the Book Fair here, then put them in my vault until your arrival.

Please don't tell us any more about how beautiful it is there. It makes staying here all the more painful.

I am glad to hear that you are writing again. You should. You have much to say, and say it so well.

Affectionate regards from Gina and me to Angie and you.

Cordially,   [JZ]

42. Frieda Lawrence to Jake Zeitlin, 12 October 1936

Text: TS UCLA

October 12, 1936

Mr. Jake Zeitlin,
614 W. 6th St.,
Los Angeles, California.

Dear Mr. Zeitlin:

With reference to our agreement of April 1, 1936, I herewith authorize its extension for an additional period of 12 months, from January 1, 1937 to January 1, 1938.

It is understood that I reserve the right to withhold from sale any of the manuscripts which I desire.

In case any of the manuscripts or letters are sold during the year, your agreed commission will apply.

Sincerely,   Frieda Lawrence

43. Harry K. Wells to Jake Zeitlin, 17 October 1936

Text: Telegram UCLA

1936 Oct 17 AM 11 06

JAKE ZEITLIN, CARE JOHN HOWELL
434 POST ST SFRAN

EXHIBITION ALL ARRANGED AT HARVARD FOR NOVEMBER VERY IMPORTANT HAVE EXHIBIT HERE WHEN COLLECTION IS COMPLETE BEFORE YOU SELL ANY ITEMS STOP WE COULD RETURN MANUSCRIPTS TO YOU BY MIDDLE OF NOVEMBER PLEASE WIRE YOUR ANSWER AT ONCE ADDRESS SIXTY FIVE LANGDON STREET CAMBRIDGE MASS

HARRY K WELLS.

44. Jake Zeitlin to Harry K. Wells, 20 October 1936

Text: TSCC UCLA

614 West 6th Street, Los Angeles, California
October 20, 1936

Mr. Harry K. Wells
65 Langdon Street
Cambridge, Massachusetts

Dear Mr. Wells:

Your telegram reached me Saturday in San Francisco and I replied immediately. Today I am at Stanford seeing the collection and talking with Mr. van Patten. I have not sold anything as yet although they are interested in several things and want a price set. A collector in San Francisco also has asked me to set prices but I have refrained. The main reason is that I think the collection should all stay together. Do you think that if Mrs. Lawrence could be induced to set a price on the lot as a whole that there is any chance of the money being raised? Before I do anything else about it I should like to hear from you.

My plans are to have the collection sent down to me in the next few days. I shall then give them a good looking over and repack and express to you. I shall also send you a list of what is included.

How sorry I am we could not meet when you were at San Cristobal. I hope there will be some reason for your coming out again soon. In the meantime, I shall await your reply.

Sincerely,   Jake Zeitlin.

45. Jake Zeitlin to Frieda Lawrence, 20 October 1936

Text: TSCC UCLA

614 W. 6th Street, Los Angeles, California
October 20, 1936

Mrs. Frieda Lawrence
Kiowa Ranch
San Cristobal, New Mexico

Dear Frieda Lawrence:

This is being written from Mr. van Patten's office. I have just been looking over the collection and it is simply overwhelming. I am confused by the problem of how to value it here and have decided to have it sent down to me before I forward it to Mr. Wells. Wells telegraphed me a few days ago and I am planning to ship it all on to him for exhibition in November (1st to 15th). In the meantime I have copied Mr. van Patten's typewritten list and shall send it on to you. Will you please indicate on it the items you wish to keep, as well as any other information that might help. Where any are unpublished to your knowledge would you indicate that in the margin? Stanford would be interested in buying some unpublished manuscript. Would you let them have the right to print it? With royalties to you, of course.

As soon as you have sent this list back to me I shall prepare a tentative price list and submit for your approval. Please return it as quickly as possible.

Harvard should really buy the whole collection and keep it intact. Would you set a price on the whole thing? There are 177 items. I understand you had some valuation fixed at one time. Lawrence's memory would be so much better served if they could be kept together.

Let me hear from you soon. I am writing Wells.

Love to you from Gina and me,   [JZ]

46. Frieda Lawrence to Jake Zeitlin, 20 October 1936
Text: MS UCLA

20. Oct 36

Dear Jake Zeitlin,

Dan Wells wants the Mss for November at Harvard. I hope it is the same to you if we bring them to Los Angeles in *January* –

He wants to buy some, so I send you his address

Harry K Wells
65 Langdon Street
Cambridge

I think it's better you make a price, I dont know enough about it.

I only know he paid 1000 d[ollars] for Lawr[ence] letters to Bertrand Russell for a few 12 or 15 letters but interesting, the same to Orioli.

Here is the contract. I hope 15% covers your work, Pollinger only wanted 10%.

To-day it tries to snow. We have killed a lamb and expect a party, but fear the road is too bad.

We are in the wilds, you know. I hope it will be possible to stay here till Xmas. I want to make a Xmas tree outside and a fire.

I have worked hard about Mss. So many have disappeared and been stolen.

Wells has already a list from Van Patten.

I wonder if people in your part of the world want to buy.

It is also better when we can talk about prices. Yes, I know, Van Patten is not keen to cooperate, *why*, do you think?

Affectionate greetings from us both to you all –

Frieda L –

[*Angelo Ravagli adds*:]
And me   Angelino

47. Harry K. Wells to Jake Zeitlin, 22 October 1936
Text: MS UCLA

65 Langdon Street, Cambridge, Massachusetts
Oct. 22, 1936

Dear Mr. Zeitlin,

Thank you for your letter. I, too, think the collection should be kept together. And I would like to have first choice. I think Frieda might name a round figure and let the whole go. That is another reason why I am eager to have the collection here for a bit. If I find I couldn't get them myself, I might be able to convince Harvard to help, providing the M.S.S. be given to the library.

So I hope you will sell nothing until I've had a chance at them. When do you think you could ship the collection off? I will pay expenses, of course.

It is too bad we did not meet in San Cristobal. But we have bought a ranch near Frieda's[1] so perhaps another time.

Thank you for your thoughtful cooperation.

Very sincerely,   Harry K. Wells

I have a list of the M.S.S. that are at Stanford.

Note

1. In 1989 Jenny Wells Vincent recalled: "When we were out riding horseback, we found and bought a ranch of 60 acres, with a house, for $2,500."

48. Frieda Lawrence to Jake Zeitlin, 23 October 1936
Text: MS UCLA

23. Oct 36

Dear Jake Zeitlin,

I am glad you are so impressed by the Mss, I not so much, so many have disappeared.

I wish Harvard would buy all the Mss, including Lady C, there are 3 complete copies, all different, 2 not published – Rosenbach[1] approached me after Lawr[ence]'s death for how much I would sell all Mss. On the spur of the moment I said 25000 Pounds – Now I think hardly enough –

I had told Wells he could have unpublished material, he would like to edit it, is so soaked in Lawr.

I have left some Mss in my will, but could change – if people wanted them.

For myself I want to keep "Hayhut in the mountains["] and ["]Chapel among the mountains."

When you send me the list, I will tell what I have left to Aldous Huxley etc – I am glad it is allright about Harvard. You would like Wells. He is energetic and very keen and intelligent.

Just a line, will write again when I hear from you –

Yours sincerely   Frieda Lawrence

[*Angelo Ravagli begins*:]

All my remember to you and Gina. We see may be for Xrismas time –

Angelino

Note
1. The dealer A. S. F. Rosenbach, who founded the Rosenbach Museum and Library in Philadelphia.

49. Jake Zeitlin to Frieda Lawrence, 29 October 1936
Text: TSCC UCLA

October 29th, 1936

Dear Frieda,

Your letter of Oct. 20th was here when I came back. I have been thinking over the matter of price and while I can fairly well estimate the worth of some of the manuscripts, it is all guesswork as regards the others.

Wells has written me and says, "If I find I can't get them myself I might be able to get Harvard to help, provided that the Mss be given to the Library. So I hope you will sell nothing until I have had a chance at them."

This sounds very favorable. I propose that you select the things on the attached list which you do not wish sold and that we name him a figure on the collection. Perhaps I will be able to go to Harvard if he indicates sufficient interest. What do you think of a price of $75,000.00. More, of course, might be realized in time by selling piecemeal but that would take several years and then the manuscripts would be dispersed. What a fine memorial it would be for Lawrence too to have them in one place.

Write me back then soon letting me know what you think of my idea for a price. Also send back the list with check marks thus (X) in front of the things you don't wish sold.

Love to you both,   [JZ]

P.S.   Your letter of the 23rd just came. 25000 pounds is a great deal of money. The question is have they that much money? I should be glad to see that much realized of course. Perhaps the best thing is to wait until we know more about the interest they show. Tell Angie we'll throw a grand Christmas party if you come.

50. Jake Zeitlin to Harry K. Wells, 31 October 1936
Text: TSCC UCLA

October 31, 1936

Mr. Harry K. Wells,
65 Langdon St.,
Cambridge, Massachusetts.

Dear Mr. Wells:
There will be some delay in getting the manuscripts off. This is, however, not due to me, since I made my promises based on those of Mr. van Patten at the Stanford University Library. He assured me that the manuscripts would be put in transit to me last Monday. I then planned to take one day for preparing a new inventory of them, and then planned to send them on immediately.

I have just called Mr. van Patten on long distance. He informed me that the manuscripts were held up until yesterday due to insurance complications, but that they are now in the express, and should reach me Monday morning.

I greatly regret this delay, and hope that you will not be too much inconvenienced.

Frieda has written me concerning the possibility of selling the complete collection with, of course, the exception of certain things that she has left in her will for Aldous Huxley, and a few other things which do not belong to her. She also plans, however, to include the three different manuscripts of *Lady Chatterley's Lover*, which are at present in Florence but which – I do not doubt – could be imported under the auspices of the University without undue inconvenience.

After the collection is on exhibition and you have had a chance to study it, we shall be better able to effect a valuation. Frieda, I know, is very enthusiastic about you and your interest in Lawrence, and would give you special consideration on that account.

I do not know when I have been so thrilled as I was the day I looked over the collection. There is such an abundance of fine material, and it is so varied.

You may be assured that there will be no further delay from my end. The manuscripts will be put in transit by Wednesday at the latest.

With kind regards,   [JZ]

51. Harry K. Wells to Jake Zeitlin, 2 November 1936
Text: Telegram UCLA

CONCORD MASS
1936 NOV 2 AM 11 29

JAKE ZEITLIN
614 WEST SIXTH ST LOSA

YOUR LETTER RECEIVED MUCH BETTER IF I CAN HAVE MANUSCRIPTS FOR WHOLE MONTH OF NOVEMBER PLEASE SEND THEM TO ME AT HARVARD COLLEGE LIBRARY CAMBRIDGE THANK YOU AGAIN

HARRY K WELLS.

52. Frieda Lawrence to Jake Zeitlin, 4 November 1936
Text: MS UCLA

4. Nov 36

Dear Jake Zeitlin,

I am waiting for a letter from Dan Wells. I was scared myself when I said to Rosenbach 25000 £s – But then I think Lady C is with "Ulysses" and (I think Lady C of *more* importance) *the* outstanding book[1] of our day –

But I think I would take 75000 dol – I am asking my children, because I consider this money theirs –

I send you a list of the Mss I left in my will to Aldous Huxley and so on –

It's still lovely and I want weather permitting to have Xmas here –
I would be glad if Harvard bought all the stuff –

All the best to you both   Frieda L –

Borderline
Eric Gill Artnonsense
David
Plumed Serpent
Jimmy and the desperate woman
Lovely Lady
St Mawr
The woman who rode away
Mornings in Mexico
Wintry Peacock

These I left in my will. I want to keep for myself

A hayhut among the mountains
A chapel among the mountains

that's *all* –

[*Angelo Ravagli begins:*]
My best regards to you and to Gina, hoping see you at Xmas Time

love   Angelino

Note
1. *the* outstanding book]   two outstanding books

53. Jake Zeitlin to Harry K. Wells, 6 November 1936

Text (abridged): TSCC UCLA

November 6, 1936

Mr. Harry K. Wells,
65 Langdon St.,
Cambridge, Massachusetts.

Dear Mr. Wells:

The Lawrence manuscripts were sent off by insured express on Wednesday morning. They should reach you by the end of this week. It was most thrilling to go through them and handle them. Somehow, I felt as if I were talking to the man, and what an astonishing man!

Really, the material should be rearranged and put up in more suitable cases. It is too fine just to be left in paper wrappers. There is such an immense amount of it, of course, that any effort to care for it adequately would be expensive. . . .

What a marvelous thing it would be to have such a collection all in one place!

I do hope that Harvard will react favorably to your idea. Let me hear from you when the manuscripts arrive. You are in for a grand treat.

Sincerely,　　[JZ]

54. Jake Zeitlin to Frieda Lawrence, 6 November 1936

Text: TSCC UCLA

November 6, 1936

Mrs. Frieda Lawrence,
Kiowa Ranch,
San Cristobal, New Mexico.

Dear Frieda Lawrence:

The manuscripts arrived last Wednesday, and I spent all afternoon and evening going through them. They are a marvellous group, and I hope that Wells can find it possible to carry out his plan.

In checking carefully with the list which Mr. van Patten sent you, I find the following differences:

1. No. 71, manuscript, "Enslaved by Civilization," seems to be a duplicate listing of No. 66.
2. No. 88, "Women are so Cocksure," seems to be a duplicate listing.

Also, there are the following items which were not listed:

1. Ms. "Making Pictures." 6 pages on carcassone stationery.
2. Corrected typescript – "Chaos and Poetry."

3. Corrected typescript – "The Last Laugh."

It is nice to know that there are some items there more than were listed originally, and I hope that not so much is missing as you have feared. They have been sent off by express, insured for $25,000 to Mr. Wells. No doubt you will hear from him direct when they arrive.

It was a grand treat to look them over, and I know that we can do very well at selling them. Naturally, I should prefer to see them stay in a group. While checking through, I made some tentative estimates of possible retail prices. Naturally, I would not offer them at these prices without your confirmation. There is time enough for us to go into this matter, but in the meantime, I have a much better conception of the material and what it should be worth.

What a pity so much good material was put into *Phoenix* as one volume. The essay on Thomas Hardy would have made an excellent separate publication, and there are other things which would have been whole books in themselves. Please do not give any one permission to publish any of Lawrence's other unpublished material without letting me discuss it with you. I think you are being very generous with some very valuable properties.

With best regards to Angie,   [JZ]

55. Harry K. Wells to Jake Zeitlin, 12 November 1936
Text: MS UCLA

75 Main Street, Concord, Mass.
Nov. 12, 1936

Dear Mr. Zeitlin –

The precious case has arrived, cargo intact.

I am in the process of checking it over very thoroughly, and I find many unlisted items – especially in the notebooks – the latter I find the most interesting.

Thank you for sending them so promptly. It will take a few days to organize them for the exhibition. It's lucky they do not have to be returned the 15th!

Harvard *is* interested. But I don't know what they will do about it.

Yours   Harry K. Wells

Please note change of address.

56. Jake Zeitlin to Frieda Lawrence, 17 November 1936
Text: TSCC UCLA

November 17, 1936

Mrs. Frieda Lawrence,
Kiowa Ranch,
San Cristobal, New Mexico.

Dear Frieda,

Mr. Wells has written me that the manuscripts arrived, and he is, of course, very much interested. He also tells me that Harvard is interested, but that he does not know yet what they will do about it.

A Mrs. Bert Campbell came into my shop yesterday. She is very much interested in Lawrence, and has started to collect his first editions. She would like to have a copy of your special edition of *Not I, But the Wind*. Would you autograph it for her – Marian Campbell – and send it to me with the bill, as soon as possible?

I hope things are well with you and Angie.

Gina sends her regards.

[JZ]

57. Jake Zeitlin to Harry K. Wells, 17 November 1936
Text: TSCC UCLA

November 17, 1936

Mr. Harry K. Wells,
75 Main St.,
Concord, Massachusetts.

Dear Mr. Wells:

I was glad to hear that the manuscripts arrived safely. I knew that there were a great many unlisted items in the notebooks and elsewhere, as you say, and I hope you will find it possible to prepare a more complete list than the one I used.

I hope your exhibition stimulates the Harvard interest as it should, and I shall be very glad to hear how it progresses.

Sincerely,   [JZ]

58. Harry K. Wells to Frieda Lawrence, 17 November [1936]

Text: Telegram HRC

CONCORD MASS NOV 17 925P

MRS FRIEDA LAWRENCE
KIOWA RANCH SAN CRISTOBAL NEAR TAOS NMEX

DEAR FRIEDA HARVARD IS ASKING YOU TO LECTURE HERE PROBABLY DECEMBER EIGHT STOP[1] THEY WILL PAY YOU ONE HUNDRED DOLLARS FOR LECTURE PLUS ALL EXPENSES INCLUDING PRIVATE ROOM ON TRAIN STOP MAIN OBJECT IS TO TALK ABOUT HARVARD BUYING THE MANUSCRIPTS STOP THEY ARE VERY INTERESTED STOP IT IS EXTREMELY IMPORTANT THAT YOU COME STOP PARTIES ARE BEING ARRANGED FOR YOU STOP YOU WILL BE TREATED ROYALLY STOP IT WILL BE THE BEST THING FOR LAWRENCE IN AMERICA STOP IT IS REALLY A SPLENDID OPPORTUNITY STOP PLEASE WIRE ME YOUR REACTIONS STOP HARVARD WILL NOTIFY YOU OFFICIALLY STOP PLEASE DO COME IT IS SO IMPORTANT BEST TO YOU

DAN

Note

1. Robert Hillyer, chairman of the Gray Committee, sent Frieda Lawrence a telegram on 18 November inviting her to speak on Lawrence's poetry.

59. Harry K. Wells to Frieda Lawrence, 21 November [1936]

Text: Telegram HRC

CONCORD MASS NOV 21 142P

MRS FRIEDA LAWRENCE
SANCRISTOBAL NMEX (NEAR TAOS)

DEAR FRIEDA WE ARE SO HAPPY THAT YOU WILL REALLY COME WE ARE COUNTING ON YOUR STAYING HERE IN CONCORD WITH US YOU WILL LIKE IT MUCH BETTER THAN IN CAMBRIDGE NOT SO STUFFY THE PRESS WILL BE HERE AND WE [C]AN TALK OVER PLANS THE LECTURE IS THE ELEVENTH SO YOU HAD BETTER LEAVE THE SIXTH OR SEVENTH PLEASE WRITE DETAILS OF YOUR PLANS I WILL WRITE TOO

DAN

60. Frieda Lawrence to Jake Zeitlin, 21 November 1936
Text: MS UCLA

21. Nov. 36

Dear Jake Zeitlin,

A long telegram from Harvard, want me to come and lecture 11. Dec for 250 dollars –

Also they are interested in buying Mss –

We leave in about a week – Dont you want to come too?

You know you are the agent – You were a prophet! I never thought of Harvard buying the Mss – like an idiot –

I am thrilled

Robert Hillyer telegraphed and Dan Wells –

Frieda Lawrence

We stay with Wells –

[*Angelo Ravagli begins*:]

I think is better you cam soon beacause we cant do enithing without you – My best to you and Gina.   Angelino

61. Jake Zeitlin to Frieda Lawrence, 24 November 1936
Text: TSCC UCLA

November 24, 1936

Mrs. Frieda Lawrence,
Kiowa Ranch,
San Cristobal, New Mexico.

Dear Frieda,

How thrilled I am to hear that Harvard wants you to come and lecture, and I am, of course, excited to hear that they are interested in buying the manuscripts.

Naturally, I want to come with you, but I must be honest and tell you my present situation. The fact is that people owe me over $6,000, and none of it is collectible until after January. In the meantime, I simply cannot spare the extra expense of the trip. I know I should be on hand, and it looks as if a sale could be effected.

Could you afford to advance me the expenses of the trip with the understanding that it would be deductible from my commissions? I know this is rather bold, but I trust you to understand.

Write me if you think this is possible. If it is not, I shall, of course, make efforts to borrow the money elsewhere, but that would be difficult.

I have very little doubt that Harvard is ripe to make a deal, and I know I should be on the ground.

With best regards, and love from Gina to Angie,

[JZ]

62. Jake Zeitlin to Frieda Lawrence, 24 December 1936
Text: TSCC UCLA

December 24, 1936

Mrs. Frieda Lawrence,
Kiowa Ranch,
San Cristobal, New Mexico.

Dear Frieda,

Tell me what happened at Harvard – I have had no word from you since my last letter, and Mr. Wells has not written me either. If they are through exhibiting the manuscripts, I should like to have them back, since I have a woman who is buying very intensively, and would take several high-priced items. I have just sold her a copy of *The Rainbow* for $150.

Best wishes to Angie. When will you be here?

Sincerely,   [JZ]

63. Jake Zeitlin to Harry K. Wells, 24 December 1936
Text: TSCC UCLA

December 24, 1936

Mr. Harry K. Wells,
75 Main St.,
Concord, Massachusetts.

Dear Mr. Wells:

I have not heard from you for some time, and I am wondering where the situation stands with regard to the Lawrence manuscripts. I should very much appreciate word from you at your earliest convenience, since I have had very urgent inquiries from one of my local customers regarding several of the important manuscripts.

With the best compliments of the season,   [JZ]

64. Harry K. Wells to Jake Zeitlin, 3 January 1937

Text: MS UCLA

75 Main Street, Concord, Mass.
Jan. 3, 1937

Dear Zeitlin,

Your letters to Frieda and to me. I answer for both of us.

For the present Frieda is not interested in selling the Lawrence M.S.S. piece by piece. She has decided to leave them at Harvard until she can dispose of them as a whole.

So far nothing has happened at Harvard – and from all indications, nothing is likely to take shape in the near future, if at all.

They are really safest in the Harvard College Library's Treasure Room. They are still on display – and will be for some time to come.

Frieda and Angelino send their regards –

Yours sincerely,   Harry K. Wells

65. Jake Zeitlin to Frieda Lawrence, 8 January 1937

Text: TSCC UCLA

January 8, 1937

Mrs. Frieda Lawrence
Kiowa Ranch
San Cristobal, New Mexico

Dear Frieda:

Enclosed is a carbon copy of a letter which I have received today from Mr. Wells. Simple as I am, I can read very well between the lines and draw my own conclusions, which are to the effect that some form of negotiation or understanding is in process between you. I hope I am mistaken, but one thing that is definitely stated is that you apparently intend to withdraw them from availability for me to offer.

If this is the case, it is contrary to our agreement and the intention of all our previous correspondence. If I am to continue to feel that you are acting in good faith with regard to our original plan, I shall have to have a letter from you personally, not from Mr. Wells telling me exactly what is going on.

The original arrangement with Mr. Wells was that he was to keep the manuscripts for the period of November. This was later extended in order to provide sufficient time for the manuscripts to be given a good showing at Harvard. At no time was anything said about keeping them there, unless Harvard wished to buy them.

I await your letter of explanation with great eagerness.

Sincerely,   [JZ]

66. Frieda Lawrence to Jake Zeitlin, 18 January 1937

Text: TS UCLA

75 Main Street, Concord, Mass.[1]

January 18, 1937

Mr. Jake Zeitlin
c/o Jake Zeitlin Inc.
614 West 6th St.
Los Angeles, California

Dear Mr. Zeitlin:

I have received your letter of January 8, 1937 in which you refer to "our agreement".

It is true that under date of April 1st and April 12th, 1936, I executed two letters prepared by you purporting to make you my agent for the purpose of negotiating for the sale of a certain manuscript, or possibly certain manuscripts, written by my husband, the late D. H. Lawrence, but I am advised that these letters do not in any sense constitute any agreement between us.

In any event, I am now writing you to advise you that as of the date hereof your agency, if any was created by said letters or either of them, is hereby revoked and terminated.

If you have any questions with regard to this situation, I will ask you to take them up with my Los Angeles counsel, Latham, Watkins and Bouchard, Suite 1112, Title Guarantee Building, Los Angeles. I may add that if I should receive any further communications from you, such communications will be immediately referred to these gentlemen as my counsel, so nothing will be gained by writing to me direct.

Yours very truly,   Frieda Lawrence

Note

1. At top of letter a handwritten note by Jake Zeitlin explains: "This was a temporary contretemps of Frieda's due to the advice of the last person she talked to. She later reversed herself – J. Z."

67. Jake Zeitlin to Latham, Watkins and Bouchard, 4 February 1937
Text: TSCC UCLA

February 4, 1937

Latham, Watkins and Bouchard
Suite 1112, Title Guarantee Bldg.
Los Angeles, California

Gentlemen:[1]

I was greatly surprised to receive, under date of January 18, 1937, a letter from Frieda Lawrence, purporting to cancel her agreement with me, whereby I was given the exclusive agency for the sale of the manuscripts of D. H. Lawrence. In this letter, Mrs. Lawrence suggests that any further correspondence should be addressed to you.

This letter is to advise you and Mrs. Lawrence that I do not acquiesce in said purported Notice of Cancellation, and on the contrary I am, and at all times past have been, willing to proceed under the terms of this agreement. And, in this connection, I wish to make it clearly understood that, in reliance upon the terms of said agreement, and in reliance upon Mrs. Lawrence's good faith in the matter, I have already devoted a great deal of time and have been to considerable expense in connection with my obligations under said agreement, and that if Mrs. Lawrence refuses to let me proceed under the agreement I shall expect to hold her responsible for the reasonable value of my services and for reimbursement for expenses incurred to this date.

Sincerely,   [JZ]

Note

1. This letter is part of a longer letter written to Jake Zeitlin on 2 February 1937 by his attorney Carey McWilliams, who added: "Having written this letter, your rights are safeguarded, and if and when Frieda Lawrence returns to California, we can sue her for the reasonable value of your services."

68. Paul R. Watkins to Jake Zeitlin, 10 February 1937
Text: TS UCLA

February 10th, 1937.

Jake Zeitlin, Inc.,
614 West Sixth Street,
Los Angeles, California.

In re: *D. H. Lawrence – Manuscripts*.

Gentlemen:

We acknowledge receipt of your letter of the 4th instant with respect to your alleged agency agreement with Mrs. Lawrence.

We regret that you take the attitude which you do and haven't the slightest doubt as to Mrs. Lawrence's right to terminate the agency. We would suggest that you consult your attorney with respect to that. We are certain, however, that if you have been put to considerable expense in connection with Mrs. Lawrence's affairs or have spent considerable time in connection therewith, that she will be willing to make some adjustment if the amount is not large. We feel sure that she will want to do that, even though she has no legal obligation to do so, if your demands are not excessive. Should you desire to discuss this with us, kindly call the writer at your convenience.

This letter is not to be deemed in any way an admission of liability to you on the part of Mrs. Lawrence but is written in an effort to adjust the controversy between you and Mrs. Lawrence and to avoid litigation.

Very truly yours,   LATHAM, WATKINS & BOUCHARD
[*signed*] Paul R. Watkins

69. Jake Zeitlin to Carey McWilliams, 15 February 1937
Text: TSCC UCLA

February 15, 1937

Mr. Carey McWilliams[1]
900 Spring Arcade Bldg.
Los Angeles, California

With reference to my outlay of time and expense in connection with the D. H. Lawrence collection of manuscripts, I can give you the following chronological account of what took place. Of course, I cannot recollect the amount of time involved, nor can I attempt to list the conversations and special thought I have given to the matter. Also, I have spent hours reading and consulting with others, in order to supplement my information on Lawrence and the value of his work.

1. Approximately March 25, 1936. Meeting with Frieda Lawrence, conversation probably two hours.
2. April 1. Mrs. Lawrence came to lunch; talked with Lawrence Clark Powell and me. Approximately four hours.
3. April 1. Letter to Nathan Van Patten, proposing that Stanford hold exhibition of D. H. Lawrence manuscripts, and suggesting that Stanford University arrange for transportation, and bringing in of material through facilities of the University.
4. April 2, 3, 4 and 5. Three days time Mr. Powell and myself preparing a transcription of manuscript of *The Rainbow*, and doing related reading. Also letters to Frank J. Hogan and Miss Virginia Warren, secretary.
5. Approximately April 7. Meeting with Frieda Lawrence. Probably three hours.
6. April 9. Letter to Mr. Van Patten.
7. April 11. Letter to Mr. Van Patten.
8. April 14. Letter of instructions to Mrs. Lawrence with regard to best method of shipment, and arranging the transportation.
9. April 27. Conversation with Frieda Lawrence.
10. April 27. Telegram to Mr. Van Patten.
11. April 28. Conference with Van Patten and Frieda Lawrence, including time spent with Mr. Van Patten. Full day.
12. May 6. Letter to Van Patten.
13. Between May 6 and May 18. Several conversations with Frieda Lawrence. Time difficult to estimate.
14. May 18. Letter to Frieda Lawrence.
15. Period between May 18 and September 4. Great deal of time spent discussing the matter and reading up on Lawrence.
16. September 8. Letter to Van Patten regarding possibilities of Harvard exhibition.
17. September 25. Letter to Dr. Powell with regard to preparing descriptive catalog of Lawrence material.
18. September 25. Letter to Van Patten with regard to cataloging Lawrence material.
19. September 28. Discussions with various Los Angeles librarians, also discussions with Miss Jane Cleveland of possibility of bringing collection to Los Angeles for month of November, especially planning to exhibit at Los Angeles Book Fair.
20. September 28. Letter to Frieda Lawrence with regard to the material.
21. September 28. Long letter to Lawrence Clark Powell discussing plans to show Lawrence collection.

22. October 5. With regard to cataloging and exhibiting at Harvard.
23. October 12. Letter to Frieda Lawrence with regard to renewal of agreement.
24. October 15. Trip to San Francisco and visit to Van Patten at Stanford. In connection with exhibition. More than 50% of my time on this trip was taken up with this exhibition, and it was primarily planned for the purpose of making the arrangements. At that time, Van Patten intimated that Stanford was interested in the purchase of several items providing that a suitable price could be set.
25. October 18. Telegram to Wells at Cambridge.
26. October 29. Letter to Mrs. Lawrence.
27. October 30. Letter to Mrs. Lawrence.
28. October 31. Long letter to Mr. Harry K. Wells.
29. November 2, 3, 4. Full time devoted by Mr. [Karl] Zamboni and myself to listing and pricing manuscripts.
30. November 6. Letter to Frieda Lawrence.
31. November 17. Letter to Frieda Lawrence.
32. November 17. Letter to Wells.
33. November 24. Letter to Frieda Lawrence.
34. December 24. Letter to Frieda Lawrence.
35. December 24. Letter to Wells.
36. January 8. Letter to Frieda Lawrence.
37. February [4]. Letter to Latham–Watkins–Bouchard.

I have telegrams and letters from Mrs. Lawrence and Mr. Wells, specifically intimating that I am the agent and that all arrangements are being made through me, and asking me to waive the plans for an exhibition of the manuscripts at Los Angeles because the possibility of Harvard's buying the collection was very favorable.

I also have a telegram from Mr. Wells requesting me not to sell anything from the collection until it has been exhibited at Harvard.

Naturally, I am sure that I have not included a good many items of time which I have spent on this matter, and of course, there is no way of measuring the amount of mental stress and disappointment, nor damage done me by Mrs. Lawrence's very curt and definitely unfriendly final letter.

Incidentally, I have written several letters to important book collectors and librarians, as well as to a large book dealer in Chicago, announcing the fact that I am agent for the Lawrence collection, and I feel that Mrs. Lawrence's premature termination of our understanding cannot be without its harmful results in my association with those people.

I shall be glad to supply additional information if you think it is necessary, and of course will be glad to elaborate all the details in the foregoing letter, which you feel are not suitably clarified.

Sincerely,   [JZ]

Note

1. Carey McWilliams received his LL.B. degree from the University of Southern California in 1927 and practised law in Los Angeles until 1938. He wrote *Ambroce Bierce: A Biography* (New York: A. & C. Boni, 1929) and several books on minority groups.

70. Jake Zeitlin to Carey McWilliams, 18 March 1937
Text: TSCC UCLA

March 18, 1937

Mr. Carey McWilliams
900 Spring Arcade Bldg.
Los Angeles, California

Dear Carey:

I am returning herewith the contracts between Mrs. Lawrence and ourselves, for revision. Following are the revisions which I have discussed with Mrs. Lawrence, and with which she is in entire agreement.

No. 1. Paragraph 4: Mrs. Lawrence is not in Los Angeles at all times, and it would greatly hamper me if I had to submit all publicity, advertising, or other printed matter regarding the collection, to her for her approval. In fact, she would rather not be concerned with this problem, and has entire confidence in my judgment and good taste as regards this.

No. 2. Paragraph 5: Upon all sales of manuscripts made outside of the United States effected directly by the party of the second part, a commission of 15% shall apply. On all sales made outside the United States by the party of the first part without the assistance of the party of the second part, a commission of 7½% shall be paid to the party of the second part.

No. 3. Paragraph 8: All of my large sales are made on credit. Universities, as well as private collectors, often make arrangements to pay over a period of time varying from thirty days to a year, since large purchases are often made out of income rather than principal. My average customer, whose credit is of the best, takes an average of 60 days to pay me, and one of my best customers[1] recently bought a twenty-two hundred dollar item from me on the basis of paying me two hundred and twenty dollars a month for ten months. Mrs. Lawrence agrees with me, that, so long as I assume full liability for the collection, the manner of credit should be left to my discretion.

No. 4. Paragrah 11: Add, "Except that the party of the second part may quote in part but not in full from any of the manuscripts for the purpose of preparing the above mentioned catalog, or any descriptions necessary to further the sale of the manuscripts."

I hope that Mr. Watkins will agree to the above revision. Mrs. Lawrence and I are both very eager to start to work on this matter without further delay, and await return of the contracts at your and his earliest convenience.

With best regards,

Sincerely,   [JZ]

Note
1. Probably T. E. Hanley.

71. Angelo Ravagli to Jake Zeitlin, 1 April 1937
Text: MS UCLA

1 April 1937

Dear Jake,

To day Frieda has sent the letter to Mr. Blake[1] and to the Wells. So you can start your work right now. We have also sent the cheque to Mrs Watkins.[2]

My love to you and Gina and thanks very much for the lovle party of last night –

The girls was very beautiful, but insignificant for me beacause I found them very could –

Yours –   Angelino

P.S.   Please send back the B[l]ake's letters until you are used them.   A

Notes
1. At the Harvard University Library.
2. At the law firm of Latham, Watkins & Bouchard.

72. Jake Zeitlin to Angelo Ravagli, 5 April 1937
Text: TSCC UCLA

April 5, 1937

Mr. Angelo Ravagglio
c/o Mrs. D. H. Lawrence
7965 Highland Trail
Hollywood, California

Dear Angie:

I am returning the two letters from Harvard which you sent me. Also carbon copies of the two letters I have just written, one to Mr. Blake and one to Mr. Wells. We shall see what happens now.

I am sorry you did not enjoy the cool young ladies. I shall provide warmer ones next time.

Sincerely, [JZ]

73. Jake Zeitlin to Robert P. Blake, 5 April 1937
Text: TSCC UCLA

April 5, 1937

Mr. Robert P. Blake
Library, Harvard University
Cambridge, Massachusetts

Dear Mr. Blake:

Mrs. Lawrence has no doubt already written you to the effect that I am representing her in the sale of the manuscripts of D. H. Lawrence.

She informs me that you have expressed an interest in acquiring this collection for Harvard, and I should like very much to continue negotiations with you. She has also shown me the appraisal prepared by Goodspeeds and Mr. Wells, in which they consider the collection worth no more than $10,000.[1]

From the work which I have already done on the manuscripts and with my knowledge of the market which exists for them, I am convinced that this figure is entirely too low, and I have at present in hand an offer far exceeding such a price.

If Harvard would be interested in acquiring the collection at a price nearer to their marketable value at the present time, I should be glad to discuss the matter with you.

I await your reply at your earliest convenience, since I have parties here interested in seeing the collection without delay, once you have relinquished it. Assuring you of my sincere desire to cooperate, I am

Yours truly, [JZ]

Note
1. See Appendix A.

74. Jake Zeitlin to Harry K. Wells, 5 April 1937
Text: TSCC UCLA

April 5, 1937

Mr. Harry K. Wells
75 Main Street
Concord, Massachusetts

Dear Mr. Wells:

I understand that Mrs. Lawrence has already written to you to the effect that we have reestablished and reenforced our agreement, and all negotiations pertaining to the sale will have to go through me.

Mrs. Lawrence has shown me the appraisal presented by you and concurred in by Goodspeeds. All I can say is, that I wish that I could buy the collection for so low a price. I understand that Harvard has been negotiating with Mrs. Lawrence regarding the purchase of the collection at a figure of $10,000.

I do not feel that I can consent to letting it go at such a price, especially in view of the fact that I have a much larger one already in hand. If Harvard is sincerely interested, I shall be glad to discuss a price more nearly in line with the figure at which they are marketable today. Unless we can get closer together, I shall have to have the collection sent back here within the next two weeks.

Since the collection was sent to you at your request, and you have assumed responsibility for its safe care and return, in your correspondence with me, I hope I may count on you to see that they are properly packed and insured, in case it becomes necessary to return them.

It is too bad that any misunderstanding or failure to cooperate should have occurred. I hope that, now that my relations with Mrs. Lawrence as regards the manuscripts have been definitely established, that you and I can continue to work together toward the end of seeing the collection stay in the place where it would be best appreciated.

Sincerely,   [JZ]

75. Harry K. Wells to Frieda Lawrence, 5 April 1937
Text (abridged): MS HRC

75 Main Street, Concord, Mass.
April 5, 1937

Dear Frieda,

. . . There has been a new legacy left to Harvard and it looks now as though your $10,000 will be forthcoming before long. I hope so. But what did you mean when you spoke in your letter of Zeitlin? How do matters stand with him now? ...

ever yours,   Dan

76. Harry K. Wells to Frieda Lawrence, 7 April 1937

Text: TS copy UCLA

April 7, 1937

Dear Frieda:

I have a letter from Zeitlin this morning saying that you "have reestablished and reenforced our agreement, and all negotiations pertaining to the sale will have to go through me." I had no idea you were hitching up with him again.

Under the circumstances, I will retire and leave the field to him. He can negotiate with Harvard – and good luck to him.

It is too bad. We were on the point of raising the $10,000. I am of the opinion you won't get any more for them at Harvard, and I doubt if you will anywhere. But that is Mr. Zeitlin's business, now.

I thought it was understood by us all that $10,000 was a low figure. You agreed to it, with reservations, only because you were willing to make personal sacrifices in order to *give* this monument for Lawrence. Angelino agreed and urged you to do it.

You are entitled, of course, to change your mind. And I understand how you feel. I'm only sorry for Lawrence's sake. It would have been a splendid tribute to him.

But perhaps you have some other institution in mind, that will pay more, and will be just as good for the purposes of keeping the collection intact. I hope so, both for your sake and for Lawrence's.

Well, Frieda, we are disappointed. But, then, that's the way it goes. I would like to hear from you again before I write to Zeitlin.

Ted and Enid and Harold[1] all write that they are still snow-bound – no plowing yet. They're worried.

Lee is taking charge of the ranch[2] and will have things in shape for us, *I hope*.

I wish Angelino would write a note. We'd like to hear from him.

Best regards to you both and please write soon.

As ever,   Dan

Zeitlin says: "I do not feel that *I* can let it go at such a price, $10,000, especially in view of the fact that *I* have a much larger offer already in hand" – If he has such an offer, he'd better accept it. Why worry in whose hands they go, money money money is all that matters. I wonder if you'll get $10,000 out of it in the long run – I hope so.

Notes
1. Ted: Ted Mackie, owner of the San Cristobal Trading Post, 1931–62. Enid: Enid Hopkin Hilton (b. 1896), who had recently come to New Mexico. Harold: Harold Hawk, brother of William Hawk; with his wife Rachel, William owned the Del Monte Ranch two miles below Frieda Lawrence's Kiowa Ranch.
2. The Valley Ranch in San Cristobal. Lee: Carlos Le Clair, caretaker of the Wells ranch.

77. Harry K. Wells to Jake Zeitlin, 15 April 1937
Text: MS UCLA

75 Main Street, Concord, Mass.
April 15, 1937

Dear Mr. Zeitlin,

I have heard from both you and Mrs. Lawrence to the effect that you are now her agent in respect to the M.S.S. now at Harvard.

My advice is that you work through me. Harvard hates agents of any sort. If you will let me know what you would consider (Angelino writes that you would like to have $15,000 for the lot), I will do the best I can.

You must realize that Harvard is *not*, as an institution "interested" in acquiring this collection; Lawrence still carries a stigma. But I have been doing my best to arouse interest enough to have them buy. That is the only way institutions will ever buy modern and untried and unclassical collections – by the pressure from an individual or individuals.

I have succeeded, through the exhibition and Frieda's lecture, and teas and parties, in arousing the interest of several individuals.

Professor Blake is not really interested. He's a diplomat and not much else. I have recently been dealing with a man closer in touch with sources. He, to a certain extent, has caught my enthusiasm. Also, you see, I hold a whip, for I intend to give my collection of M.S.S. and letters to the institution, if any, which acquires the M.S.S.[1]

So I think, as you suggested, we had better work together. And as I say I think the best way is for me to deal directly with Harvard, and you *use* me as your unofficial agent here. Of course, I expect nothing in exchange, so you can rest assured on that point.

Everybody knows that $10,000, and even $15,000, is ridiculously low as a price for the collection. But few will offer as much, not to say more.

No one knows better than I do how invaluable some of those M.S.S. are. I have read through most of them very carefully.

Personally, I think, and in this I am in accord with Gabriel Wells of New York and Goodspeed of Boston, that you and Mrs. Lawrence will make more by selling as a whole than piece by piece. This way you get a lump sum – the other, the money would dribble in and be gone without notice.

Anyway, please let me hear from you on these points.

I think you'd make a mistake to go ahead on your own at Harvard. I have professors and students lined up supporting the scheme etc. It takes time and effort to build up feeling in an institution.

But it's your business and just say the word. Either we do or do not cooperate.

Yours sincerely,   Harry K. Wells

Note
1. In October 1943, however, Ben Abramson of the Argus Book Shop, Chicago, offered for sale, in List No. 827, a large collection of D. H. Lawrence's work, including autograph letters and postcards, drawings, manuscripts, and typescripts. The head-note states: "This collection was gathered by Mr. Harry K. Wells on a pilgrimage to the Lawrence country in England, Germany, Austria and Italy." In 1989 Jenny Wells Vincent recalled: "I'm sure that [his D. H. Lawrence collection] is what he lived on, because he didn't have very much income after he left [San Cristobal] in 1943." His father, who inherited Wells Brothers Construction Company in Chicago, had gone bankrupt in 1936. "He lost everything in the depression, and the family sold their home in Hubbard Woods, Illinois, and moved to Lake Geneva, Wisconsin, where Dan's mother and aunt owned a home."

78. Robert P. Blake to Jake Zeitlin, 15 April 1937
Text: TS UCLA

Library of Harvard University, Cambridge, Massachusetts
April 15, 1937.

Jake Zeitlin, Inc.,
614 West Sixth St.,
Los Angeles, California.

Dear Mr. Zeitlin:-

I received yours of April 5th some days since. I note that you consider the present appraisal too low, and consequently would be glad to know what you think would be a more adequate figure. At the same time I should like to point out that the previous appraiser[1] is one of the most experienced persons along these lines that we have in the country.

Hoping to hear from you at your convenience, I am

Very truly yours,   Robert P. Blake, Director

Note
1. See Letter 74.

79. Angelo Ravagli to Jake Zeitlin, 19 April 1937
Text: MS UCLA

Monday 19 of April 1937

Dear Jake,

Here is the Well's letter – The [letter] is too personal and is better after you have read it to send it bak – So is come the time to go bak to the Ranch, and I am offly sorry that we can plane on other evining togeter – It would be for another time –

My love to you and to Gina.

Sincerly yours.   Angelino

P.S.   Good lok for seling the m.m.ss.

80. Jake Zeitlin to Robert P. Blake, 20 April 1937
Text: TSCC UCLA

April 20, 1937

Dr. Robert P. Blake
Harvard University Library
Cambridge, Massachusetts

Dear Dr. Blake:

Your letter of April 15 arrived yesterday morning. I am well aware of the competence of Goodspeed's as appraisers, but would consider them a great deal better qualified in the field of American historical material and American first editions than in such matters as the manuscripts of D. H. Lawrence. I should, moreover, like to point out to you the fact that the appraisal was not strictly one of value, but rather one of sentimental understanding in that connection.

Perhaps I had better quote from Mr. Wells' recent letter to Mrs. Lawrence: " .... It was understood by us all that $10,000. was a low figure, agreed to with reservations...." Also his letter to me in which he says, "Everybody knows that $10,000. and even $15,000. is ridiculously low as a price for the collection...."

As an instance of how low your valuation is, let me refer to several items on the list:[1] No. 4, "Paul Morel," and No. 6, *The Rainbow*. The total value set upon these two by your appraiser is a thousand dollars. In my estimation, the two together have a value of from seven to ten thousand dollars. No. 43, *The Captain's Doll*, and No. 44, *The Woman Who Rode Away*, are appraised at a total value of $235.00. I consider the two together worth between eight hundred and one thousand dollars.

The above are not imaginative fancies, but are based on what I have been able to get for similar manuscripts, and the valuations which I have discussed with my present prospective purchasers. Based upon a careful estimate of the individual items, I have appraised the collection as having a minimum value of $40,000. I have no doubt that this figure could be reached if I should undertake to sell the items individually.

Since talking the matter over with Mrs. Lawrence, she has decided that she would be agreeable to letting the collection go to Harvard at a special price of $25,000. This sum would not have to be paid all at once. In fact, any reasonable form of extended payment would be agreeable. We would, however, have to have your decision within a fortnight, since the other parties with whom we are negotiating may be leaving the country before very long.

I do hope that we will be able to come to agreeable terms, since so much has already been done at Harvard to identify your interest in the collection.

Sincerely,   [JZ]

Note
1.   See Appendix A for the Wellses' appraisal to which Jake Zeitlin refers.

81. Jake Zeitlin to Angelo Ravagli, 20 April 1937
Text: TSCC UCLA

April 20, 1937

Mr. Antonio Ravagglio
c/o Mrs. Frieda Lawrence
7965 Highland Trail
Hollywood, California

Dear Angie:

Here is the letter back. I am also enclosing a carbon copy of the letter which I am sending to Mr. Wells.

I still hope that there will be some way for us to get together before you and Frieda go [back to the Kiowa Ranch].

Sincerely,   [JZ]

82. Jake Zeitlin to Harry K. Wells, 20 April 1937
Text: TSCC UCLA

April 20, 1937

Mr. Harry K. Wells
75 Main Street
Concord, Massachusetts

Dear Mr. Wells:

Your letter arrived this morning just as I was about to respond to a letter I received yesterday from Dr. Blake.

I am naturally very much interested in cooperating with you, and in view of the fine spirit which your letter indicates, I want you to continue to assist in negotiations. Frankly, however, in view of the way in which I was left out of the matter back in December, and the obligation I feel I owe to Frieda, I cannot completely leave all negotiations in your hands, and I therefore propose that we team together in an attack on both flanks, as it were.

You are quite right in agreeing that $10,000. or even $15,000. is a ridiculous figure for such an important collection. I don't know how Angelo could have told you $15,000. would be acceptable, since that price had never been mentioned by Frieda or myself in conversation. My own appraisal comes to between forty and fifty thousand dollars, and I would, under no circumstance, consent to letting the collection go for less than the $25,000. which I have named as a figure in my letter to Professor Blake. I haven't the slightest doubt of our getting this price.

Your intense interest and active work on behalf of the collection certainly should result in seeing it stay at Harvard, where you can have the best access to it. I am enclosing a carbon copy of the letter which I am sending to Dr. Blake. All my negotiations will be carried out in the open, and I want yours to be done in the same way. In the end, I think such tactics will bear the best results.

As I explained in my letter to Dr. Blake, some indication of what can be done must be given to me within the next two weeks, since the parties I am dealing with may be sailing abroad between now and the 15th of May.

Thank you again for your letter and your fine spirit. Here's luck to our project.

Sincerely,   [JZ]

P.S.: Before the collection was sent to Harvard, I had promised an exhibition of it here. Do you think Harvard would be agreeable to letting the collection come here for a month, if they should acquire it?

83. Robert P. Blake to Jake Zeitlin, 27 April 1937

Text: TS UCLA

Library of Harvard University, Cambridge, Massachusetts

April 27, 1937.

Jake Zeitlin, Inc.,
614 West Sixth Street,
Los Angeles, California.

Dear Mr. Zeitlin:-

Yours of April 20th sent by air mail was received some days back. I have considered carefully the proposal which you make in it and have talked with the persons here in the University who are most interested in the matter. The figure of $25,000 which you make for the collection would be too great a drain on our rather limited resources and there appear to be no benefactors who would be able to advance a sum of this magnitude. Consequently I feel that we shall have reluctantly to withdraw from the picture.

Very truly yours,   Robert P. Blake, Director

84. Jake Zeitlin to Frieda Lawrence, 1 May 1937

Text: TSCC UCLA

May 1, 1937

Mrs. Frieda Lawrence
Kiowa Ranch
San Cristobal, New Mexico

Dear Frieda:

I am enclosing a carbon copy of a letter which I have just received from Dr. Blake of Harvard. So far, Mr. Wells has not replied to my last letter, and I am writing him to ask if he concurs in Dr. Blake's decision. If this is the case, I am asking him to forward the manuscripts back here to me, so that Dr. Powell can start work on them without delay.

I don't think you need to feel badly if Harvard does not accept them at $25,000. It would still be foolish to sell for less.

I hope that you and Angie arrived safely and are enjoying the return. Mickey McGeary called me this morning, and said that she was sorry to have missed you.

Gina sends her regards with mine.

Cordially,   [JZ]

85. Jake Zeitlin to Jacob Blanck, 1 May 1937
Text: TSCC UCLA

May 1, 1937

Mr. Jacob Blanck
3 West 46th Street
New York, New York

Dear Mr. Blanck:

I think it might be of interest to you in your rare book section to announce that we are now the agents for the sale of the manuscripts of D. H. Lawrence. The collection which we have to offer is the one which was exhibited at Bumpus several years ago and at Harvard last December. It includes most of the manuscripts of Lawrence's novels, including many early drafts, and also a number of his important notebooks and other very wonderful material.

We would prefer to sell the collection as a whole, in order that it might be kept intact and remain a memorial to Lawrence. Lawrence Clark Powell is coming down from the University of California at Berkeley in June to prepare a detailed and annotated catalogue. We look upon this as a considerable event.

Harvard has been negotiating for the collection with us, but it appears that unless they can raise more funds than they have so far gotten up, it will have to come back here to us for sale. Of course, the best thing that could happen would be for Harvard's alumni to raise in contributions the amount necessary for the purchase of the collection, and we have not entirely given up hope that it can be done.

If you have any ideas regarding this, I should be glad to hear from you. A brief descriptive checklist has already been prepared, and I would be glad to send it to you if you are interested.

With cordial regards,

Sincerely,   [JZ]

86. Jake Zeitlin to Harry K. Wells, 1 May 1937
Text: TSCC UCLA

May 1, 1937

Mr. Harry K. Wells
75 Main Street
Concord, Massachusetts

Dear Mr. Wells:

Yesterday I received a letter from Dr. Robert P. Blake, carbon copy of which I am enclosing to you. Do you think that this is the last word? If so, will you please arrange to have the manuscripts packed and returned to me by insured express without delay, since I am anxious to have them here by the 15th of May. Of course, if you see any possibilities of a change in attitude, let me know.

Sincerely,   [JZ]

87. Frieda Lawrence to Jake Zeitlin, 10 May 1937

Text: MS UCLA

Monday 10th May 37

Dear Jake Zeitlin,

No, I dont fret either if Harvard is not willing – Some book-sellers from Chicago "Dunlop" were here this afternoon and they also said how first editions were very high –

So we might sell some and do as we please – I will write to Dan Wells to send the Mss to you –

Then I might have some here too later on, when you have shown them –

It is only just getting warm and Angelino is terribly busy, so much to do –

All good luck to you –

Our best to Gina and you –

Yours   F –

[*Angelo Ravagli begins*:]

Dear Jake: The Cole book and magazines have not arrived – I wonder why –

88. Jake Zeitlin to Harry K. Wells, 11 May 1937

Text: Telegram copy UCLA

MAY 11 1937

HARRY K WELLS
75 MAIN STREET
CONCORD, MASSACHUSETTS

PLEASE ADVISE STATUS OF LAWRENCE MANUSCRIPTS ARE YOU RETURNING WIRE REPLY

ZEITLIN

89. Jake Zeitlin to Robert P. Blake, 12 May 1937
Text: TSCC UCLA

May 12, 1937

Dr. Robert P. Blake, Librarian
Harvard University Library
Cambridge, Massachusetts

Dear Dr. Blake:

I have delayed responding to your letter of April 27, in which you inform me that you did not find yourself in a position to purchase the D. H. Lawrence collection of manuscripts. I was naturally very sorry to hear of your decision, and before accepting it as final, I had hoped to have some word from our mutual friend, Mr. Wells, who wrote me some time ago expressing his intense desire to see the collection remain at Harvard.

If no new factors have developed which might cause you to alter your decision, I should like very much to have the collection forwarded to me here as quickly as possible. Mr. Wells, who requested that the collection be sent in the first place, will, I am sure, be glad to cooperate in having it returned, although I am also certain that he will do so with great regret. The opportunity for securing this collection for the Harvard of the future, as well as for the Harvard of today, is one that I am sure you are not passing by lightly. I do hope that you have found some last-moment rescuer.

I await further word from you with interest, and if you have entirely given up hope, I earnestly beg you to lose no time to see the collection started on its way back here.

Sincerely,   [JZ]

90. Jake Zeitlin to Frieda Lawrence, 13 May 1937
Text: TSCC UCLA

May 13, 1937

Mrs. Frieda Lawrence
Kiowa Ranch
San Cristobal, New Mexico

Dear Frieda:

Your letter arrived this morning. Dan Wells must have a peeve at me because I haven't heard a word from him since I responded to his long letter. Yesterday I sent him a wire asking what the final decision was regarding the manuscripts, and asked him to wire a reply, but none has come. I hope he is not being a bad sport.

I can't understand why the books[1] have not reached you. They were sent by express on April 29. It may be that they are at the nearest express office. I will send a tracer.

It is getting hot here.

When do you expect Aldous Huxley? Be sure and let me know, and if he should come before you can notify me, be sure and tell him that I can get him a very good motion picture contract if he would be interested.

Regards to Angie.

Sincerely,   [JZ]

Note
1. See postscript to Letter 87.

91. Harry K. Wells to Frieda Lawrence, 20 May 1937

Text (abridged): MS HRC

75 Main Street, Concord, Mass.
May 20, 1937

Dear Frieda,

Your letter. I am glad you are not disappointed that Harvard pooped out on us. It doesn't matter so terribly much. It would have been nice, but I guess it was just too good a thing. . . .

I have not yet sent the Mss back to Zeitlin. Blake is still undecided. But they will probably go off in the next few days.

I have an exam on June 8th,[1] so it will be the middle of the month before we can get to N. M. . . .

As ever   Dan

Note
1. Wells was briefly a graduate student in philosophy at Harvard University.

92. Jake Zeitlin to Harry K. Wells, 21 May 1937
Text: TSCC UCLA

May 21, 1937

Mr. Harry K. Wells
75 Main Street
Concord, Massachusetts

Dear Mr. Wells:
The other day, May 11, I sent you a telegram as follows:

> PLEASE ADVISE STATUS OF LAWRENCE MANUSCRIPTS
> ARE YOU RETURNING WIRE REPLY

I have also not heard from you in reply to my recent letter. Since you know the situation, and are aware of the fact that a delay in having the collection back here may affect the possibilities of my disposing of the collection as promptly as I had hoped, I have been counting on you to cooperate in either keeping me informed or sending the collection back.

Won't you please take the trouble to write me air-mail without delay, as I must have word of how matters are going, and when the collection can be expected back here.

Sincerely,   [JZ]

93. Harry K. Wells to Jake Zeitlin, 22 May 1937
Text: Telegram UCLA

CONCORD MASS
1937 MAY 22 AM 10 44

JAKE ZEITLIN
614 WEST SIXTH ST LOSA

THE MANUSCRIPTS ARE BEING SENT TO YOU TODAY TOO BAD

H K WELLS.

94. Excerpt from *Publishers' Weekly*, 22 May 1937

"News from the Rare Book Shops" – Jacob Blanck

From the Bookshop of Jake Zeitlin, Inc. (Los Angeles, Cal.), comes the following bulletin: "We have just been appointed agents for the manuscripts of D. H. Lawrence. The collection which we offer is the one exhibited at Bumpus several years ago and at Harvard last December. It includes most of the manuscripts of Lawrence's novels, including many early drafts, and also a number of his important notebooks and other material. A brief descriptive checklist has already been prepared, and although it has not been put in type it may be consulted by those interested in the works of this author."

95. Lawrence Clark Powell to Jake Zeitlin, 28 May 1937
Text: TSCC UCLA

10956 Strathmore Drive, Westwood
May 28, 1937

Mr Jake Zeitlin
Jake Zeitlin Inc.
Los Angeles

Dear Jake:

This letter will serve as my summing up of the several letters and conversations between us during the past year and our concluding verbal agreement of yesterday.

I have studied the check-list of 124 D. H. Lawrence manuscripts. I propose to make you a descriptive-literary-sales-catalog of these manuscripts, the prime purpose of which will be to create buying interest in the items. My method will be twofold: first, a brief physical description of each manuscript; second, the circumstances (as far as I am able to determine them) of the composition of each piece, its special history, and a picture of its relative position in the great world of Lawrence's complete works.

In addition to writing the catalog, I propose to prepare it for the printer and see it through press, including proof-reading, etc. Finally, I will cooperate with you in preparing a mailing-list to which copies will be sent. This will include the important libraries in all parts of the world, as well as people of means who were Lawrence's friends or are interested in his work.

We have estimated this to be at least a month's work. Whether it be a little more or less, my price to you for the complete job is $100.00, plus an expense allowance of $15.00 to pay my transportation between Westwood and the California Bank and your shop, and later to and from the printer's – making a total of $115.00. I suggest that this sum be paid me in two installments: half upon your okay of my typescript for the printer, the balance upon receipt from printer of completed catalog.

A word regarding my fitness to do this particular job. As you know, I have been studying Lawrence's books and personality for nearly eight years. In this time I have acquired a notable collection of Lawrenciana, numbering more than 50 volumes, and including virtually everything Lawrence wrote, plus 14 books about him in English, French and German. It is the most complete Lawrence collection in the West, and one of the largest anywhere not excepting the British Museum.

In addition, I have gone over Lawrence's trail in several countries, from the place of his birth in Eastwood, Nottinghamshire, to the Villa Mirenda near Florence where he wrote *Lady Chatterley*, and finally to the place of his death and first burial in Vence on the French Riviera near Nice. I have either met or corresponded with the important people in his life, including Frieda, Middleton Murry, Catherine Carswell, Mabel Luhan, Richard Aldington, etc.

I am confident that I could catalog these 124 items in a way that would be instrumental in their sale, and which would bring your shop the finest kind of publicity and prestige among the trade, libraries, scholars and collectors. With a foreword by Aldous Huxley (which you tell me is assured), our work should take an important place in the literature about Lawrence.

Inasmuch as I am awaiting a call which I hope will take me east upon library work in midsummer, I believe it would be advisable to start work as soon as possible on the catalog. I suggest the first of June as a good time to begin.

I await the confirmation of you and your board of directors upon the foregoing.

Yours faithfully,   [LCP]

96. Jake Zeitlin to Lawrence Clark Powell, 1 June 1937
Text: TS UCLA

Jake Zeitlin, Inc., 614 West Sixth Street, Los Angeles
June 1, 1937

Dr. Lawrence Clark Powell
10956 Strathmore Drive
West Los Angeles, California

Dear Dr. Powell:

This will acknowledge receipt of your letter of May 28 with reference to the cataloging of the D. H. Lawrence manuscripts. It will also serve as an acceptance of the terms therein set forth.

Sincerely,   Jake Zeitlin

97. Ben Abramson to Jake Zeitlin, 1 June 1937

Text: TS UCLA

The Argus Book Shop, Inc., 333 South Dearborn Street, Chicago
June 1 ** 1937

Jake Zeitlin, Inc.
614 West 6th Street
Los Angeles, California

Gentlemen:

Please send us a list of the D. H. Lawrence items which you have for sale, together with prices and discounts.

Yours very truly,   Ben Abramson

98. Jake Zeitlin to Robert P. Blake, 2 June 1937

Text: TSCC UCLA

June 2, 1937

Dr. Robert P. Blake, Director
Harvard University Library
Cambridge, Massachusetts

Dear Dr. Blake:

The D. H. Lawrence manuscripts have arrived, and are being checked over. I have no doubt that our checking will conform to yours, and that everything will be satisfactory, but will of course notify you in case there are any discrepancies.

I have had no word from Mr. Wells or yourself previous to the return of these manuscripts indicating that there was any possibility of your decision to relinquish the manuscripts being changed.

I should very much appreciate further word from you, since it might be of value in the future.

Sincerely,   [JZ]

99. Jake Zeitlin to Harry K. Wells, 2 June 1937
Text: TSCC UCLA

June 2, 1937

Mr. Harry K. Wells
75 Main Street
Concord, Massachusetts

Dear Mr. Wells:

The manuscripts have arrived and are now in our vault, where Dr. Lawrence Clark Powell is at work on them. It is our plan to prepare a complete annotated catalog. As soon as it is completed, I shall certainly send one on to you.

I would appreciate hearing from you at greater length regarding the close of the negotiations at Harvard. I have had no word from you since I responded to your letter, and I hardly feel that your curt telegram was in any way informative.

Won't you take the time to sit down and let me know more about what transpired?

Sincerely,   [JZ]

100. Jake Zeitlin to Frieda Lawrence, 2 June 1937
Text: TSCC UCLA

June 2, 1937

Mrs. Frieda Lawrence
Kiowa Ranch
San Cristobal, New Mexico

Dear Frieda:

The manuscripts have been returned by Harvard and are now in the bank, where Lawrence Powell is at work describing and cataloging them. He is very enthusiastic, and I know will do a beautiful job.

Be sure and let me know when you expect Aldous Huxley. I am very anxious to have him do a foreword for the catalog, and I should think that he would enjoy doing it. We intend to get out a beautifully printed booklet. Ward Ritchie will probably print it, and it will in every way be consistent with the quality of Lawrence's material.

I hope that you and Angie are well and are enjoying the ranch. Regards from Gina.

Cordially,   [JZ]

101. Jake Zeitlin to Frieda Lawrence, 8 June 1937
Text: TSCC UCLA

June 8, 1937

Mrs. Frieda Lawrence
Kiowa Ranch
San Cristobal, New Mexico

Dear Frieda:

Glad to have your note.[1] Although the manuscripts have already been returned, I have an idea that they have not given up hope entirely, and we will be hearing from Harvard again. They certainly are fools to let the collection go.

I am glad to hear that Huxley is going to stay at your place for the summer. As soon as he is settled, I should like to come out there for a few days, so you might let me know when it is convenient for you.

In the meantime, I should like very much to see what can be done in Hollywood with his work. Would you ask him to write me a letter giving me the authority to offer his work for motion picture purposes for a period, say, of six months. It can specify that any arrangements that I might make will be subject to his confirmation and of course I will not close anything without first referring to him in detail.

Last night we went to a commencement ceremony at Occidental College, where Robinson Jeffers was given an honorary degree of Doctor of Literature. Una and the boys were there and we had quite a talk.

Gina sends her regards with mine. Best to Angie.

Cordially,   [JZ]

Note
1. Note not recovered.

102. Jake Zeitlin to Ben Abramson, 24 June 1937
Text: TSCC UCLA

June 24, 1937

Mr. Ben Abramson
Argus Book Shop
333 South Dearborn Street
Chicago, Illinois

Dear Ben:

Your letter of June 4 inquiring about the D. H. Lawrence manuscripts has remained unanswered because I have wanted to write you in full detail about them. After going over the collection, I found that it contained a great deal more material than was listed in the original check list, and I have therefore put Dr. Lawrence Clark Powell to work preparing a complete catalog. This will be ready in about two more weeks, and I shall be glad to send a copy of it on to you.

We would prefer to sell the collection as a whole, and if you should be interested, I could quote you a very good price for it, one that would justify your buying it complete and breaking it up and offering it to your customers.

It is really a magnificent thing. Frieda has asked Aldous Huxley to write a preface to the list, and if we don't sell it as a whole, we shall issue a handsomely printed catalogue.

I wish you were coming out here soon. We might be able to work up a very good deal together, and this job is certainly worthy of your talents. How have you been, and why are you irked with me? Virginia Maremont was in a few days ago and said you seemed to disapprove of me. I should be very sorry if this were so, since I still look upon you as my original mentor and inspiration in all things bookish.

Sincerely,   [JZ]

103. Jake Zeitlin to Philip C. Duschnes, 24 June 1937
Text: TSCC UCLA

June 24, 1937

Philip C. Duschnes
507 Fifth Avenue
New York City, New York

Dear Sir:

Since announcing the fact that the D. H. Lawrence manuscripts are for sale, we have found that the collection contains a great deal more material than our original check list included. I am therefore having a complete new catalog of the material prepared by Lawrence Clark Powell, and this will be completed in about two more weeks. As soon as it is done I shall send a typewritten copy on to you. Thank you very much for your inquiry. I hope we can cooperate to our mutual advantage.

Sincerely,   [JZ]

104. Bertram Rota to Jake Zeitlin, 29 June 1937
Text: MS UCLA

June 29/37

Dear Mr. Zeitlin

Mr L. C. Powell tells me that you have the Lawrence MSS for disposal. One of my customers[1] is a keen Lawrence collector and very likely to be interested. Could you let me have early information about the material available and the prices? I feel sure that some business would result if the figures are not unreasonable.

Yours very truly,   Bertram Rota.

Note
1.   George Lazarus, a member of the London Stock Exchange.

105. Jake Zeitlin to Frieda Lawrence, 7 July 1937
Text: TSCC UCLA

July 7, 1937

Mrs. Frieda Lawrence
Kiowa Ranch
San Cristobal, New Mexico

Dear Frieda:

Lawrence Powell has just finished preparing the complete catalogue of the Lawrence Manuscripts. I am mailing a copy of the typescript to you today in order that you may read it over and see if it pleases you. Now, there are several matters that have to be taken up in connection with it before I can send it to the printers:

1.   Will you show the manuscript to Aldous Huxley and ask him if he would care to write a preface for it? Tell him we intend to have it very beautifully printed and to reproduce two or three of the manuscript pages in facsimile. It would be a very nice touch if Huxley could give us his imprimatur.

2.   You gave me a list one time of the manuscripts which you leave in your will. Following are the titles:

Borderline
Eric-Gill: Art Nonsense
David
The Plumed Serpent

Jimmy and the Desperate Woman
St. Mawr
Lovely Lady
The Woman Who Rode Away
Mornings in Mexico
Wintry Peacock

You also specified that you wanted to keep for yourself "A Chapel Among the Mountains." You also mentioned "A Hay Hut Among the Mountains," which was neither inventoried by Harvard nor seen by myself. If these manuscripts are withdrawn from the collection, the value will be immensely reduced. I think it would be better, for Lawrence's sake, for them to remain if the collection is sold intact. Would you consider changing your original will, or in some other way making it possible not to have to leave these out?

3.   Mr. Powell has found it advantageous to quote from the writings of a number of different authors on Lawrence. A list of those is attached.[1] In order to be safe against possible infringement of copyright, it would be wise to get permission from these various authors and publishers. Would you like to write them yourself? If not, send us the names and addresses of those whom you know, and we will get in touch with them. This is a matter which must not be neglected nor postponed, since it would be unwise to proceed with the printing of the material unless we had these permissions. In several instances, we quote from books published by the Viking Press. Is it necessary to get additional copyright permission from them, or do you have the authority to grant this?

I am proceeding to prepare a price list on the separate items, and shall write you about a proposed price for the collection as a whole. This, however, must wait until I hear from you in regard to those not to be included.

I hope you will be pleased with the manuscript. I am very happy with it. Write me fully without delay. If there are any questions you have, send them on. I don't believe it will be very complicated to take care of things by correspondence.

Please give my regards to Angie. Gina, who has had poison ivy for the past two weeks, sends her love, somewhat dampened just now by a complete covering of wet packs in which she is sitting.

Cordially,   [JZ]

Note
1.   The list of 14 titles has been omitted.

106. Ben Abramson to Jake Zeitlin, 10 July 1937

Text (abridged): TS UCLA

The Argus Book Shop, Inc., 333 South Dearborn Street, Chicago
July 10, 1937

Dear Jake:

Thanks for your letter of 24 June.

I look forward to receiving the catalogue of Lawrence material but don't think I will be able to sell the collection as a whole, because I think the amount asked will be staggering. Only an institution could afford such a purchase. If, however, it is dispersed separately, I am sure that I will be able to sell some of the material. . . .

For myself, I have little leisure. A huge correspondence, the magazine, and customers during the day, and a wife and daughter occupy my time, pleasantly. I must confess that these last see little of me. Mollie is mainly away; she was in Mexico two years ago for seven months, and this year for three. Deborah was away at school and is now at camp for the summer. Some day, not too distant, I hope I will be able to take a Sabbatical year, to rest, to learn, and to remember. Maybe I will be able to renew old friendships and reunite old ties which time has severed, and to think of books as a means of enjoyment rather than as merchandise for sale. . . . [1]

Note
1. Remainder of letter missing.

107. Jake Zeitlin to Frieda Lawrence, 10 July 1937

Text: TSCC UCLA

July 10, 1937

Mrs. Frieda Lawrence
Kiowa Ranch
San Cristobal, New Mexico

Dear Frieda:

I am leaving here Sunday afternoon to drive to Texas. I expect to get there about Wednesday, and stay about three days. From there I drive to Denver, when I shall stay one day, and then come down by way of Taos.

If everything goes well, and according to schedule, I should be in Taos on Wednesday, July 23. Judith will be with me, [1] and we shall probably stay two days.

I want to see you and Angie, and to meet Aldous Huxley and talk with him. Much as Gina would like to come, her condition doesn't warrant her facing the heat of the trip. She is very unhappy because she cannot call on you.

If, for any reason, you won't be at the ranch, or think it better for me to come at some other time, write me care of Sam Zeitlin, 708 Tenth Avenue, Forth Worth, Texas.

Hasta la vista,   [JZ]

Note

1. Judith, Jake's daughter, did not accompany him.

108. Memorandum in Jake Zeitlin's Hand, [*c.* 24 July 1937]

Text: MS UCLA

[*Probably a summary of Jake Zeitlin's conversation with Frieda Lawrence at the Kiowa Ranch*]

1. Send Ms. of "Laura Phillipine" to Frieda, make slipcase
2. If collection can be sold complete do not reserve any. If not reserve *St. Mawr* for Huxley, "Wintry Peacock" for Medley (Frieda's Lawyer).
3. Dan Wells has addresses of authors quoted
4. Must have permission from Viking Press.
5. Make price of Cat. 75 cents
6. Ask $30,000. for collection.

109. Frieda Lawrence to Jake Zeitlin, 3 August 1937

Text: MS UCLA

San Cristobal, N. M.
Aug 3, 1937.

Jake Zeitlin
614 W. 6th St,
Los Angeles, Calif.

Dear Mr. Zeitlin,

This will confirm my permission for you to quote from any of D. H. Lawrence's or my own writings in the descriptive catalog of his manuscripts which you are preparing.

Sincerely   Frieda Lawrence

110. Jake Zeitlin to Ben Abramson, 10 August 1937
Text: TSCC UCLA

August 10, 1937[1]

Mr. Ben Abramson
333 South Dearborn Street
Chicago, Illinois

Dear Ben:

Dr. Lawrence Clark Powell has just completed the typescript description of the D. H. Lawrence manuscripts. It is quite an extensive and detailed study of the manuscripts, and, I think, constitutes a significant Lawrence item in itself. It is my intention to publish this in beautiful format, with typography by Ward Ritchie. Aldous Huxley has agreed to write a foreword for it.

I am sending you a copy of this typescript. The printed catalogue will not be out for another month. It will run to about one hundred pages of printed text, and I do not intend to print the prices with the catalogue, but rather to issue the price list as a separate supplement to those interested. I am sending you this list in advance, so that you can make any selections that you wish out of it in time enough for me to indicate what items have been reserved or sold, in the catalogue, when we publish it.

Unfortunately my commission is so small and my expenses are so great that I will not be able to allow you any discount on the prices quoted, but I will protect you by not publishing the prices on any of the items you buy. This will leave you free to set any price you wish on the items your customers might be interested in.

Naturally I should like very much to sell the collection as a whole. It would constitute a great source of material for the graduate student of some university. Why don't you try the University of Chicago? Hutchins is a live wire. I want $30,000. for the collection as a whole.

This list is going out to only about five dealers, some in England. I suggest that you let me know as quickly as possible what interests you, and I hope that you will find several items desirable.

With best regards,

Sincerely,   [JZ]

Note
1.   The same letter was sent on 12 August 1937 to Bertram Rota in London.

111. Jake Zeitlin to Harold Jay Snyder, 11 August 1937
Text: TSCC UCLA

August 11, 1937

Mr. Harold J. Snyder
1335 Eastman Park Way
Brooklyn, New York

Dear Mr. Snyder:

A few days ago, while visiting Mrs. Lawrence at San Cristobal, I had an interesting talk with Mr. H. K. Wells. He told me that you still have a good deal of Lawrence material which you are offering for sale.

I should like very much to have a list of any items you still have. Also I should be grateful if you could send me a copy of the catalogue you once got out of the D. H. Lawrence material.[1] It was one of the best prepared catalogues I ever saw, and the one I had was borrowed by some admirer whose intensity of admiration was greater than his ethics.

I should be glad to hear from you.

Sincerely,   [JZ]

Note
1. "A Catalogue of English and American First Editions, 1911–1932, of D. H. Lawrence" (152 items), issued October 1932.

112. Jake Zeitlin to Frieda Lawrence, 12 August 1937
Text: TSCC UCLA

August 12, 1937

Mrs. Frieda Lawrence
Kiowa Ranch
San Cristobal, New Mexico

Dear Frieda and Angie:

I arrived in Los Angeles last Saturday morning quite exhausted by driving straight through from Albuquerque to L. A. in twenty hours. The first of this week I have spent in the confusion of all that developed while I was away, and this is the first chance I have had to write and thank you for the memorable and glorious time you gave me at the ranch.

The printing of the catalogue is going forward, and I hope to have more to report on the manuscripts soon. In the meantime, please forgive this brief note. I shall write you more before long.

With greetings from Gina to both of you,

Cordially,   [JZ]

113. Angelo Ravagli to Jake Zeitlin, 12 August 1937
Text: MS UCLA

12 August 1937[1]

Dear Jake

Hope you got home safely – Here is you cheque for the bill – very best to you and to Gina from me and from Frieda

Angelino.

Note
1. The note is written on Jake's bill of 1 August 1937 for $2.38.

114. Lawrence Clark Powell to Catherine Carswell, 30 August 1937
Text: TSCC UCLA

August 30, 1937

Catherine Carswell
17 Keats Grove
London, N.W.3

Dear Mrs. Carswell:

I have just completed a descriptive catalog of the manuscripts of D. H. Lawrence. This firm has undertaken to sell them for the benefit of Mrs Lawrence. She has asked me to write for your permission to quote a few passages from your *Savage Pilgrimage*. May we have such permission? A copy of the catalog will be sent you as soon as ready. Aldous Huxley has written a foreword to it. Your courtesy will be greatly appreciated.

Perhaps you will remember the two visits I paid you in the spring of 1933? I was the young American with the beard! You were very kind to me then, I remember. I hope we will meet again sometime.

Yours cordially,   Lawrence Clark Powell

115. Frieda Lawrence to Jake Zeitlin, 2 September 1937
Text: MS UCLA

Kiowa
2. Sept 37

Dear Jake,

I hope your affairs are going all right. Please send the Mss of Laura Philippine as *soon as you can*. Is'nt Aldous's foreword nice? The Huxleys have gone to Hollywood. I miss them –

Best wishes to you both   Frieda

[*Angelo Ravagli begins*:]
Dear Jake,

The check you gave Frieda $10.00 and cashed at Mackies store came back "insufficient funds." Will you please send me another check at once –

My love to you and to Gina

Sincerely   Angelino

116. Bertram Rota to Jake Zeitlin, 4 September 1937
Text: Telegram UCLA

1937 SEP 4 AM 3 35

LC JABBERWOCK LOSA

SEND LAWRENCE TWENTYTHREE THIRTYTWO THIRTYSIX THIRTYEIGHT THIRTY-NINE FORTYFOUR FORTYFIVE ROTA.[1]

JABBERWOCK ROTA.

Note
1. The order is for "The Old Adam", "Daughters of the Vicar", "The Border Line", "The Last Laugh", "Glad Ghosts", "Rawdon's Roof", and "The Rocking-Horse Winner". See Appendix B.

117. Jake Zeitlin to Harry K. Wells, 4 September 1937

Text: Telegram UCLA

SEPTEMBER 4, 1937

HARRY K WELLS
75 MAIN STREET
CONCORD, MASSACHUSETTS

I HAVE JUST HAD CABLE ORDER FROM LONDON PRIOR TO PUBLICATION OF CATALOG FOR ONE THOUSAND DOLLARS WORTH OF LAWRENCE MANUSCRIPTS BEFORE SENDING WOULD LIKE YOUR FINAL ADVICE THIS IS LAST CALL FOR COMPLETE COLLECTION AT TWENTY FIVE THOUSAND DOLLARS PLEASE WIRE REPLY

JAKE ZEITLIN

118. Jake Zeitlin to Frieda Lawrence, 9 September 1937

Text: TSCC UCLA

September 9, 1937

Mrs. Frieda Lawrence
Kiowa Ranch
San Cristobal, New Mexico

Dear Frieda:

Since writing you yesterday I have given considerable additional thought to the question of whether we should break up the collection of manuscripts or continue to try to sell it as a lot. In addition to that, I have had a talk with one of my important customers and that also has changed the complexion of things.

I have at last come to the conclusion that we would do better to break the collection up and sell it piece by piece. In the first place, I know we can get more for it, and in the second place, we can get action right away from people who might not care to wait very long.

In my interview with my customer[1] this morning, he asked me to reserve the following items:

No.   8. [TYPESCRIPT OF] LADY CHATTERLEY
"   9: APROPOS OF LADY CHATTERLEY
"   10: PORNOGRAPHY AND OBSCENITY
"   11: THE FOX
"   113: INTRODUCTION TO PAINTINGS

He is agreeable to paying a lump sum for the lot of twenty-two hundred dollars. He wants them held here until January 1 and at that time he will commence payment. This man is one of my best customers and highly reliable. It is his usual custom to pay in installments. He is very trustworthy and has always made his payments on time.

I suggest we accept his offer. If you are in agreement with me, please sign and return the enclosed memorandum since, according to the terms of my contract, it is necessary for me to have your written consent for any deviations from the strict terms of the agreement.

This sale, coupled with the order I have from England for seven hundred dollars worth of the manuscripts,[2] makes a total of twenty-nine hundred dollars worth of stuff sold, without any real effort having been made as yet. I think this is pretty good for a start, don't you?

Please give my regards to Angie.

Sincerely,   [JZ]

Notes
1. T. E. Hanley.
2. See Letter 116.

119. Harry K. Wells to Jake Zeitlin, 11 September 1937
Text: Telegram UCLA

CONCORD MASS
1937 SEP 11 AM 9 41

JAKE ZEITLIN
614 WEST SIXTH ST LOSA

ONLY NOW RECEIVED YOUR WIRE SPENT LAST WEEK RIDING ACROSS COUNTRY DIFFICULTY IS THAT NO ONE IS AT HARVARD THIS EARLY PERHAPS YOU HAD BETTER ACCEPT LONDON OFFER THOUGH I COULD WISH THAT NOTHING BE DONE UNTIL YOU CAME ON HERE BUT IT IS UP TO YOU

DAN WELLS.

120. Frieda Lawrence to Jake Zeitlin, 13 September 1937
Text: MS UCLA

Kiowa.
13. Sept. 37

Dear Jake Zeitlin,

I had your letter, but you dont say *how* much your man pays a month from the first of Jan. If it's 5 "dollars" a week it will be a nuisance. And the 700 dollars worth of Mss for England, you dont say which you have in mind. Write back quickly and tell me and I will send you the authorisation. Ask him your customer, that I would like to know about the installments now.

Yes, I agree, it is better for both of us to break up the collection – Some day if an institution wants to buy it they can pay more for it and serve them right.

Dont forget to send me the Mss of "Laura Phillippine". I promised it.

The Huxleys are in Hollywood and I want to hear from them and I hope you can do something for them too. Dan Wells, who has "finished" with his phase of Lawrence,[1] he admires the "machine" now and wants to make a "mechanised unit" of his ranch would also like to sell the Lawrence Mss he bought. He has some *very* interesting Bertie Russell letters and Pino Orioli's. [*insertion*: notebooks. They were really mine] he paid each a 1000 dollars.

Yours sincerely   Frieda –

[*Angelo Ravagli begins*:]
My regards to you and to Gina,   Angelino

Note
1. Rosalind Wells, who married Harry K. Wells in 1959, has explained that the Viking Press had encouraged him to write a new biography of Lawrence, then, after he started work, cooled because the market seemed glutted, thus precipitating the end of his Lawrence "phase" (conversation with the editor, 21 August 1989).

121. Catherine Carswell to Lawrence Clark Powell, 16 September 1937
Text: TS UCLA

35 Gloucester Crescent, London. N.W.1.
16.9.37

Dear Mr. Powell;

About your D. H. Lawrence catalog and the quotations from my *Savage Pilgrimage*. After replying to your letter of the other day, it struck me that I ought to have referred you to my American publisher, Messrs Harcourt Brace, besides giving you my personal permission. I suppose, in fact, that, so far as any copyright is concerned, this is theirs and not mine. But as you are, of course, fully informed on all such matters, no doubt you wished only to obtain my permission before making the more formal request to them. Not long ago Professor De Lancey Ferguson wanted passages from the same book for a students' text book he was compiling, and he also wrote first to me and afterwards to Harcourt Brace. They gave permission, but I think they also made a charge. In any case, their permission is necessary. I do not doubt they will give it.

I wish you all success with your sales of the MSS. The catalog should be most interesting.

Yours cordially,   Catherine Carswell.

122. Jake Zeitlin to Bertram Rota, 17 September 1937

Text: TSCC UCLA

September 17, 1937

Mr. Bertram Rota
Bodley House, Vigo Street
London W.1, England

Dear Mr. Rota:

Your cable ordering a number of the Lawrence manuscripts arrived a few days ago. I am having to delay shipment on these a little while because the collection is being considered for purchase en bloc. I should have a decision on this matter within a week, and as soon as I do I shall either cable you that they are unavailable, or forward them without further delay.

Incidentally, Mrs. Lawrence tells me that the Aga Khan[1] would be a good prospect to try on the manuscripts. Do you have any way of getting in touch with him?

Sincerely,   [JZ]

Note
1. The Aga Khan had visited Lawrence at the Ad Astra Sanatorium a few days before the author's death on 2 March 1930.

123. Jake Zeitlin to Frieda Lawrence, 18 September 1937
Text: TSCC UCLA

September 18, 1937

Mrs. Frieda Lawrence
Kiowa Ranch
San Cristobal, New Mexico

Dear Frieda:

My customer [T. E. Hanley] usually pays for such large purchases in ten equal payments which would mean that in this case he would pay $220.00 a month for ten months. This has been his usual custom and I do not think that arrangements will be different in the case of your manuscripts, although he did not tell me definitely what his plans were. He is a very rich Eastern man who has bought thousands of dollars from me in the past, and always in the same manner. I am sure we are safe in leaving the terms of payment to him, as he usually gets everything paid for in advance of the agreed time.

The manuscripts ordered from England[1] are:

	No.	12:	OLD ADAM[2]
	ʹʹ	32:	DAUGHTERS OF THE VICAR
	ʹʹ	36:	THE BORDERLINE
	ʹʹ	38:	LAST LAUGH
	ʹʹ	39:	GLAD GHOSTS
	ʹʹ	44:	RAWDON'S ROOF
	ʹʹ	45:	ROCKING HORSE WINNER

I have, since writing you, also had orders for the following:

| | No. | 43: | SMILE |
| | ʹʹ | 60: | PUBLISHED PANSIES |

Also from Albert Bender in San Francisco I have an order for

| | No. | 62: | FOUR HOLOGRAPH POEMS |
| | ʹʹ | 63: | SIX UNPUBLISHED POEMS |

Mr. Bender, as you know, is a friend of the Jeffers[es] and one of the loveliest men in the world. He would like to reprint the SIX UNPUBLISHED POEMS for the Book Club of California. I hope you will grant him permission to do so.

"Laura Phillipine" must have reached you by now. So far I have been unsuccessful of getting hold of the Huxleys. Where are they staying? Mr. Geller has been very anxious to reach them, as well as his lecture agent, and nobody seems to know where to find him.

Dan Wells's manuscripts sound interesting and I should like to know more about them. Do not believe I would want to switch my efforts from selling yours for a while, anyhow.

It looks like we are off to a fair start on the sale of the manuscripts. I think more orders will be coming through in the next few days. As it is now, we have over three thousand dollars worth sold, with very little effort, and I do not think that is bad.

Best regards to Angie and yourself.

Cordially,   [JZ]

Notes
1. By Bertram Rota for the collector George Lazarus.
2. Should read *No. 23* instead of *No. 12*.

124. Frieda Lawrence to Jake Zeitlin, [21? September 1937]

Text: MS UCLA

Kiowa Ranch
15. Sept 37[1]

Dear Jake Zeitlin,

All right, go ahead – Angelino and I thought you had made a detailed pricelist of the Mss for us, but could'nt find it.

It is interesting to see *what* different people want.

I am glad you are'nt short of money.

My agent Curtis Brown wrote that[2] there was going to be an exhibition of the Lawr[ence] Mss at *Yale* – and they wanted to place the unpublished ones – I wonder what story they got hold of –

It's lovely now, autumn peace and sunny –

With our best to you   Frieda L –

You have'nt sent us a catalogue – do please – also to "Carl Weeks" Des Moines Iowa he is "Armand" cosmetics and rich and has Lawrence Mss – Had your last letter, sounds all very good. Yes, Bender can have poems for publication –

Aldous address

1425½ N Cresant Heights Boulevard West Hollywood –

And also, please, send a list of prices of[3] Mss – We compared the sold ones with the Goodspeed ones – It *would* have been a mistake to sell to Harvard –

[*Angelo Ravagli begins:*]

My best to you and to Gina

Angelino

Notes
1. Misdated. This letter replies directly to Letter 123.
2. that] that you
3. of] of the

125. Jake Zeitlin to Harry K. Wells, 21 September 1937

Text: TSCC UCLA

September 21, 1937

Mr. H. K. Wells
75 Main Street
Concord, Massachusetts

Dear Dan Wells:

Since receiving your telegram I have had three more orders for Lawrence manuscripts. This now makes a total of over three thousand dollars in orders before the printed catalog has even been issued. I have in all sent out about five lists.

Upon discussing the matter with Frieda, we have decided that it would be better to take advantage of the sales in hand rather than wait. I am dreadfully sorry because I know how hard you have tried to see Harvard get the collection. Still, there should be a number of items listed separately that you might want. Why don't you let me know which you should like to have?

This is certainly the greatest opportunity for any Lawrence lover that will ever come. I think you understand why the situation makes it advisable to not keep the collection together any longer.

Please give my regards to Mrs. Wells. I hope you will be coming to California some day and will not forget to see me.

Cordially, [JZ]

126. Frieda Lawrence to Stefano Manara, 23 September 1937

Text: TSCC HRC

Kiowa Ranch, San Cristobal – New Mexico
23 Settembre 1937

Caro Avvocato Manara,

Rispondo alla sua lettera diretta al Capitano. Egli mi ha spiegato le sue intenzioni riguardo il procedimento che ella vorrebbe seguire nella nota causa, ma se a lei non dispiace la mia intenzione sarebbe invece, sempreché lo ritenga possibile – che lei prima di intentare una causa penale cercasse di avvicinare l'Orioli e lei come mio fiduciario chiedere direttamente la restituzione dei manoscritti e degli altri oggetti che diró in seguito. Se po[i] l'Orioli cercasse di menare il can per l'aia o ne ottenesse addirittura un rifiuto allora potrebbe senz'altro farlo citare per appropriazione indebita. Non le parrebbe una buona via da seguire?

Oggi stesso telegraferó a mia sorella che deve essere giunta da pochi giorni a New York per conoscere l'indirizzo di sua figlia Marianne Frau Von Eckart che abita in Italia, o almeno vi abitava, perché fu a lei che l'Orioli, pur avendo Marianne una richiesta scritta da me, l'Orioli senza negare il possesso dei manoscritti in questione, si schermí dicendo che era troppa responsabilitá il consegnarli ad una terza persona e che ad ogni modo uno di essi – e non sapeva quale – apparteneva a lui. Ció che è assolutamente falso. Cosi non appena avró l'indirizzo di Marianne glielo ecomunicheró immediatamente ond'ella possa chedere a lei direttamente tutte quelle informazioni del caso ed avere cosí la prova che detti manoscritti erano e sono effettivamente in suo possesso. Ormai che detti manoscritti erano in di lui consegna lo sa tutto il mondo, tutti i miei amici, i miein agenti di Londra, di Parigi, di quí ecct. e non credo che all'Orioli riesca facile il negarlo. Resta il fatto che egli li abbia a li faccia parire, ma a lui non fá nulla il timore della galera? Non credo che voglia correre questo rischio.

Spero inoltre che la mia procura le sia giunta completa senza aver bisogno di altre formalitá onde ella possa agire immediatamente. Questa mia sollecituèine ad agire é suggerita dal timore che l'Orioli essendo in Francia con l'amico Duglas possa vendere quei manoscritti che senza esagerare costituiscono una vera fortuna.

Ed ora cercheró di darle le informazioni che desidera.

Se ricordo bene, consegnai all'Orioli in piena fiducia e senza richiederne ricevuta, considerandolo un fedele amico mio e di mio marito, nel 1931 credo e non ricordo il mese al mio rito[r]no da Bandol a Firenze.

La ragione della consegna fu suggerita dal fatto che l'Orioli mi espresse l'intenzione di voler pubblicare due dei detti manoscritti non mai pubblicati ed anche perché io viaggiando all'estero temevo che essi mi venissero confiscati alla frontiera. Perché, com'Ella sa lo stesso libro della "Lady Chatterley's Lover" in molte Nazioni ne é proibita la pubblicazione integrale, se si eccettua la Francia ed il Sud America.

Lasciai a lui in perfetta buona fede anche un baule con molte cose dentro, di queste ricordo che vi erano molte lettere, taccuini, promemoria, fotografie di mio marito, nonché diversa mia corrispondenza, oggetti questi che lui (Orioli) pur non avendone alcun diritto di possesso ha irregolarmente venduti per l'importo di mille dolla[r]i ad un certo sign. Dan Wells residente in Concord, Mass. Detto baule con gli oggetti menzionati credo che rimanesse nell'abitazione dell'Orioli ancora all'epoca che mio marito era in vita e precisamente quando ci trasferimmo da Villa Mirenda (Firenze) a Bandol (Francia) nel 1928? Non ricordo bene, che per ragioni del nostro continuo viaggiare non si ebbe mai occasione di ritirare, anche perché ci si credeva in buone mani.

Per convincere il Magistrato della possessione di tali cose, non saprei che altre prove addurre, se non che:

1) un elenco degli oggetti acquistati dal Sign. Wells dal quale elenco sará facile dimostrare come tutti qu[e]i documenti fossero di carattere personale mio e di mio marito e niente affatto di pertinenza del Pino. Ma ció per provare unicamente come l'Orioli fosse in possesso realmente di tali cose e non per fargli una causa per essi, giacché ormai non ne varrebbe la pena e perché a me interessano i detti manoscritti. Nel caso che ció possa essegli [esserle] utile scriveró oggi stesso al Dan Wells affinché mi mandi l'elenco degli oggetti che acquistó circa due anni fa dal Pino, e non appena mi giungerá gliela manderó.

2) Le informazioni che potrá avere da mia nipote e per la quale faró seguire l'indirizzo fra qualche giorno. Nel caso che essa non abitasse piú in Italia potrá scriverle egualmente in Italiano, dove si trova forse in Germania perché lo scrive e lo parla bene – facendole in breve la storia di quanto accade e richiedendole le informazioni che le abbisognano.

L'Orioli ha inoltre una edizione di lusso speciale in pergamena l'unica in tutto il mondo della Lady Chatterley con dedica di mio marito a me che da sola puó valere un capitale ed altri libri, che non ricordo, pure di valore, che vorrei mi venissero restituiti assieme ai manoscritti.

Il fatto che l'Orioli ad una mia lettera scrittagli l'inverno scorso da Concord, Mass. e nella quale fra l'altro mi ripromettevo di dare a lui una percentuale sulla vendita dei manoscritti qualora li avesse consegnati al detto Dan Wells nel caso si fosse recato in Italia per ritirarli, come allora sembrava, non ha mai dato risposta, mi fa pensare che egli non sia piú l'Orioli che credevo, e che altresí non goda piú di quella riputazione che m'ero immaginata.

La mia offerta di una percentuale sulla eventuale vendita dei manoscritti era dettata semplicemente dal cuore, sapendolo a corto di denaro, ma non perché l'Orioli possa vantare alcun diritto su di essi. Ma poiché egli ora mi si presenta sotto un'altra veste, non ho piú nessuna intenzione di gratificarlo, ma bensí di ingiungergli di restituirmi il mal tolto o con le buone o con la forza.

Caro avvocato, mi sono di molto dilungata nella sola speranza di riuscire a spiegarmi il piú chiaramente possibile. Non appena avrá tutte le informazioni necessarie proceda il più sollecitamente possibile scegliendo la via che crederá migliore. Mi stia bene e con tanti saluti mi creda

[*Translation*:]

Dear Advocate Manara,

I am replying to your letter addressed to the Captain.[1] He has explained to me your intentions regarding the procedure you would like to follow in the well-known case, but, if you do not mind, my preference would be rather – provided you consider it possible – that before bringing a criminal case you try to contact Orioli and that, as my representative, you ask him directly for the restitution of the manuscripts[2] and other items I shall mention below. In case Orioli tried to beat about the bush, or even if you had a refusal from him, then you could, without doubt, have him sued for embezzlement. Don't you think this is a good way to proceed?

This very day I shall telegraph my sister,[3] who must have arrived in New York a few days ago, in order to get the address of her daughter Marianne von Eckart who lives in Italy, or at least who lived there, because, although Marianne had a request written by me, Orioli rebuffed her – without denying his possession of the manuscripts in question – by saying that it was too much responsibility to hand them over to a third party and that anyway one of them – he did not know which – belonged to him. This is absolutely false. Therefore, as soon as I have Marianne's address, I shall immediately make it known to you so that you can ask her directly all the information about the case and in this way have the proof that the said manuscripts were and are in effect in Orioli's possession. By now everybody knows that the said manuscripts were in his care – all my friends and my agents in London, Paris, here, etc., know it – and I do not think it can be easy for Orioli to deny it. What remains is the fact that he has them and that he can produce them. But is he not afraid of prison? I do not think that he wants to run this risk.

I also hope that you have received my full proxy, without needing further formalities, so that you may act immediately. This concern of mine is aroused by my fear that Orioli, being in France with his friend Douglas,[4] may sell those MSS that, with no exaggeration, are a real fortune.

And now I shall try to give you the information that you want.

If I remember correctly, I gave Orioli [the manuscripts] in full trust and without asking for a receipt, considering him a faithful friend of mine and my husband's. I think it was in 1931, but I cannot remember which month, when I returned from Bandol to Florence.

The reasons for the consignment are that Orioli expressed to me his intention to publish two of the said manuscripts[5] never before published and also that, since I was going abroad, I was afraid they might be confiscated at the border. Because, as you know, in many nations the uncensored publication of the book *Lady Chatterley's Lover* is prohibited, with the exception of France and South America.

In perfect good faith I also left with him a trunk with many things inside – among them, I remember, were many letters, notebooks, memoranda, photographs of my husband, not to mention several letters of mine – all objects that he, Orioli, although he had no right of possession, has improperly sold for the sum of $1000 to a Mr. Dan Wells, who lives in Concord, Mass.[6] The said trunk with the mentioned items was, I think, still in Orioli's house when my husband was alive and certainly when we moved from the Villa Mirenda (Florence) to Bandol (France) in 1928. I do not remember [the dates] well. Because of our continuous travels, we never had an opportunity to collect the trunk; but we also thought we were in good hands.

To convince the Magistrate of Orioli's possession of these things, I do not know what kind of further proofs I might provide, except for the following:

1) one list of the items purchased by Mr. Wells. From that list it will be easy to demonstrate that all those documents were of a personal nature, mine and my husband's, and not in any way Pino's concern. All of this only goes to prove how Orioli really had those things in his hands. But it would not be worthwhile to bring a case against him to recover them, since by now it would not be worth it and since I am now concerned with the said manuscripts. If this list may be useful to you, I shall write this very day to Dan Wells so that he may send me the list of the objects he purchased from Pino about two years ago, and as soon as I receive it I shall send it on to you.

2) the information you will be able to have from my niece, whose address I shall send in a few days. If she no longer lives in Italy, you can write to her in Italian all the same, where she lives now, perhaps in Germany, since she can write and speak it well, giving her a brief summary of what is happening and asking her for the information you need.

Orioli also has a special and precious parchment edition of *Lady Chatterley* (the only one in all the world) with a dedication to me by my husband, which on its own is worth a fortune, and other books that I do not remember, also valuable, which I would like to have back along with the manuscripts.

The fact that Orioli never replied to a letter I wrote to him last winter from Concord, Mass. – in which, among other things, I proposed to give him a percentage on the sale of the manuscripts if he handed them over to the said Dan Wells in case Dan went to Italy to collect them – gives me reason to believe that he is not any more the Orioli I thought he was, and that, moreover, he does not enjoy any longer the reputation I had imagined.

My offer of a percentage on the possible sale of the manuscripts was simply suggested by my heart, because I knew that Orioli was short of money, but not because he has any right to them. But since he appears now in a different guise, I have no intention of gratifying him any more, but rather of demanding that he return the loot by fair means or foul.

Dear advocate, I have gone on so long only in the hope that I make myself as clear as possible. As soon as you have all the necessary information, proceed as promptly as possible, choosing the way you believe is best. Take care, and with my best regards, yours sincerely

Notes

1. Angelo Ravagli.
2. Of *Lady Chatterley's Lover*.
3. Else Jaffe.
4. Norman Douglas.
5. The first and second versions of *Lady Chatterley's Lover*, composed 1926–7 at the Villa Mirenda near Florence.
6. Jenny Wells Vincent remembers that she and her husband Dan "were living in Cornwall at the time – March of 1936. Dan made a special trip, by himself, to Italy to see Orioli in Florence. When he returned he brought with him '160 letters and all sorts of odds and ends' (I quote from my diary of March 27, 1936). He paid 200 pounds for this collection, which is undoubtedly what Frieda refers to" (letter to the editor, 13 October 1989).

127. Jake Zeitlin to Frieda Lawrence, 25 September 1937
Text: TSCC UCLA

September 25, 1937

Mrs. Frieda Lawrence
Kiowa Ranch
San Cristobal, New Mexico

Dear Mrs. Lawrence:

Thanks for sending the authorization. I am sorry to have to return it, but it would not be legal without your dating it and Angelino signing as witness.

I don't know how Curtis Brown got the idea that there is going to be an exhibition at Yale. Nothing has been mentioned to me at all.

No printed catalogue has been gotten out. I have not been able to afford the cost. In the meantime, I am sending you a typewritten copy of the catalogue and the price list, which you can use for reference. The printed catalogue will cost about three hundred dollars to get out and I am too short of funds to put up the money for a little while.

Thanks for giving me the name of Carl Weeks at Des Moines, Iowa. I shall see that he gets a copy of the typewritten list and a copy of the catalogue later. I shall also write him a letter.

Albert Bender will be delighted to have your permission to publish the poems. I have seen Aldous Huxley three times. He came in one afternoon and the next day we had a long interview with Geller, followed by luncheon last Thursday at the Paramount Studios with Idwal Jones and Anna May Wong.[1] We are to have dinner at Paul Jordan Smith's house this coming Thursday night.

Yes, you are right about selling to Harvard. If things continue as they are going we should have ten thousand dollars out of the collection by the end of the year, and still retain some of the best items.

Best regards to Angie. Your few words about the ranch make me want to get in my car and dash back up there.

Cordially,   [JZ]

Note
1. Anna May Wong (1907–61), American actress of Chinese parentage who starred in 50 films, including *Shanghai Express* (1932). Lawrence and Frieda saw her screen performance in *The Thief of Baghdad* (1924).

128. Angelo Ravagli to Jake Zeitlin, 28 September 1937
Text: MS UCLA

Kiowa Ranch, San Cristobal, N.M.
28 September 1937

Dear Jake –

Here is the authorization with my signt and the date – I hope you can go along very well now –

We need the price list only – because the typewritten of the catalogue we have already.

Is to bad you can not print the catalogue, but I hope in a wile you are able to do so –

I hope you and Gina and the children are well –

My regards to you both –

Sincerely yours,   Angelino –

P.S.   Frieda is well – but to busy to write –

129. Frieda Lawrence to Jake Zeitlin, 28 September 1937

Text: TS UCLA

Date 28 September 1937

Mr. Jake Zeitlin
614 West Sixth Street
Los Angeles, California

Dear Mr. Zeitlin:

I herewith authorize you to make a special price of twenty-two hundred dollars ($2,200.00) to your customer for the following five manuscripts of D. H. Lawrence:

No.	8:	LADY CHATTERLEY Typescript
No.	9:	A PROPOS OF LADY CHATTERLEY
''	10:	PORNOGRAPHY AND OBSCENITY
''	11:	THE FOX
''	113:	INTRODUCTION TO PAINTINGS

I understand that they are to be held until January 1, 1938, and billed to your customer at that time, and that payment will be made in a number of installments, terms of which are to be agreed upon at that time.

Of course I understand you are assuming responsibility for the ultimate payment of the full amount, less your commission.

Witness: Angelo Ravagli.   Signed: Frieda Lawrence

130. Bertram Rota to Jake Zeitlin, 28 September 1937

Text (abridged): TS UCLA

Bodley House, Vigo Street, London, W.1
28th September, 1937

Messrs Jake Zeitlin, Inc.,
614, West 6th Street,
Los Angeles,
Cal., U.S.A.

Dear Mr. Zeitlin,

I was glad to have your letter of September 17th, as I was beginning to wonder if my cable had miscarried. It would be well if the collection were kept en bloc, of course, but it is probably too extensive for that. I know of no particularly easy approach to the Aga Khan, nor have I heard of his buying material of this sort. I look forward to hearing further from you as soon as possible and to receive the manuscripts selected if the collection is not sold intact. . . .

Yours sincerely,   Bertram Rota

131. Jake Zeitlin to Frieda Lawrence, 16 October 1937
Text: TSCC UCLA

October 16, 1937

Mrs. Frieda Lawrence
Kiowa Ranch
San Cristobal, New Mexico

Dear Frieda:

I have exciting news for you. We are going to hold an exhibition of the Lawrence manuscripts at the Los Angeles Public Library from November 1 to November 20. A very fine committee of sponsors has been formed and everyone is very enthusiastic.

Aldous Huxley has agreed to be present on the night of the formal opening, which will be November 2, and to speak on Lawrence. We have also gotten together enough money to print the catalogue in very handsome form and Ward Ritchie is starting to work on it right away.

The one thing lacking would be your presence. The committee wants you to be on hand at the opening and to be introduced and say a few words. Please sit down and write me without delay and let me know if this would be at all possible. I know that you and Angie like to leave Taos during the cold weather and I hope it will be convenient for you to come. We want to make an announcement as soon as possible, so I hope you can send me word without delay. Could you also send a copy of the painting and perhaps the imprinted piece of the pegasus which Lawrence did?

I hope you will be pleased with the plans. Aldous seems to be most enthusiastic. The Huxleys have been in touch with me quite a lot and we have been having some very good times. Did you hear him speak over the radio Thursday night?

Regards to Angie.

Cordially,   [JZ]

132. Jake Zeitlin to Ben Abramson, 20 October 1937
Text (abridged): TSCC UCLA

October 20, 1937

Mr. Ben Abramson
333 South Dearborn Avenue
Chicago, Illinois

Dear Mr. Abramson:
    . . . Don't wait too long for the decision on the Lawrence manuscripts. I have a good prospect for the sale of all of them in one lot but have told

him that I cannot reserve anything. The prices are low and you ought to be able to act quickly.

By the way, I am printing an eighty-page catalogue with an introduction by Aldous Huxley. Ward Ritchie is doing the printing and it will be a very handsome item. I cannot afford to distribute them free and am planning to ask 75¢ apiece. How many copies do you want?

Cordially,   [JZ]

133. Stefano Manara to Frieda Lawrence, 20 October 1937
Text: Telegram UCLA

FIRENZE 1000
OCT 20 1937

MRS LAWRENCE
KIOWA RANCH
SANCRISTOBAL
TAOS JCT, NMEX

MANOSCRITTI RICUPERATI[1]

MANARA

Note
1. "Manuscripts recovered".

134. Bertram Rota to Jake Zeitlin, 27 October 1937.
Text: TS UCLA

Bodley House, Vigo Street, London, W.1
27th October, 1937.

Messrs Jake Zeitlin, Inc.,
614, West 6th Street,
Los Angeles, Cal.,
U.S.A.

Dear Mr. Zeitlin,

The parcel of D. H. Lawrence manuscripts arrived this morning and although the seven items it contained were quite satisfactory in general I hasten to point out that two of the supplementary pieces described in your list were missing. Item 38 "The Last Laugh" consisted of the twenty-four page holograph manuscript only and lacked the twenty-one page corrected typescript. Item 39 "Glad Ghosts" contained the sixty-nine page holograph manuscript only and lacked the several odd pages of manuscript of an early version. I trust that these pieces can be found at your shop, as it is certain that they were not lost in transit. The parcel arrived here quite securely packed and sealed.

Although the most important material has reached me safely I naturally cannot ask my client to complete the purchase until he has all the items catalogued and I therefore look forward to receiving the two missing pieces as soon as possible.

Yours sincerely,   Bertram Rota

135. Jake Zeitlin to Frieda Lawrence, 1 November 1937

Text: TSCC UCLA

November 1, 1937

Mrs. Frieda Lawrence
Kiowa Ranch
San Cristobal, New Mexico

Dear Frieda:

The Lawrence exhibition is going to be put on at the Library and will open tomorrow night. Aldous will fortunately be here and will be able to speak. We expect a large number of people and I know you will be present in name for neither Aldous nor I can speak long without mentioning you.

I have just remembered that the terms of our contract require written permission from you for this exhibition. Would you mind sending me a brief statement to the effect that you are agreeable to my placing the manuscripts of Lawrence on exhibition at the Los Angeles Public Library? The catalogue is in the press and may be ready by Tuesday. As soon as we have some copies I shall send you about ten. Ward Ritchie is doing it and I think you will agree that it is a beautiful job.

Enclosed is a copy of a letter I have just received from Albert Bender in which he speaks of his desire to have Grabhorn print a group of unpublished Pansies and six unpublished poems, described as items sixty-one and sixty-three in our list. I hope you will agree to write a short foreword. Albert Bender is such a nice man that I am sure you could never refuse him anything he asked for if you knew him.

I understand that Mr. Weeks is not interested in buying the manuscript collection, the head of the fiction department of the Los Angeles

Public Library tells me. It seems that she got in touch with him as soon as she heard that the exhibition was going on. Of course I shall send him a catalogue as soon as it comes out and perhaps this will stimulate his interest over again. You will hear from me again after the opening of the exhibition, since I know you will want to have a report on what takes place.

With kindest regards to Angelo.

Sincerely,   [JZ]

136. Althea Warren to Jake Zeitlin, 4 November 1937
Text: TS UCLA

Los Angeles Public Library
530 South Hope Street, Los Angeles, California
November 4, 1937

Mr. Jake Zeitlin
614 West Sixth Street
Los Angeles, California

My dear Mr. Zeitlin:

The Board of Library Commissioners wish to acknowledge your gracious courtesy in placing the name of the Los Angeles Library as imprint on the descriptive catalog of the manuscripts of D. H. Lawrence. It is certainly an honor to be in any way associated with such a piece of printing. The Library is glad of the opportunity to distribute the review copies, as Mr. Powell has asked us to.

In regard to the D. H. Lawrence manuscripts, it is felt by the Board that the owner of the manuscripts should be the one to sign a statement that the Library is not responsible for fire and theft while the manuscripts are in this building, all reasonable protection being granted them. Will you get Mrs. Lawrence's signature on the enclosed waiver of responsibility?

I hope you were pleased with the success of the meeting Tuesday evening. All speakers seem to me most delightful, and if only the audience could have been reduced by half it would have needed no improvement!

Most sincerely yours,   Althea Warren, City Librarian[1]

Note
1. Althea Warren was head of the Los Angeles Public Library, 1933–47.

137. Frieda Lawrence to Jake Zeitlin, 5 November 1937
Text: MS UCLA

Kiowa
5. Nov 37

Dear Jake,

Of course I am pleased about the exhibition and above all I am thankful not to have sold to stingy Harvard.

It is good of Aldous to help so much. I thought his foreword was very charming. Have they gone?

I also have a piece of good news. You remember Orioli had the 3 Lady C's. Then he would not part with them to my grief. I thought he was a real friend, but Douglas, who is quite without morals and never liked Lawrence must have worked on him.

So I was afraid to loose these 3 Mss. Angelino's step-father-in-law[1] is a fine old lawyer and *got* the Mss from Pino. So Angelino will bring them in the spring. You find a person for them. The two unprinted Lady C's are *very* interesting and different, but I fear the Viking has the rights. But could one not sell a few interesting chapters?

I forgot who told me, that the Mss of the printed Lady C looses in value because there are two more Mss, but they are so different and not so "improper."

I shall like to hear your report very much and see the catalogue.

You heard that the occidental college is doing "David," very pleasing thought.

It is still awfully beautiful and sunny. Kindest wishes – Angelino is in Denver. He has a great scheme of making pottery – learning in Italy this winter.

Frieda L

I want you to give Aldous the Mss of *St Mawr*, and for Witter Bynner "None of That."

Note
1. Stefano Manara.

138. Frieda Lawrence to Jake Zeitlin, 8 November 1937
Text: MS UCLA

Kiowa Ranch
8. November 37

Dear Jake Zeitlin,

This is to say that I am very glad that you are making an exhibition of the Lawrence Mss in Los Angeles.

Sincerely yours   Frieda Lawrence

139. Jake Zeitlin to Flora Belle Ludington, 9 November 1937
Text: TSCC UCLA

November 9, 1937

Miss Florabelle Ludington
Mount Holyoke College
South Hadley, Massachusetts

Dear Florabelle:

I am sending you today two copies of the new catalogue I have just published of the collection of Lawrence manuscripts now being exhibited at the Los Angeles Public Library. It is a grand collection and really ought to be kept all together. We had quite an affair at the opening of the exhibition. I introduced Aldous Huxley and Huxley spoke very brilliantly about Lawrence as he knew him. I thought of you and regretted that you were not here to do a similar job by the manuscripts at Mills [College].

Do you think there would be any interest in them at Mount Holyoke? If so let me know. It might be that I could send a substantial group to you for an exhibition.

Lots has happened to me but it is all of a nature that cannot be transmitted in a letter. I wish I could have a long talk with you. It would do me good.

Please sit down and write me about yourself, if you can forgive me my long silence.

With best regards to you.

Cordially,   [JZ]

140. Jake Zeitlin to Robert Gordon Sproul, 9 November 1937
Text: TSCC UCLA

November 9, 1937

Dr. Robert Gordon Sproul
University of California
405 Hilgard Avenue
Los Angeles, California

Dear Dr. Sproul:

I am sending you with my compliments a copy of the catalogue of the manuscripts of D. H. Lawrence which I have just gotten out. This is a very important collection and is very excellent source material for students of contemporary literature as well as others such as investigators into the psychology of creative writing.

We are very anxious to try to keep this collection intact as well as highly desirous of having it remain in California. Aldous Huxley, whom I had hoped you could meet when he spoke the other night at the library here laid much emphasis upon the great value that such a collection of material would have in a place like this: "Crawling with education," as he said.

If you have any ideas or suggestions concerning the collection, I shall be very happy to hear from you.

Sincerely,   [JZ]

141. Frieda Lawrence to Jake Zeitlin, 12 November 1937
Text: MS UCLA

12. Nov. 37

Dear Jake Zeitlin,

I am just as pleased as a peacock with that catalogue. What you wrote is very fine. Also Aldous and Mr Powell.

I feel for the first time in America something is happening about Lawrence in a truly enthusiastic Lawrence spirit. I feel at last he is coming alive in America. It takes a long time.

When I think that years ago I asked the Viking to make an exhibition and they did'nt do it.

I still hope to get the books away from Viking. They want *14000* dollars and I have'nt got it and the modern library wont pay so much.[1]

There *are'nt* any publishers, if not Houghton Mifflin, who wanted to do an edition de luxe.

Let me know if anybody wants to buy.

I also promised "Eric Gill" that unfinished review of Lawrence's. Write and tell me more.

Yours ever   Frieda L –

You must be pleased too, I liked so much what you wrote.

[*Angelo Ravagli begins*:]

Bravo Jak this time you did a very grand Jobe. I congratulate you and with your assistants – Dear Jake when you can, will you ask Mr. Twadowsky three copy of three play that Frieda gave to him last winter and send here? Thanks very much – my regards to Gina and bravo again to you

Angelino

Note
1. See Letter 158.

142. Frieda Lawrence to Lawrence Clark Powell, 12. November 1937
Text: MS UCLA

Kiowa Ranch
12. Nov. 37

Dear Mr Powell,

It is a long time since anything gave me as much pleasure as that catalogue. It seems to be alive with Lawrence, you really did a beautiful work.

I very much wish I could have come. But I am enjoying the conviction that for the first time in America, something truly alive is happening about Lawrence, with that exhibition and the play.

I thank you very sincerely for your part of the show! If it does'nt bore you, write me more details.

Lawrence would have enjoyed your catalogue. You just got the humanly significant bits. It is real fun to read it, to me anyhow.

With very kind regards   Frieda Lawrence

Would you send a catalog to my son

Montague Weekley
29 Barrowgate Rd
Chiswick
London W 4

I have given my copies away already –

143. Jake Zeitlin to Bertram Rota, 15 November 1937
Text: TSCC UCLA

November 15, 1937

Mr. Bertram Rota
Bodley House, Vigo Street
London, W.1, England

Dear Mr. Rota:

My apologies and regrets at having left out the two supplementary pieces. I can assure you that I was not intentionally withholding them and I was quite surprised to discover they had not been included.

They are being sent to you today and I hope that your customer will be pleased with them on their arrival.

No doubt you have by now received a copy of the printed catalogue of the manuscripts. These are being sold retail at 75¢ each and I am allowing one third off to dealers. If you have any special customers whom you think are good prospects for the manuscripts, I shall be glad to supply you with as many extra catalogues as you might desire. I am sure that if they are properly placed they will bring more sales and I see no reason why you cannot handle them. The inserted supplementary price list can, of course, be taken out. I am sending it to practically no one except one or two dealers in England, such as Maggs [Brothers] and Sawyers. If you have any suggestions or ideas as to how we might effectively further the sale of the manuscripts I would be most grateful.

Sincerely,   [JZ]

144. Willard Johnson to Jake Zeitlin, 17 November 1937
Text: TS UCLA

laughing horse, taos, new mexico
November 17th, 1937

Jake Zeitlin, Esq.,
614 West 6th Street,
Los Angeles, California.

Dear Jake Zeitlin:

At Frieda Lawrence's yesterday, I saw your catalogue of the exhibition of D. H. Lawrence's manuscripts, and would like to have one or two for myself. Will you please let me know how much they sell for, or whether I must write to the Los Angeles Public Library about getting copies?

Mrs. Lawrence and I were also talking about one of the manuscripts – a fragment of a play called "Altitude" (No. 68 in the catalogue) and she says that I may print it in the *Laughing Horse* since it is not likely to be of enough public interest to publish elsewhere. Could you have a copy of this manuscript made for me? Or will it be necessary to wait until after the exhibit is over? In any case, you will probably hear from her also, corroborating this request.

Incidentally, may I congratulate you on the catalogue. It is a beautiful piece of work, typographically, and quite as interesting biographically as some of the more pretentious biographies!

Yours sincerely,   Spud Johnson

145. Jake Zeitlin to Frieda Lawrence, 17 November 1937
Text: TSCC UCLA

November 17, 1937

Mrs. Frieda Lawrence
Kiowa Ranch
San Cristobal, New Mexico

Dear Frieda:

Your satisfaction at the way the exhibition has gone off and the way the catalogue came out has given me a great deal of pleasure. I am glad to have been able to contribute my part towards seeing that Lawrence is recognized as he should be. My admiration for the significance of his work has grown immensely as I have come in closer contact with it. He is certainly coming alive in America and I think that in the years to come his significance will grow to proportions comparable to that of religion.

I should like to know more about the situation regarding the books with Viking Press. Do they want to release all American publishing rights on Lawrence for fourteen thousand dollars or is that what they want for the prints [plates] and all stock in print? I might be able to find a publisher who would more aggressively promote him. I do think that the idea of an edition de-luxe would find interest with some publisher. My first idea is that it should be done in England by some firm like Gollancz, Chatto and Windus or Heinemann. Shall I get in touch with some of the publishers I know and see what they might care to do?

Thanks for the kind words about my foreword. Aldous's introduction is really a very highly illuminating and sympathetic piece and will, I believe, do a great deal of good. I gave Aldous the manuscript of *St. Mawr* the other night at dinner. He was very happy to have it. Shall I send "None of That" to Witter Bynner? He didn't stay over here and I understand that he is now back in Santa Fe. Also where do you want me to send the Eric Gill review? If you have his address I shall be glad to send it on.

That is very grand news about your getting *Lady Chatterley* back. I know you had despaired of ever getting the other manuscripts. By all means get them to me at the earliest possible moment. The man who bought the corrected typescript[1] would be interested in these also and I think that a very good price for the lot could be had. I doubt if the unprinted chapters would have any special publishing value but I will talk it over with Larry Powell. He might be interested in editing these. Do you think they might be brought over before the spring when Angelo returns? Would you also get hold of the specially printed copies of *Lady Chatterley*? As you know, I am most anxious to have one of these for a customer.

The affair at the library was very grand. Many people came to hear Aldous talk. In fact, only about one half of those who came could get in the hall. The exhibition is attracting a great many people. Some are coming from out of town to see it. I know that there has never been a literary exhibition here to compare with it in importance and public interest.

Let me know more about Angie's project. I hope it is successful. Also I should be interested to hear how you are feeling. Maria and Aldous have told me you have bought another ranch.[2] Please be careful and don't overstep yourself. I should hate to see you assume financial obligations for any property or enterprise that might endanger your means.

As you might know I have always wanted to have one of the Lawrence manuscripts for myself but my means will never allow me to buy one. If you ever feel like making a present of another one of them I wish you would keep me in mind. My particular favorite of course is *The Escaped Cock* but that would be too important a thing. Next to that comes *Apocalypse* which I believe will some day be the gospel for the followers of Lawrence. That too is too important an item for you to make a present of. The third thing in my classification of desirability is item 117 entitled "Three Essays on Love."

By the way, I want to get out a Christmas card on which I print a quotation from Lawrence. I want to use the final paragraph from *Apocalypse* which starts "What man most passionately wants is his living wholeness." In all it consists of about eleven lines. May I have your permission to reprint these?

Please give Angelo my kindest regards. Tell him I wish every success for him in his new undertaking. I have no doubt of his ability and aggressiveness and I am sure that I would not hesitate to trust any undertaking to his hands. My love to both of you.

Cordially,   [JZ]

Notes
1. T. E. Hanley.
2. Los Pinos in El Prado, New Mexico.

146. Flora Belle Ludington to Jake Zeitlin, 19 November 1937

Text (abridged): MS UCLA

Mount Holyoke College, South Hadley, Massachusetts
Nov. 19, 1937.

Dear Jake –

Your Lawrence catalogue is simply lovely – how well Ward Ritchie did by you and what chances have I for two more copies? One for the library, for I can't bear to part with the one which came and one for Bacon Collamore a Hartford collector who turned up for my exhibit in the spring? Or you might like to send it to him direct – address 85 Pearl Street, Hartford. He has a good collection of Lawrence firsts and some mss. if I remember rightly, is vice-president of a Fire Insurance money and must spend several thousand dollars a year on books.

How I wish I might have been to your opening and heard and met Huxley whom I admire no end. – Somehow life in South Hadley is very sheltered, more so than Mills [College] by far.

Now as to an exhibit of Lawrence mss. I'd love to have one – could, I think, gather in a few outsiders who might be interested in purchase (Collamore for one and Carroll Wilson another) – and our own students would love to see them. When would you suggest our having them? Jan, Feb or March appeals most to me but you could decide upon that. We would carry suitable insurance and can show in locked cases. (Have 3 good ones.) . . .

Greetings always – Flora Belle

147. Jake Zeitlin to Philip C. Duschnes, 20 November 1937

Text: TSCC UCLA

November 20, 1937

Mr. Philip Duschnes
507 Fifth Avenue
New York City, New York

Dear Mr. Duschnes:

Praise from you for our Lawrence catalogue is something I highly value, especially since I have so long admired the style of your own catalogues.[1] We have been getting some very interesting responses from [it] and it is the kind of thing that a book-seller must do once in a while in order to feel justified in his calling.

Unfortunately Mrs. Lawrence is only allowing me fifteen percent commission on the manuscripts and out of that I have to pay all expenses. You can see that on that basis I can hardly afford to allow any discount. However, if you can get anyone interested in a group of the items I think that some satisfactory terms could be reached.

I am sending you four copies of the catalogue by today's mail. I appreciate your interest in distributing them and I hope you do effect some sales.

With kindest regards.

Sincerely,   [JZ]

Note
1. Duschnes had praised the catalogue in his letter of 18 November 1937, saying: "This is a most handsome presentation and your good self and Ward Ritchie deserve the highest compliments."

148. Herbert Faulkner West to Jake Zeitlin, 20 November 1937
Text: MS UCLA

Dartmouth College, Hanover, New Hampshire
Nov. 20/37

Thanks for what you said about my book.[1] I have not yet received the Lawrence catalogues but when I do I shall take the matter up with our library. Much as they want original material they seldom have funds to get it unless some wealthy alumnus will provide it.

I should be glad to receive your catalogues myself though my expenditures can not be great. I had a notice from Hanover, Mass. about some printed matter so perhaps you addressed the catalogues to the wrong state. I send the postage there and shall get them next week.

Yours,   H. F. West

Note
1. *Modern Book Collecting for the Impecunious Amateur* (Boston: Little, Brown, 1936).

149. Frieda Lawrence to Jake Zeitlin, 21 November 1937
Text: MS UCLA

Kiowa
21. Nov 37

Dear Jake Zeitlin,

Have'nt we got a lot of irons in the fire! I answer your letter right away.

The Vikings, I dont like them, want 14000 for all American rights, plates and stock. I know they dont think much of Lawrence and ought to sell cheese, not books. It was Houghton Mifflin's idea to make an edition de luxe. In England it's allright, Heinemann, Frere Reeves, a director very enthusiastic and a friend.

You will love the Lady C Mss, they are perfect. I wish Mr Powell could edit them, but so far Viking has all rights and I dont want them to do it.

There is only one parchment bound copy of Lady C, printed on blue handmade paper, an inscription to me from Lawrence "One for the dame, none for the little boy, that cries down the lane." There was only this one for me, none for him.

The 3 Lady C's are quite different. I remember a very amusing, sarcastic, common people tea-party with salmon and buns and cakes and tinned fruit, jams etc. The first Lady C is my favorite, more romantic it was in the last version he wanted to "rub" it in. When I said, "why do you use those words so on purpose?" He said: ["]Well, they shant get away with it as they did with Blake, they will have it, that his is only mysticism and symbols."

I fear it is not safe to send the Mss, they wont suspect Angelino. The other two Lady Cs are'nt even typed.

Please send Bynner "None of That." I could'nt find it in the list. It is about Mabel, when he hated her. I dont know Eric Gill's address, will ask Pollinger. Also the man [Robert] Byron wanted his review, promised me a persian rug, but I never got it.

We will see about an Mss for you. How things go.

Yes, do send[1] the Xmas card and send me one.

Everybody loves the catalog, if you have a few to spare send them me.

Angelino runs round picking up bits of clay for his future pottery.

Maria H[uxley] came for two days, a telegram from Aldous, that Gerald [Heard] has dislocated a shoulder and Aldous has to lecture alone.

The practical Angie also remarked that Lawrence's Mss are specially valuable, as nobody writes by hand anymore.

Carl Weeks' Xmas card is Lorenzo's chapel here. He is coming to Los Angeles soon.

Thank you for the cheque. Do people want to buy?

I also like the Thomas Hardy essay very much and [the essay on] education. I think I will not sell the Thomas Hardy, I remember so well, when he wrote it, so full of beans. (Price too low, I think.)

Maria says, you are marrying again. Do we know her?[2]

Write again. I asked them to send you my mother's letters to L[awrence] from the bank in England. All I have here are a lot of postcards, shall I send them? I also want to give Mr Powell a small Mss later on –

Many greetings from us both. No, it is'nt so stupid to have bought that place, I can stay there in winter, here I cant. It is cold already, but beautiful. "Smile" is Murry and Catherine.

Such a muddle of a letter!

I do *want* to get rid of Viking.

Ever yours   Frieda L –

With Bender is again the complication with Viking.

[*Angelo Ravagli begins*:]

P.S.   Dear Jake, according to your recent about divorce, try to have a divorce also with the Viking Press, but you have to found the husband first, like you did I hope!!

love   Angelino.

Notes

1.   send]   print
2.   A reference to Josephine Ver Brugge.

150. Herbert Faulkner West to Jake Zeitlin, 23 November 1937

Text: MS UCLA

Dartmouth College, Hanover, N.H.
Nov. 23, 1937

Dear Mr. Zeitlin:–

To-day I received a copy of "The Manuscripts of D. H. Lawrence" – a magnificent catalogue. (It had been sent by error of address to Hanover, Massachusetts.) Many thanks.

I shall take it to our librarian and talk to him about the possibility of acquiring something and see whether or not he knows of any wealthy alumnus who might buy it in part for the college.

A private collector I know might be interested. In fact I know he has one of the Lawrence's manuscripts – I believe it is *Sea and Sardinia*. His name is Richard H. Mandel, Mt. Kisco, New York. Let him know what you have and the prices. His wife might give him one for Christmas and he might want some of them himself.

I should like to have seen the exhibition.

The creative process at work is a strange and miraculous thing. Lawrence was unquestionably a genius, if, withal, a sick one.

That's a magnificent collection – and for a man with sufficient means it should be a glorious opportunity.

Very sincerely yours,   Herbert F. West

151. Hon. Dorothy Brett to Jake Zeitlin, 23 November 1937
Text: TS UCLA

Box 214   Taos   New Mexico
Nov 23 1937

Dear Sir

Having read your catalogue of the Lawrence Manuscripts I thought you might be interested to know that I intend to sell mine. ... I am anxious to help with the education of some children that need a good education ... and as Lawrence suffered all his life from his education I think he would like to have these letters of his written to me sold for that purpose. ... Therefore if you could put me in touch with any one interested in collecting such things I would be much obliged ... I would like to get about $35 a letter. ... I have nearly 100. ...

Yrs sincerely   D E Brett[1]

Note

1. Sean Hignett explains that "Brett had been pursued some years earlier by a young man from Harvard [almost certainly Harry K. Wells] who wanted to photocopy the Lawrence letters ... for publication as part of a research thesis. The Lawrence letters were, in fact, in a tin box in Stieglitz's keeping in New York where Brett had taken them, along with her Lawrence manuscripts, when Stieglitz had asked if he could read them. She warned Stieglitz not to allow the Harvard student any access and then, later, in the summer of 1936, twice asked Stieglitz to return the letters to her in New Mexico but, for some reason, Stieglitz ignored her request and held on to them. It was not, in fact, until after the death of Stieglitz in 1946 that the Lawrence letters and manuscripts were finally returned to Brett by Georgia O'Keefe.... [On 11 July 1938] Brett had written again to Stieglitz asking him to try to find a buyer for both Lawrence's and Katherine's letters, the proceeds of which, she said, she wanted to use to educate Rachel Hawk's children. The best offer Brett managed to obtain then for Lawrence's letters was $100 and so they remained in her possession until 1951 when ... she sold them ... to the University of Cincinnati" (*Brett: From Bloomsbury to New Mexico* (New York: Franklin Watts, 1983) p. 232). The letters were published as "D. H. Lawrence and Frieda Lawrence: Letters to Dorothy Brett", *D. H. Lawrence Review*, 9 (1976) pp. 1–116.

152. Frieda Lawrence to Lawrence Clark Powell, 26 November 1937
Text: MS UCLA

Kiowa
26. Nov 37

Dear Mr Powell,

Thank you very much for the catalogs, they came to-day – Many people wanted one.

The Guggenheim people are wrong, the real books on Lawrence have'nt begun yet. I will tell you, when you come, what will seem interesting to you – I mean you will have to ask – The Jeffers were here to lunch yesterday, what a lovable person he is!

Are you sure my recommendation would be any use? Of course I will gladly do it.

With very kind wishes

Sincerely   Frieda Lawrence

153. Jake Zeitlin to Bennett A. Cerf, 30 November 1937

Text: TSCC UCLA

November 30, 1937

Mr. Bennett A. Cerf
Random House, Inc.
20 East 57th Street
New York City, New York

Dear Bennett:

Thanks for the kind words about the catalogue. The exhibition has evoked a great deal of interest and we have had thousands of visitors. It is astonishing what a following Lawrence has. His public is continuing to grow and I think the time will come when he will be regarded as a sort of a prophet, something more than a literary name.

Frieda Lawrence has just written me that she would like to see someone take over the American publishing rights of Lawrence's works. She is not entirely happy with the Viking connection and she tells me that all of the rights, plates and stock on hand at Viking could be purchased at what appears to me to be a very low figure. Houghton-Mifflin have approached her with the suggestion of bringing out a collected edition, and she has asked me what I think about it. In my opinion, Random House is the logical publisher for Lawrence and I think you could do a very swell job both by him and yourselves.

A collected edition of Lawrence edited by Lawrence Clark Powell, who edited the manuscript catalogue and who, I think, is the best-equipped man to do such a job, would find a big market right now. There is a great need for a standard edition. Libraries would all go for it and a good many Lawrence readers who have isolated volumes of his works would, I think, want everything, if the complete set could be published at a moderate price.

Frieda has written me that they have located the other three manu-scripts of *Lady Chatterley's Lover* in Italy and that she has gotten possession of them. They are being brought over this fall. She says:

"The 3 Lady C's are quite different. I remember a very amusing, sarcastic, common people tea-party with salmon and buns and cakes and tinned fruit, jams etc. The first Lady C is my favorite, more romantic it was in the last version he wanted to 'rub' it in. When I said why do you use those words so on purpose? He said: 'Well, they shant get away with it as they did with Blake, they will have it, that his is only mysticism and symbols.' . . . The other two Lady C's aren't even typed."

I am sure that the announcement of the publishing of a complete collated version by you, and you are the only publisher who could get away with it in America, would create a very big demand. Frieda has authorized me to see what can be done in this connection and I should like very much to discuss it with you further. You may be sure that I would heartily cooperate with you if you were to consider taking over the publishing of Lawrence and I think I could contribute some very constructive ideas.

We should keep in touch more and cooperate better. While my troubles are not over my business is better and I could dispose of a good many Random House books. I realize that your attitude is based upon reports you have been receiving but I think we are both losing business through not getting together. Will you be coming to California soon? A good talk between us might do us both good.

With kindest regards.

Sincerely,   [JZ]

154. Jake Zeitlin to Richard Mandel, 1 December 1937
Text: TSCC UCLA

December 1, 1937

Mr. Richard Mandel:
Mount Kisco, New York

Dear Mr. Mandel:
Dr. Herbert Faulkner West has given me your name and suggested that I send you a catalogue of the manuscripts of D. H. Lawrence which I have in my possession at this time. Dr. West has been very kind in his praise of the catalogue as well as in his enthusiastic appreciation of Lawrence. He tells me that you have one of Lawrence's manuscripts, possibly *Sea and Sardinia*. I should be interested to know if this is the case, since according to Frieda Lawrence, who has only the corrected typescript, described as item 77 in the catalogue, Lawrence destroyed it.

The significance of Lawrence is just commencing to be realized and I think the full effect of his greatness will not be felt for another twenty-five years. Certainly all of the most distinguished people of our day agree with Dr. West that Lawrence was unquestionably a genius.

I hope you will find something you would care to have in the collection and I should be glad to hear from you if you are further interested.

Sincerely,   [JZ]

155. Jake Zeitlin to H. B. Collamore, 1 December 1937
Text: TSCC UCLA

December 1, 1937

Mr. Bacon Collamore
85 Pearl Street
Hartford, Connecticut

Dear Mr. Collamore:

At the suggestion of my friend, Miss Flora Belle Ludington, of Mount Holyoke College, I have sent you a copy of my catalogue of the manuscripts of D. H. Lawrence. I hope that you have received it in good order and I should be very glad to have your comments.

Miss Luddington tells me that you are a collector of Lawrence first editions and have some of his manuscripts. I am interested in keeping track of Lawrence's manuscripts and would appreciate knowing what you have of his.

Should you care to see any of the items described in the catalogue I would be very glad to send them on for consideration. This is a rare opportunity to have one's choice from among the manuscripts of the one acknowledged literary genius of our time.

Dr. Herbert Faulkner West of Dartmouth has just written me a most enthusiastic letter expressing his admiration for Lawrence. I really wish it were possible for the collection to be kept intact. It would provide such marvelous source material for students of the creative process. Mrs. Lawrence would be agreeable to a considerable reduction in price if the purchase of the collection as a whole were possible. Could you offer any suggestions?

I would be most appreciative of any expression of interest from you.

Sincerely,   [JZ]

156. Jake Zeitlin to Herbert Faulkner West, 1 December 1937
Text: TSCC UCLA

December 1, 1937

Dr. Herbert Faulkner West
Dartmouth College
Hanover, New Hampshire

Dear Dr. West:

Yours is one of the most gracious and appreciative letters I have received concerning the catalogue and I am most pleased to have so pleasant a response. I hope your conference with the librarian yields good results. Best of all I should like to see you get the complete collection. What a great mine it would be for the student of the creative process.

At least you should have one of the significant items. My own preference is for #4, *The Rainbow*; #19, *The Escaped Cock* (the second part is an entirely unpublished version); #22, "Odour of Chrysanthemums"; #64, *Last Poems* (which contains that magnificent threnody "I sing of autumn and the falling fruits," equal in my mind to the highest flight of Whitman in "When lilacs last in the dooryard bloomed"); #85, "Four Essays on the Novel"; #102, "Reviews"; #110, *Apocalypse*; #117, "Three Essays on Love"; and #118, "Holograph Notebook," totaling 161 pages entirely in his hand and containing all varieties of Lawrence's writing. If I were having my choice, it would be from among these.

Thanks for giving me the name of Mr. Mandel. I have sent him one of the catalogues; also written him a letter in which I have taken the liberty of saying that the catalogue was sent at your suggestion.

I wish you could have seen the exhibition, better even have been present the night Huxley talked on Lawrence. He had some very illuminating things to say about him, not only as a genius but as a very cheerful, sunny man. It must have been inspiring to know Lawrence.

In case too many of the items do not go right away I might arrange to send a group of them to you for exhibition. I am already discussing the matter with Miss Florabelle Ludington of Mount Holyoke College. It might be that we could send it on a small circuit. Last November and December it was shown at Harvard. Harvard had a good chance to buy the collection but they missed through trying to be too shrewd.

Thanks again for your kind and interesting response. I hope I may hear from you further. If you or your librarian would care to have any of the items sent on approval, I should be happy to oblige.

Sincerely,   [JZ]

157. Jake Zeitlin to Hon. Dorothy Brett, 1 December 1937
Text: TSCC UCLA

December 1, 1937

The Hon. Dorothy Brett
Box 214
Taos, New Mexico

Dear Miss Brett:

I am very glad to hear from you and am interested to note that you would consider selling the letters Lawrence wrote to you. It is hard to say what they are worth. A lot depends upon the contents of the individual letters and whether or not they are all published.

If it were possible for you to send them to me by insured parcel post I would take very good care of them and make a study of their possibilities for sale. I would then be in a position to give you some estimate of value and see whether or not one of my customers might care for them. If there are a great many unpublished letters the value could be more than if the majority have been published.

Frieda Lawrence, Maria Huxley or anyone else who knows us both can assure you that I would be entirely responsible for your letters and not make use of them if you cared to send them to me for consideration.

I shall be very glad to hear from you.

Sincerely,   [JZ]

158. Bennett A. Cerf to Jake Zeitlin, 2 December 1937
Text: TS UCLA

At proof stage, permission to publish this letter was refused. Answering Jake Zeitlin's letter of 30 November 1937, Bennett Cerf describes Frieda Lawrence's visit to him in the early spring, then explains that Random House, hoping to purchase from the Viking Press in New York the rights to all of Lawrence's books, halted negotiations when a high price was set – $14000, according to Letter 141.

159. Stefano Manara to Frieda Lawrence, 2 December 1937
Text: TS HRC

Savona, 2/XII/1937–XVI

Gentile Signora Frieda LAWRENCE
Kiova Ranch – S. Cristobal
Nuovo Messico

Mi è giunta regolarmente la di lei pregiata lettera 12 scorso mese, e sono ben lieto che ella sia rimasta contenta dell'esito da me e dall' Avv. Rolla ottenuto nella pratica Orioli. – Questi rimase un po' sorpreso, quando di primo mattino per due volte andammo da lui, e gli esponemmo quanto gli richiedevamo. Ma quando lesse la procura che ella mi aveva fatto – e la lesse sull'originale, comprese che sarebbe stata inutile una sua opposizione, perché capì che non eravamo andati da lui con la sola procura, ma avremmo certamente predisposto in senso di legge contro ogni eventuale rifiuto. E allora fece buon viso a cattiva sorte; e ci consegnò i pregiati manoscritti.

Ora questi li ho depositati in casa del Cap. Ravagli ove stanno sicuri e a di lei disposizione.

Intanto la ringrazio, anche a nome dell'Avv. Rolla, di quanto accluso nella detta di lei lettera, e che è un compenso molto generoso per quello che abbiamo fatto.

Quì si sta ora attendendo l'arrivo del Cap. Ravagli, che speriamo farà buon viaggio.

Mi ha fatto molto piacere sentire che ella farà prossimamente un viaggio a Londra; e ci facciamo l'augurio che nell'occasione faccia una punta anche a Savona, ove ella, speriamo, abbia simpatici ricordi, per vedere il suo Figlioccio, gli amici, e per dar modo a me di ringraziarla personalmente della fiducia dimostratami pel ricupero dei preziosi manoscritti, e della generosità con cui mi ha ricompensato. Ciò ella potrebbe fare, progettando il di lei ritorno da Londra in America venendo ad imbarcarsi a Genova. A lei non pesano questi viaggi, che a me farebbero impressione. Veda dunque di accontentare il desiderio della famiglia Ravagli e mio.

La ringrazio poi anche dell'invito fattomi di venire costì per tante passeggiate su codesti bei monti. Ma vi sono due difficoltà insormontabili: il gran mare che ci divide, e . . . . . l'età mia quasi ottuagenaria. Mi credo quindi scusato da lei, se non aderisco al di lei invito.

Termino ora, ringraziandola nuovamente di quanto ha fatto per me, e con devoti ossequi me le professo.

Dev. mo:

Manara Stefano

P.S. – Se la presente le ginugesse quando il Cap. Ravagli fosse ancora presso di lei, vorrà salutarlo per me.

[*Translation*:]

Savona, 2 December 1937

Dear Mrs. Frieda LAWRENCE
Kiowa Ranch – S. Cristobal
New Mexico

Your letter of the 12th of last month has arrived, and I am very glad that you were pleased with the result achieved by the advocate Rolla and myself in the Orioli matter. – Orioli was a little surprised when twice we went to see him, first thing in the morning, and explained what we wanted. But when he read the power of attorney that you had granted me – and he read it in the original – he realized that any opposition on his part would be useless; in fact, he realized that we went to him not only with the power of attorney but would certainly have arranged something, according to the law, against any possible refusal. So then he put on a good face and handed over the precious manuscripts.[1]

Now I have left them at Captain Ravagli's house where they are safe and at your disposal.

In the meantime I thank you, also in advocate Rolla's name, for what was enclosed in your letter; it is a very generous reward for what we did.

Here we are waiting now for Captain Ravagli's arrival and hope he will have a good journey.

I was very pleased to hear that you will make a trip to London in the near future, and we hope that on that occasion you will also stop in Savona, of which we trust you have fine memories, to see your godson and your friends, and to allow me to thank you in person for the trust you showed in me regarding the precious manuscripts that I recovered and for the generosity with which you rewarded me.

You could do that if, when you plan your return from London to America, you come to Genoa and sail from here. You are not worried about such journeys, which would frighten me, so please try to meet the wishes of the Ravagli family and mine.

I also thank you for your invitation to come there and take lots of walks on those beautiful mountains. But there are two insurmountable difficulties: the big ocean that separates us, and . . . my almost octogenarian age. So, I hope you will forgive me if I don't accept your invitation.

I close by thanking you again for what you did for me, and with my best regards I remain

Yours sincerely   Manara Stefano

P.S.   If you receive this letter while Captain Ravagli is still with you, please give him my regards.

Note

1.   Of *Lady Chatterley's Lover*.

160. Bertram Rota to Jake Zeitlin, 3 December 1937

Text: TS UCLA

Bodley House, Vigo Street, London W.1
December 3rd 1937.

Messrs Jake Zeitlin, Inc.,
614 West Sixth Street,
Los Angeles, U.S.A.

Dear Mr. Zeitlin,

Many thanks for the two pieces of Lawrence material which were required to complete my order and which have now arrived safely. I am submitting the lot to my customer at once and will send you a cheque as soon as I have his approval. Thank you also for the printed catalogue of the Lawrence manuscripts. Allow me to congratulate you on a very attractive piece of work. With one exception my wealthiest Lawrence clients are in the United States and will probably see the catalogue there, but if you would send me two or three more copies I would be glad to send them to possible buyers. You may be sure that I will do all I can to dispose of some more of the manuscripts, and to this end I wonder if you would care to put an advertisement in the *Times literary supplement,* which is the best medium for such things. The circulation is about 80,000 and space costs £1.10.0 per inch. One inch would suffice to announce that the collection is for sale and that catalogues are obtainable from me. If you think it worth while doing this kindly let me know and send me a supply of anything up to fifty catalogues on consignment. Nothing might result, but I should be hopeful of making sales, and any one item would repay the outlay.

Yours sincerely, Bertram Rota

161. Jake Zeitlin to Frieda Lawrence, 4 December 1937

Text: TSCC UCLA

December 4, 1937

Mrs. Frieda Lawrence
Kiowa Ranch
San Cristobal, New Mexico

Dear Frieda:

Albert Bender of the Book Club of California is pleased to have your permission to publish the four unpublished poems of Lawrence which he is planning to buy from the manuscript collection.

Would you, for my sake, agree to write a brief introduction when they are ready to put the poems in print? Please write me about this as soon as possible.

I shall write you about several things at greater length soon. Maria Huxley must have misunderstood my interest in someone. It is much too premature for me to consider marrying anyone. I am still married to Gina, although proceedings are under way now and it looks as if we were through.

Kindest regards.

Cordially, [JZ]

162. Jake Zeitlin to Bertram Rota, 4 December 1937

Text (abridged): TSCC UCLA

December 4, 1937

Mr. Bertram Rota
Bodley House, Vigo Street
London W.1, England

Dear Mr. Rota:
    . . . What first editions of D. H. Lawrence do you have? Please send
me a complete list, if possible. I should like a fine first of the limited
edition of *Lady Chatterley*; also a couple of the paintings. With regard to
the latter, if you pick up one at around three pounds send it on without
consulting me.
    With kindest regards.

Sincerely,   [JZ]

163. Frieda Lawrence to Jake Zeitlin, 6 December 1937

Text: MS UCLA

Central Park Court, W Central at 11th Street
Albuquerque NM
6 Dec 37

Dear Jake Zeitlin,
    Will you please send this to Charley Chaplin, I dont know his address
and please dont mind the bother.
    I am here for two months, the ranch got too cold; Angelino left
yesterday for Italy.
    Will you also please send me the Mss of New Mexico.[1] I want to give it
to Christine Hughes, she was a good friend of L[awrence]'s and mine.
    I want to write, while Angelino is away. I hope I can.

Yours   Frieda L –

Note
1.   No. 71 in the Powell catalogue.

164. Ted Stevenson to Frieda Lawrence, and Frieda Lawrence to Jake Zeitlin, 7 December 1937

Text (abridged): TS followed by MS UCLA

117 East 17 St., New York City
7 Dec., 1937

Dear Frieda:

The other night I was with Hal[1] and Cliff, and we talked affectionately of you, and as one does at such times I said, "I want to write to Frieda." But one rarely follows up those simple and natural impulses unless something else arises to give us a shove. And now something has, so I take no credit for coming through here.

About the end of January – possibly in February – the League of American Writers is holding an auction sale of manuscripts, the proceeds of which are to go to the Medical Bureau and the North American Committee for Aid to Spanish Democracy. We have only just begun to collect donations of manuscripts, but so far we have not had a single refusal, and we already have items by Barbusse, Rolland, Thomas Mann, Albert Einstein, Havelock Ellis, Lincoln Steffens, H. G. Wells, and several lesser writers. It would be a great boost for the project if we could have something by Lawrence – even if only a fragment. Tentatively I suggest that very early play of his about the mining family which I read at your house. But that was very early work, and perhaps the MS has disappeared? Then the pages of *Sea and Sardinia* contained many of his most passionate utterances on the subject of oppression and would have a special appeal to people who are trying to help the Spanish victims of invasion. But these are only suggestions in case you do see your way to giving us something. I repeat, a fragment would be grand enough.

You may, if you like, set a price below which you would not care to part with the item. I do not mean that any part of the price would go to you – for all manuscripts are out and out donations – but many persons hesitate to give something unless they have assurance that its contribution to Spain will be substantial.

It occurs to me also that you might have a letter of Katherine Mansfield not too precious to part with, and that you might have suggestions for us where other material might be obtainable. [*Frieda notes*: I have nothing except a song-book –]   We are planning a sale that will be definitely of interest to professional collectors as well as to those who primarily want to help Spain. By the way, you understand that you do *not* part with publication rights when you give away manuscript. If you should give us something as yet unpublished, you would still retain the right to keep a copy and to publish it as you pleased. . . .

Greetings to Angelino and best of good wishes to you always.

Ted Stevenson

If you decide to send us something, perhaps you had better address it:

Manuscript Sale Committee
League of American Writers
381 Fourth Ave.
New York, N.Y.

There is a safe in the office, and the material will be better cared for there. Or, if you send it to me, I'll take it to the office right away.

[*Frieda Lawrence writes to Jake*:]

I am sending this on to you. Will you send some *small* thing? Ted Stevenson is a communist by thought, not by blood. I was thrilled to get your letter from Putnam's.[2] I am writing hard. You are very kind to me. – Angelino is almost in Italy. I can work here and see few people, a triumph for me – you never read *Merrild*'s book, it is so good – He has not found an American publisher. I wonder if Putnam's would look at it – Routledge in London are doing it.

About you – Gina – I think it is right, though it's always hard. But I felt you were'nt the man for her and she not the woman for you!

A merry Xmas to you! I may turn up in Hollywood. Send me please a copy of those poems I am to write something for, it may give me a cue –

Ever yours   Frieda

Notes
1. Witter Bynner (1881–1968).
2. The letter of 6 December 1937 asks to see "anything that Frieda Lawrence has written".

165. Herbert Faulkner West to Jake Zeitlin, 7 December 1937
Text: MS UCLA

Dartmouth College, Hanover, N.H.
Dec. 7. 1937

Dear Mr. Zeitlin:-

I have spoken to Mr. Harold E. Rugg – assistant librarian and custodian of rare books and manuscripts.

He tells me that he has written for a catalogue and that as soon as possible after Christmas vacation he will write you as regards exhibits, etc.

We have a fine library – and there is, of course, a great interest in D. H. Lawrence. It's just a question of how to get money to buy rare

1. Jake Zeitlin, about 1970.

2. Knud Merrild, Del Monte Ranch, New Mexico, 1922–3.

3. D. H. Lawrence and Frieda Lawrence, Chapala, Mexico, 1923.

4. Frieda Lawrence, San Cristobal, New Mexico, 1937.

5. Angelo Ravagli, San Cristobal, New Mexico, 1937.

6. (*foreground*) Harry K. Wells, San Cristobal, New Mexico, 1937; (*background*) Charles Ferguson, Wells's Harvard classmate.

7. Thomas E. Hanley, 1940.

8. Frieda Lawrence
   Ravagli (passport
   photograph),
   Houston, Texas,
   21 May 1952.

9. Lawrence Clark
   Powell, Tucson,
   Arizona, 1987.

manuscripts, etc. I think that if we saw some of it – and exhibited it – we might be able to get somebody interested in getting something for the library, but I have a feeling that only a great and rich library could buy it complete.

I know that Mr. Mandel could afford certain items if he wanted them. I, also, am the "impecunious amateur."

You'll hear from us later on and many thanks for your good letter.

Send me any of your own catalogues as they come out, please.

Yours sincerely,   Herbert F. West

166. Jake Zeitlin to Charles Chaplin, 8 December 1937

Text: TSCC UCLA

December 8, 1937

Mr. Charles Chaplin
1103 Cove Way
Beverly Hills, California

Dear Mr. Chaplin:

Frieda Lawrence sent me the enclosed letter and poem of Lawrence's and has asked me to forward them to you.

I should have liked to deliver them in person and to have added my compliments to hers. Some time I hope for the opportunity of a personal meeting.

Sincerely,   [JZ]

167. Jake Zeitlin to Frieda Lawrence, 9 December 1937

Text: TSCC UCLA

December 9, 1937

Mrs. Frieda Lawrence
Central Park Court
W. Central at 11th Street
Albuquerque, New Mexico

Dear Frieda:

Your letter and poem for Charles Chaplin arrived and I have forwarded them to him. No doubt you will have some reply direct.

I am glad you are out of the cold. Albuquerque is a beautiful place. If you get very lonely come on here. I am sure there are many people who would be happy to see you during the winter.

The manuscript of "New Mexico" will be sent to you in a few days. Do try to write if you can. You can see from the letter I sent you a few days ago the publishers are anxious to have something of yours and I am sure it would sell. You have lived so much and have so much to remember and to tell others.

Cordially,   [JZ]

168. Jake Zeitlin to Frieda Lawrence, 9 December 1937

Text: TSCC UCLA

December 9, 1937

Mrs. Frieda Lawrence
Central Park Court
W. Central at 11th Street
Albuquerque, New Mexico

Dear Frieda:

I am enclosing a copy of the letter I just received from the Macmillan Company. They would be very glad to see anything you might be writing and I am sure it would be worth your while to submit something.

With kindest regards.

Sincerely,   [JZ]

169. Frieda Lawrence to Lawrence Clark Powell, 10 December 1937

Text: MS UCLA

Central Park Court, W Central 11th Street, Albuquerque
10 Dec 37

Dear Mr Powell,

It was charming of you to send me all those things –

I was of course so interested. I return your review and enclose this from "John Bull" that will interest you, I still cant see it without rage. Horatio Bottomley this guardian of purity who wrote the attack was in prison for swindling small people out of their savings![1] But we had the fun anyhow!

I think you are a very modest person, you get things *done*! But perhaps you are'nt so modest inside!

What fascinates you about Lawrence you dont quite know yet – but you will find out – His significance lies – I dont know where, in the spring of a person, right from an unknown source.

I cant describe it. As for politics he had to approach everything from a human angle.

Please send me those two articles back –

I hope you will come and talk to me –

Thank you very much for your thought and the trouble you took –

I saw the Jeffers at the ranch –

Sincerely yours   Frieda Lawrence

Note

1. "Famous Novelist's Shameful Book: a Landmark in Evil", *John Bull*, 20 October 1928, p. 11. The article attacked *Lady Chatterley's Lover* as "the most evil outpouring that has ever besmirched the literature of our country". Horatio Bottomley (1860–1933), editor of the weekly journal *John Bull* (1906–29), was convicted of fraud in 1922 and sentenced to seven years in prison.

170. Bertram Rota to Jake Zeitlin, 17 December 1937

Text: TS UCLA

Bodley House, Vigo Street, London W.1
December 17th 1937.

Jake Zeitlin, Inc.,
614 West Sixth Street,
Los Angeles, U.S.A.

Dear Mr. Zeitlin,

Thank you for your letter of December 4th. I attach a quotation of most of the D. H. Lawrence first editions which are now in stock here, but as many others are constantly passing through my hands I would be very glad to receive lists of any titles you particularly require.

I have a nice clean copy of the first edition of *Lady Chatterley's Lover*, limited to 1,000 signed copies, privately printed, which I could supply at £4.10.0 net. Your price of £3.0.0 is rather low for the *Paintings*, but I will see what I can do. Both these books, however, could only be sent at your risk. I should be glad to know if you have imported them safely or if you will know of their being stopped.

I have pleasure in enclosing my cheque for the 700 dollars due to you for the Lawrence manuscripts, less the £7.0.0 (or 35 dollars) due to me for *The Crock of Gold* and *Zuleika Dobson*.

I am glad to be able to order another Lawrence manuscript. If it is available please send me item 24, "The Witch à la Mode". If this has gone please substitute item 37 "Jimmy and the Desperate Woman". I hope you will be able to send the former. I hope the catalogue is going well and should be glad to know what remains available, for future reference.

With kind regards,

Yours sincerely,   Bertram Rota

171. Frieda Lawrence to Knud Merrild, 18 December 1937
Text (abridged): MS HRC

18. Dec 1937

Dear, dear Merrild,

. . . Now, Merrild, I think you had best send me a copy of your book.[1] I will give it to *Zeitlin*, he has had a very successful Mss exhibition at Los Angeles library with your picture of Lawrence. I am sending you the beautiful catalogue. Zeitlin is a good honest man. Putnam's, a good oldfashioned publisher wants to do my book, Zeitlin wrote me. Why not yours? Zeitlin will help you – . . .

I have bought the Maltzahn place 4 miles from Taos, do you know it? Angelino has a grand scheme of making *pottery*. He will learn in Italy hard this winter[2] and begin next spring. You see I can stay at the Maltzahn place in winter, the ranch is too cold and high and snowy. . . .

Ever your old friend   Frieda

Notes
1. *A Poet and Two Painters.*
2. Angelo Ravagli had gone to visit his family.

172. Jake Zeitlin to Bertram Rota, 18 December 1937
Text: TSCC UCLA

December 18, 1937

Mr. Bertram Rota
Bodley House, Vigo Street
London, W.1, England

Dear Mr. Rota:

I am very glad to get your letter and to know that the two pieces of Lawrence material arrived and that your order is now satisfactorily completed. I shall look forward to your draft as soon as possible since I am sure your customer will be happy to have the manuscripts.

Your suggestion that I should advertise in the *Times Literary Supplement* sounds very good and I shall be glad to pay for one insertion of an advertisement at the rate you mention.

I am forwarding you ten catalogues by today's mail. My supply is limited but I should be glad to send you more if your demand and interest justifies it. If for any reason you need them in a rush I should be glad to have you cable me.

Incidentally, I eagerly await your quotations on any firsts of Lawrence or Huxley. With best wishes for the season,

Sincerely,   [JZ]

173. Ben Abramson to Jake Zeitlin, 22 December 1937
Text: TS UCLA

The Argus Book Shop, 333 South Dearborn, Chicago
22 December 1937

Jake Zeitlin, Esq
614 West 6th Street
Los Angeles, California

Dear Jake:

Some years ago I bought from Frances Steloff, of the Gotham Book Mart, a number of Lawrence manuscripts.

Among these were included three versions, two in his hand and one in type, of the introduction to one of the psychoanalysis volumes, as well as the typescript, corrected, of *Sea and Sardinia*.

This last I sold to Richard Mandel who tells me now that he has heard from you that his is not authentic. If that is what you said I think you are mistaken, but I don't know, certainly. I do know that the holograph material was absolutely authentic, and it is only reasonable to suppose that the *Sea and Sardinia* manuscript was too.

I should like to have a photostat of a page or two of the manuscript which you have, pages which carry the greatest number of corrections in Lawrence's hand, so that Mr. Mandel can compare them with what he has. Whatever expenses are incurred I will, of course, pay.

If you will arrange to have the photostats made just as soon as possible, I will be very much obliged to you.

I hope you prosper and are well, and that your New Year will be filled with the world's good.

Sincerely yours,   Ben

174. Jake Zeitlin to H. B. Collamore, 24 December 1937
Text: TSCC UCLA

December 24, 1937

Mr. H. B. Collamore
95 Pearl Street
Hartford, Connecticut

Dear Mr. Collamore:

I am glad to hear that you received my Lawrence catalogue and am very happy to know that you found it so interesting. If it were not too much trouble, I should appreciate your letting me know what Lawrence manuscripts you own.

I do wish it were possible for you to get the two Lawrence items you mentioned. Item No. 118, a notebook, is especially interesting to me since it contains almost a complete cross section of all the different varieties of Lawrence's writings. Why don't you let me send them to you to look over and if you decide to take them terms of postponed payment according to your own convenience could be arranged. Orders are coming in for different items in the catalogue quite steadily and some of the best ones promise to be gone very shortly. Mrs. Lawrence is permitting me to arrange terms according to my own ideas and even if you wished to take six months to take care of the manuscripts I am sure that it would be agreeable.

The one referred to, the manuscript of *Sons and Lovers* that was offered to you, must have been the one Lawrence gave to Mabel Luhan in exchange for the ranch. As I understand it that is no longer for sale. Several versions of the same novel were written by Lawrence, since, as Huxley states in his preface to the catalogue, "He could never revise, but rather preferred to write the whole thing in a continuous stream of inspiration."

I should be very glad to hear from you again and in the meantime send you the most cordial greetings of the season.

Sincerely,   [JZ]

175. Jake Zeitlin to Willard Johnson, 27 December 1937
Text: TSCC UCLA

December 27, 1937

Mr. Spud Johnson
Taos, New Mexico

Dear Spud:

I have been a long time responding to your request for a transcript of "Altitude." Here it is now and I hope you will see that I get a copy of the *Laughing Horse* in which it appears.[1]

The Lawrence manuscript catalogue sells at seventy-five cents and I would suggest that you write to the Los Angeles Public Library for copies.

When in New Mexico this summer I tried to look you up but you seemed to be somewhere else. I should be very glad to hear from you and take up our contact again. If you ever come back to Los Angeles I shall feel slighted if you don't look me up.

With kindest regards.

Sincerely,   [JZ]

Note
1. Willard ("Spud") Johnson (1877–1968) edited the *Laughing Horse*, 1922–39. "Altitude" was published in *Laughing Horse*, no. 20 (Summer 1938) pp. 12–35.

176. Jake Zeitlin to Ben Abramson, 27 December 1937
Text: TSCC UCLA

December 27, 1937

Mr. Ben Abramson
333 South Dearborn Street
Chicago, Illinois

Dear Ben:

I had no intention of shaking Mr. Mandel's faith in the *Sea and Sardinia* typescript which you speak of. My interest was in finding out whether there was a holograph version of the manuscript in existence, since Mrs. Lawrence makes it quite clear that the original holograph manuscript was destroyed. There is nothing in my letter which states that Mr. Mandel's manuscript is not authentic and I had certainly no wish to make such a statement. No doubt there could be two corrected type-scripts of *Sea and Sardinia*, and it is very likely that Mr. Mandel has the one other than that described in my catalogue. I am wondering if the facsimile of a page from *The Rainbow* which appears in my catalogue between pages eight and nine will not be satisfactory enough? That is quite characteristic of Lawrence's later hand and of his manner of correction. There is no reason why the manuscript you sold Mr. Mandel should not be authentic. I am writing him today to correct whatever impression my letter may have made. Please be assured that I will be glad to cooperate in every way.

Frankly I am disappointed in your not wishing to make an effort on the Lawrence manuscripts which I have. Your letter of some time ago has remained unanswered because I did not want to express that disappointment. You of all people should be able to do more with such things, first, because I know you are enthusiastic about Lawrence and second because you must be in contact with many people who already have been prepared and to whom you need do very little else than notify that you have the items available. Mrs. Lawrence has authorized me to make a special reduction in price where a group of the manuscripts are purchased. Why don't you look the catalogue over again and see if you don't want to make a real purchase and then put over a real drive on them?

There is much to tell about myself but little that a letter can convey. I live intensely both physically and in the imagination. My direction seems to be shaken just now because of marital difficulties. I think I am at the beginning of a new cycle and I hope that it is on the upward turn of the wheel.

Bookselling from a street shop pleases me less and less. I seem to function better under conditions of a person-to-person relationship amidst quieter surroundings. I don't seem to be a quantity merchandiser nor an executive capable of managing a group of subordinates, so as to get the most out of them. If things go right, I shall close my down-town shop the first of the year and move out to an old ivy-covered barn off Wilshire Boulevard. It has living quarters upstairs and plenty of space below for a large book room and print gallery. I have an idea that the issuing of regular catalogues, the writing of lots of letters and the quiet pursuit of the business that I know can be had if I just go after it will help me more both in cash and happiness than the frantic confused way of doing business that a down-town shop seems to impose on me.

It will be good to see you. If you ever take a few days off and want to do something different, why not make a flying trip out here? There is much to educate and divert you in this part of the world now.

May your new year be full of good things, long sunny talks, perhaps like those we had on the truck in Texas.[1] May it bring you wealth and happiness and some satisfaction for the creative ache of which I know you still have memories.

Sincerely,   [JZ]

Note
1. In 1919.

177. Jake Zeitlin to Richard Mandel, 27 December 1937

Text (abridged): TSCC UCLA

December 27, 1937

Mr. Richard Mandel
Mount Kisco, New York

Dear Mr. Mandel:

Mr. Ben Abramson has written to me that my letter to you has caused some question to occur in your mind as to the authenticity of the manuscript he sold you.

I am sorry if this is the case. Perhaps I was not careful enough in my phrasing. What I meant to ask was if you could possibly have an original holograph manuscript of *Sea and Sardinia* in your possession. I wanted to determine if Frieda Lawrence might have been mistaken in her statement about the original having been destroyed[1] or if a second original manuscript were in existence. . . .

With the best regards of the season, I am

Sincerely,   [JZ]

Note
1. By Lawrence himself.

178. Jake Zeitlin to Frieda Lawrence, 5 January 1938

Text: TSCC UCLA

January 5, 1938

Mrs. Frieda Lawrence
Central Park Court
West Central at 11th Street
Albuquerque, New Mexico

Dear Frieda:

Mr. Hanley, to whom we agreed to sell the group of manuscripts consisting of *Lady Chatterley*,[1] *The Fox*, and "Introduction to Painting," "Pornography and Obscenity" and "A Propos of *Lady Chatterley*" has just written me that due to large demands on his income he will not be able to take the whole group.

Mr. Hanley offers, however, to take *Lady Chatterley*, *The Fox* and "Introduction to Painting" at a total price of $1900, payable in monthly payments beginning the end of February.

I believe we should accept this compromise especially since I think he would pay a very fine figure for the other three manuscripts of *Lady Chatterley* when they come over and since the existence of these three manuscripts would considerably reduce the value of the typescript.

I must let my customer know immediately. Will you please fill in the enclosed note giving me your authorization for this change in the price by return mail so that no time will be lost.

I hope you enjoyed a good holiday season.

Sincerely,   [JZ]

Note
1. The typescript.

179. Frieda Lawrence to Jake Zeitlin, 5 January 1938
Text: TS UCLA

January 5, 1938

Mr. Jake Zeitlin
614 West Sixth Street
Los Angeles, California

Dear Mr. Zeitlin:

I herewith authorize you to accept a revised price of $1900 on the group of manuscripts listed as follows:

LADY CHATTERLEY

THE FOX

INTRODUCTION TO PAINTING

Sincerely,

_____   _____

Witness[1]   Frieda Lawrence

Note
1. Elizabeth Moore Cottam witnessed the agreement.

180. Frieda Lawrence to Jake Zeitlin, 6 January 1938
Text: MS UCLA

Central Park Court, W Central 11th Street, Albuquerque
6. Jan 38

Dear Jake Zeitlin,

Here is the signature – I hope you are careful about English customers, I remember that some of them did not pay for *Lady Chatterleys*, I mean firms.[1]

Also I had promised my very good lawyer, who won my suit for me against Lawrence's family, when they did'nt let me have any money, to give him: Goose Fair and "Wintry Peacock." His address is – C. D. Medley esq, 36 Lincoln's Inn Fields, London W C II. Please send him these two Mss – I owe it to him –

Soon I will send about half of my book to Macmillan. I enjoy writing it –

Hope you are well – Have they paid yet for those stories, that you sold to England?[2]

Angie is in Italy, the Huxleys in the north and they feel cold –

Ever yours   F. L –

Notes
1. Shortly after the novel was published in July 1928, William Jackson and Stevens & Brown refused to accept the total of 108 copies they had ordered.
2. See Letter 116.

181. Jake Zeitlin to Frieda Lawrence, 8 January 1938
Text: TSCC UCLA

January 8, 1938

Mrs. Frieda Lawrence
Central Park Court
West Central at 11th Street
Albuquerque, New Mexico

Dear Frieda:

Your authorization arrived this morning and I am forwarding the manuscripts to my customer today. I am also carrying out your written instructions with regard to "Goose Fair" and "Wintry Peacock" which are being sent today accompanied by a letter to Mr. Medley. I tell him in the letter that you will no doubt write him concerning these manuscripts. I hope you do not have to give away any more of these manuscripts because you will be reducing the amount left to sell. However, I know you know what is best. I am still hoping that you will find something around that you would care to let me have.

You may be sure that I am very careful about my English customer. The man [Bertram Rota] to whom the Lawrence manuscripts were sent is entirely reliable, and I expect to forward you a remittance within the next ten days.

I hope you are finding the weather in Albuquerque pleasant. If you are thinking of coming to Los Angeles please let me know in advance. I shall be glad to do everything possible to make you comfortable.

I am glad to hear that you have about half of your manuscript finished and are sending it to Macmillan. If it were possible I should like to read it before it goes on. I might be able to make a useful suggestion or two.

With the kindest regards.

Sincerely,   [JZ]

182. Jake Zeitlin to C. D. Medley, 8 January 1938
Text: TSCC UCLA

January 8, 1938

Mr. C. D. Medley
36 Lincoln's Inn Fields
London, W.6 II, England

Dear Mr. Medley:

At the request of Mrs. Frieda Lawrence I am forwarding to you today two of the manuscripts of D. H. Lawrence. She has instructed me to send these to you and will no doubt write you concerning them. I would appreciate your sending me a letter acknowledging their receipt since I have to account to Mrs. Lawrence for all of the manuscripts which I have.

Sincerely,   [JZ]

183. Jake Zeitlin to Mabel Dodge Luhan, 8 January 1938
Text: TSCC UCLA

January 8, 1938

Mrs. Mabel Dodge Luhan
Taos, New Mexico

Dear Mrs. Luhan:

I have recently heard that you wish to sell the manuscript of D. H. Lawrence's *Sons and Lovers*. As you probably know I have in my possession most of the other manuscripts of Lawrence including an early version of *Sons and Lovers* entitled *Paul Morel*.

One of my customers is considering buying this manuscript and might also be in the market for the manuscript you have if you do not want too much for it. While I am not in a position to make a firm offer I am wondering if you would care to accept $1500.00 for this manuscript. That is the price I am asking for *Paul Morel* and I have an idea that I could pay you that much net for your manuscript should you care to consider selling it.

I should appreciate a response from you at your earliest convenience since the client whom I have in mind may be leaving Southern California before long.

With sincere regards.

Very truly yours,   [JZ]

184. Jake Zeitlin to Bertram Rota, 8 January 1938
Text: TSCC UCLA

January 8, 1938

Mr. Bertram Rota
Bodley House, Vigo Street
London, W.1, England

Dear Mr. Rota:

I am very glad to have your letter and remittance covering the Lawrence manuscripts. Unfortunately "The Witch a La Mode" has been sold but the manuscript of "Jimmy and the Desperate Woman" is still here and this is being sent to you today. I hope you will find it satisfactory. Before long I shall send you a list of what remains available but would rather wait a little longer since several items are under reserve and I shall not know whether they are sold or not for another possible two weeks.

I suggest you send me the copy of *Lady Chatterley's Lover* which you quote at 4.0.0. Could you have someone who is coming over to this country bring it with them? I am attaching an order covering a number of the D. H. Lawrence items from your list. I hope they are all still available and look forward to receiving them in good shape. Is there a separate printing of D. H. Lawrence's *Essays on Paintings* or *An Introduction* to his book of paintings which deals mainly with Cezanne. If there is such a thing printed in English, I should like to have some copies.

At this time I should like to express my appreciation for the very charming Christmas booklet you got up. Literature will lose a very fine talent if you do not continue to write. Why not do a book of such essays? Most books by book dealers in the past have been a little too heavy on the business side. I think you could do one that would be altogether in the terms of charm and fine books and fine writing.

With the best regards and best wishes for the new year.

Sincerely,   [JZ]

185. Mabel Dodge Luhan to Jake Zeitlin, 11 January 1938
Text: MS UCLA

The Alvarado, Albuquerque, N.M.
Jan. 11

Dear Mr. Zeitlin –

Please take up the matter of the mms of *Sons and Lovers* – D. H. Lawrence – with Dr. A. A. Brill at 88 Central Park West. New York City. The mms is now in his possession. Of course – as you probably know, this is the original and complete hand written mms of the book and $1500 is a low offer for it.[1]

Sincerely –   Mabel Dodge Luhan

Note
1. On 31 August 1924 Lawrence wrote to his sister, Margaret King: "Mabel Luhan bought the [Kiowa Ranch] for $1200 six years ago, and let it go to rack and ruin. Now she traded it to Frieda for the MS. of *Sons and Lovers*. Every one is very mad with me for giving that MS. The ranch was worth only about $1000, and the MS of *Sons and Lovers* worth three or four thousand – so everybody says. But I don't care" (*The Letters of D. H. Lawrence*, vol. 5, ed. James T. Boulton and Lindeth Vasey (Cambridge: Cambridge University Press, 1989) p. 111).

186. Bertram Rota to Jake Zeitlin, 12 January 1938
Text: TS UCLA

Bodley House, Vigo Street, London W.1
January 12th 1938.

Messrs Jake Zeitlin, Inc.,
614, W. 6th Street,
Los Angeles
Cal., U.S.A.

Dear Mr. Zeitlin,

I am glad to be about to send you another small order from the Lawrence catalogue. Please send me item No. 40. "Sun", and if that is sold No. 41. "More Modern Love" or No. 27. "New Eve and Old Adam" *or* No. 25. "Strike Pay". These are priced at 50 dollars each. I want only one at the present and I hope that the first is available.

I have not yet put the advertisement in the "Times Literary Supplement" for you, as I have no catalogues here yet, but immediately they arrive the notice will appear.

Yours very truly,   Bertram Rota

187. Jake Zeitlin to Dr. A. A. Brill, 13 January 1938
Text: TSCC UCLA

January 13, 1938

Dr. A. A. Brill
88 Central Park West
New York City, New York

Dear Dr. Brill:

Mabel Dodge Luhan has suggested that I write to you concerning the manuscript of *Sons and Lovers* by D. H. Lawrence which she tells me is now in your possession. As you probably know I have in my possession most of the other manuscripts of Lawrence, including an early version of *Sons and Lovers* entitled *Paul Morel*.

One of my customers is considering buying this manuscript and might also be in the market for the manuscript you have if you do not want too much for it. While I am not in a position to make a firm offer I am wondering if you would care to accept $1500.00 for this manuscript. That is the price I am asking for *Paul Morel* and I have an idea that I could pay you that much net for your manuscript should you care to consider selling it.

I should appreciate a response from you at your earliest convenience since the client who I have in mind may be leaving Southern California before long.

Very truly yours,   [JZ]

188. Frieda Lawrence to Lawrence Clark Powell, 14 January 1938
Text: MS UCLA

Albuquerque
14. Jan 38

Dear Mr Powell,

No, this Mss is the second draught. I dont know what happened to the missing pages.

This Mss is particularly interesting because *Miriam*,[1] if you will notice, has written some remarks, very revealing.

Lawrence had sent her the Mss and she hated it and was hurt.

But for anybody who is really interested it ought to be particularly interesting.

Mabel Luhan gave the final Mss to Dr Brill, who I believe and as far as I know still has it –

I dont remember what pages Miriam wrote on, towards the end, but Dan Wells and I got so excited, when we saw her writing –
It makes it such a piece of life –

In haste yours,　　Frieda Lawrence

Note
1. See Letter 40, n. 1.

189. Dr. A. A. Brill to Jake Zeitlin, 18 January 1938
Text: TS UCLA

88 Central Park West, New York
January 18, 1938

Mr. Jake Zeitlin
614 West 6th St.
Los Angeles, Cal.

My dear Mr. Zeitlin:

Replying to your letter of the 13th inst., I beg to say that I would certainly not consider any such offer as $1500 for my manuscript. When I acquired it, which was long before Lawrence died, it cost me much more than that.[1]

Cordially yours,　　A. A. Brill

Note
1. A. A. Brill, M.D. (1874–1948), gave the manuscript to his wife K. Rose Owen Brill, M.D. (1877–1963); she, in turn, gave it to their son, Edmund R. Brill (b. 1914), who sold it to the University of California at Berkeley in 1963 Edmund Brill remembers that, "After my father got the manuscripts he was advised by literary friends to have appraisals made and to verify their identity. . . . The offers were all very low, even for that historical period, and so were all rejected. My father felt that we should keep the manuscripts until Lawrence's work was more appreciated. Eventually, my mother gave them to me to do with as I pleased. I had several rare papers dealers look at them but preferred to let a scholarly center which showed great interest buy them" (letter to the editor, 14 April 1990). The University of California paid $17,000 for the manuscript.

190. Lawrence Clark Powell to Jake Zeitlin, 18 January 1938

Text (abridged): TSCC UCLA

Los Angeles
January 18, 1938

Mr Jake Zeitlin
614 West Sixth Street
Los Angeles

Dear Mr. Zeitlin:

Since cataloging the manuscript of D. H. Lawrence's *Sons and Lovers* I have been giving it more detailed study. It is apparently the earliest extant version of this great novel; its title here is "Paul Morel", after the hero. Lawrence wrote a total of four separate drafts of the novel. As you know, he always rewrote a story in its entirety, rather than patched and pieced it with corrections. According to Mrs Lawrence, this is the second version. All others save the final have disappeared; it was given by Lawrence to Mabel Luhan, who in turn gave it to Doctor Brill, the psychoanalyst. While the final version was written in Bavaria and Italy, after Lawrence's elopement with Frieda, this earlier manuscript came into being during 1911 when he was teaching school in the London suburb of Croydon.

This early draft differs considerably from the published novel. The character Lawrence called Miriam is in the story, but placed in a bourgeois setting, in the same family from which he later took Alvina Houghton of *The Lost Girl*. He placed Miriam in this household as a sort of foundling, and it is there that Paul Morel makes her acquaintance.

Another point of variance is the presence in the early draft of a non-conformist minister whose sermons the mother helps to compose, and who acts as a foil to the brutal husband.

It is however in the treatment of Lawrence's father that the most striking difference occurs. In this unpublished version Arthur Morel in a drunken rage accidentally kills one of his sons, is sent to prison, and dies soon after his release. Thus young Lawrence took vengeance on his crude and lusty father. Having accomplished this katharsis Lawrence in the published book kept it free from such melodrama and allowed his father, in slow sad decline, to outlive his mother. I have pointed out in the Catalog of Mss. that Lawrence in later life expressed the desire to rewrite *Sons and Lovers* in order to give his father fairer treatment.

One of the unpublished version's sections is a marvelously sensitive account of one of Lawrence's childhood pets, Adolphus the rabbit. Omitted from the published book this sketch was rewritten and published in a periodical, and finally collected in *Phoenix*.[1]

·   ·   ·

Aside from its own great intrinsic literary merit the chief interest and value of this manuscript lies in its many differences from the published version of the novel. Anyone can buy for a dollar the printed book, but this early draft is absolutely unique and unpublished. It is an important document in the history of English literature and in the evolution of D. H. Lawrence's genius as revealed in the creation of his masterpiece, *Sons and Lovers*.

COLLATION

Chapter I   Antecedents: pp. 1–7.
       II   Missing
       III   Final pp. only: 73–88.
       IV   Paul Morel's First Glimpses of Life: 85–125.
       V   Acquaintances: 125–176.
       VI   Launched: 176–207.
       VII   Love: 207–284.
       VIII   Calamity: 284–330.
       IX   Attraction: incomplete: first pp. only: 330–5.

The rest of the manuscript, except for a single page numbered 353, is missing; Mrs Lawrence writes me that she does not know what became of it.

Also present is a four page fragment of what I believe to be the first version of the novel. It is on the same ruled notebook paper and the handwriting resembles closely that of the story "Odour of Chrysanthemums", which was written early in 1910.

Lawrence Clark Powell

Note

1. The sketch was published as "Adolf", in *Phoenix: The Posthumous Papers of D. H. Lawrence*, ed. Edward D. McDonald (New York: Viking, 1968) pp. 7–13.

191. Jake Zeitlin to Frieda Lawrence, 20 January 1938
Text: TSCC UCLA

January 20, 1938

Mrs. Frieda Lawrence
Central Park Court
West Central at 11th Street
Albuquerque, New Mexico

Dear Frieda:

I am enclosing the typewritten copies of the manuscript poems which Albert Bender has bought and which he intends to have Grabhorn print in a beautiful format as soon as he has your introduction. In his letter to me he says:

"The printing of these poems without Mrs. Lawrence's comments will be insufficient. I know she can add much of human interest as well as information (concerning the composition) and I would like her to have absolute freedom in the length, breadth and choice of her material."

I hope that you are enjoying the winter in Albuquerque and that you are not finding it too cold. The movies are still considering Aldous's story but there has been some delay in their arriving at a decision.

Much has happened to me in my life that I wish I could talk with you about. Maybe you will be coming down to Los Angeles before long? With the kindest regards.

Sincerely,   [JZ]

192. Frieda Lawrence to Jake Zeitlin, 29 January 1938

Text: MS UCLA

29. Jan. 38

Dear Jake,

I hope what I wrote will do – I would like to keep the poems, I mean the type, but return typists slips.

Powell wrote you might sell the Mss of "Sons and Lovers". I hope it is to a nice person, because of the Miriam bits in it. I wish I were rich, then I would have a huge fire of all his Mss, that's what he would have liked, you know he hated the personal touch. But I daresay he wanted me to have the money.[1]

Another thing: Among the Mss are there his letters to me and my mother? Pollinger says they are. I hope so –

My book is coming along, lively and colorful, I think, but a bit like telegrams.

Quite soon I will send you some of it –

What have you been up to? Dont get into ar y tight corners in living.

Maria wrote they are coming this way again. On the *fourth* I go to the new place in Taos, dont forget.

"Los Pinos" Taos. N M

Angie is working hard at his pottery. 10 hours a day.

I hope to come and see "David". Then I will see you.

Routledge have taken Merrild's "Lawrence and the Danes".

Kindest regards   F –

If you can make what I wrote a little less uncouth, do so –

Note

1. Frieda Lawrence wrote to Angelo Ravagli, also on 29 January 1938 (MS UCLA): "Zeitlin sent me 500 dollars and more is coming next month and he *may* sell the Mss of *Sons and Lovers*."

193. Bertram Rota to Jake Zeitlin, 29 January 1938

Text: TS UCLA

Bodley House, Vigo Street, London W.1
January 29th 1938.

Messrs Jake Zeitlin, Inc.,
614 West Street,
Los Angeles,
Cal., U.S.A.

Dear Mr. Zeitlin,

I am glad to hear that the manuscript of "Jimmie and the Desperate Woman" is on its way and I look forward to receiving both this and the other manuscript which I ordered later. The Lawrence catalogues have not yet come in.

I am afraid I do not know anyone who is coming as far as Los Angeles and could bring the copy of *Lady Chatterley's Lover* with him. Do you think it safe to trust it to the mails? As I said, I could only send it at the buyer's risk. The order for other D. H. Lawrence items from my list which you spoke of enclosing was not included with your letter, but I trust to have this by the next mail. There has been no separate edition of Lawrence's introduction to his "Paintings".

Many thanks for the kind things you say about my little Christmas booklet. I enjoy producing these trifles occasionally for my friends but they are too ephemeral for the dignity of stiff covers. I sometimes promise myself enough leisure to attempt something more lasting, but you probably know very well what happens to booksellers' dreams of leisure.

With kind regards,

Yours sincerely,   Bertram Rota

194. Jake Zeitlin to Frieda Lawrence, 1 February 1938
Text: TSCC UCLA

February 1, 1938

Mrs. Frieda Lawrence
"Los Pinos" Ranch
Taos, New Mexico

Dear Frieda:

The preface is excellent and I know that Albert Bender will be pleased with it. It tells a great deal about Lawrence and the way he wrote as well as reminding one that Lawrence was an Englishman.

This morning I called Mr. Powell to check up with him regarding the letters to you and your mother from Lawrence. He confirms my remembrance that they were not in the packing case and are not here now. Mr. Wells did not list them among the things which he sent back to me and I remember when I first opened the box upon its arrival here that they were not enclosed. Perhaps Mr. Pollinger has them filed. I think you should write him again.

Send me what you can of your new book as soon as possible. I am most eager to see it. If it is like the other things you have done I am sure everyone will like it. You have a way of making everyone feel like a personal friend in your writing.

There is much to tell about myself but little that a letter can make clear. Most of my tight corners are financial right now. Personally I am having more contentment and quiet in life than I have ever known.

Yes, Aldous wrote that they are on the way out here again and that they would stop by the ranch. I shall drop them a note care of you in a few days. Isn't it cold in Taos now? I shan't forget the address, Los Pinos, and I hope to send you more money before long. Angie sent me a postcard from Italy. How long does he plan to stay there? I know you must miss him and will be glad to have him back. Congratulations to Merrild on *Lawrence and the Danes*. I know it must be a good book. Now we have to find an American publisher for it. I wish I could afford to be a decent publisher. I would certainly try to bring it out. Your writing needs no revision from me. It is excellent for its purpose, I think.

Best regards.

Sincerely,   [JZ]

195. Frieda Lawrence to Jake Zeitlin, [mid-February? 1938]
Text: MS UCLA

Los Pinos, Taos, New Mexico

Dear Jake Zeitlin,

Thank you for the cheque. I wonder how your life is coming along.

Angelino is bringing the two unpublished versions of Lady C from Italy. I dont know whether Viking or Knopf has the publishing rights.

They ought to be published, they are not so improper and I love them and dont know, what to do about it.

Angelino gave the Mss to an English missionary he knows to type. The missionary brought them back and said he had no time! I dont wonder.

Do you see Aldous?

I come to Hollywood on the 23rd of May for the performance of David.[1]

I am in my new place,[2] lovely too, on the sagebrush with *such* a view. The house is charming.

Angelino starts back next month on the Rex, the 6th –

He lives for his pottery and I hope he makes a success of it –

I get so sick, sick to the bone of their jeering in England at Lawrence and his dark gods I wish the dark gods would bite them.

The man who was paying every month[3] will do so soon, I hope, I want to build a bathroom here with that money. We will bring the Lady Chatterley Mss to you when we come.

Soon my book is finished and I will send it you and you tell me what you think of it and what I am to do with it.

I feel a kind of slowly coming Lawrence wave in this country –

Very sincerely   Frieda

Notes
1. At Occidental College.
2. Los Pinos.
3. T. E. Hanley.

196. Ben Abramson to Jake Zeitlin, 16 February 1938

Text: TS UCLA

333 South Dearborn, Chicago
16 February 1938

Jake Zeitlin, Esq
614 West 6th Street
Los Angeles, California

Dear Jake:

Richard Mandel returned the Lawrence manuscript to me. I examined it carefully, and the annotations are certainly in Lawrence's hand. If you have a chance to talk to Frieda, please find out about this second copy for me, will you?

None of it is carbon, although there are two kinds of typewriting on it, the first and last part were done on a European machine, the middle part on an American one.

Polifka was here and I talked with her. She told me little more than you have told me about yourself. I hope that some day when you are in an autobiographical mood, you will write me a long letter.

Sincerely yours,   Ben
for THE ARGUS BOOK SHOP, INC.

197. Jake Zeitlin to Bertram Rota, 17 February 1938

Text: TSCC UCLA

February 17, 1938

Mr. Bertram Rota
Bodley House, Vigo Street
London, W.1, England

Dear Mr. Rota:

With reference to the *Lady Chatterley's Lover* it would not be necessary for whoever brings it over to come as far as Los Angeles. They could have it wrapped at any bookstore in New York, such as Dave Randall, [a manager] at Scribner's, and they would send it on to me by express the rest of the way. I am sure someone might be glad to do that. Otherwise I do not think it is safe to send it since I am sure it will be stopped at the customs.

I am enclosing another copy of the order for the Aldous Huxley first editions. I recall now that Lawrence's introduction to his paintings was published in a small book of some other title, something like "Cezanne". Perhaps that will help you locate it.

You are quite right about what happens to booksellers' dreams of leisure. Most of our masterpieces are composed in the form of sales letters.

I am seeing a great deal of one of your admirers, Frank Armstrong. Last week his sister [Jean] came up from Palm Springs and we all had dinner together. They are both very charming and tell me nice things about you.

No doubt you have received by now the other manuscript, "Strike Pay." This was the only one left in the group you mentioned in your letter of February 12. The catalogues seem to have gone astray so I am sending you another group.

Sincerely,   [JZ]

198. Jake Zeitlin to Ben Abramson, 21 February 1938
Text: TSCC UCLA

February 21, 1938

Mr. Ben Abramson
333 South Dearborn
Chicago, Illinois

Dear Ben:

I am sorry to hear that Richard Mandel returned the Lawrence manuscript to you. Frieda Lawrence will not be here for a month or so, perhaps longer. If in the meantime you would care to have me verify the annotations I will be glad for you to send the manuscript on, or part of the manuscript, and I will gladly write you a note about it as well as get Larry Powell to describe it in detail.

There is very little that I can tell you about myself without going into lengthy elaboration. I certainly wish you were here so I could talk to you. Last night I sat up until midnight with Carl Sandburg. Of course you were the topic of much of our conversation. Sunday before last I rode up to San Francisco on the train with Bob Wachsman. Saturday Ben Abramson was meat for more talk with Frank Armstrong. Your name is mentioned to me more frequently than that of any other one person, I think.

When I write my autobiography "Abramson, Ben" will take up a long portion of the index. Best regards.

Cordially,   [JZ]

199. Bertram Rota to Jake Zeitlin, 15 March 1938

Text (abridged): TS UCLA

Bodley House, Vigo Street, London, W.1
March 15th 1938.

Messrs Jake Zeitlin, Inc.,
Los Angeles. U.S.A.

Dear Mr. Zeitlin,

I do not know of anyone visiting the United States shortly whom I could ask to take the Lawrence book and post it to you from New York. If an opportunity occurs I will use it, but otherwise we must let the matter drop.

Thank you for the duplicate of your order for a few Huxley books. I had the original of this, however; what I never received was an order from my Lawrence list. You spoke of enclosing an order for *Lawrence*, but perhaps this was a slip for 'Huxley'. I do not know "Cezanne" or whatever book it is in which Lawrence's essay on painting is reprinted, but I will make further enquiries. The "Strike Pay" manuscript arrived safely and I will send you a remittance as soon as possible. As you cannot allow any discount on these things my profit is so microscopic that I really need to collect before remitting. Anyway, we will not be unreasonably long. . . .

Yours sincerely,   Bertram Rota

200. Frieda Lawrence to Kathryn Herbig, 26 April 1938

Text: TS copy UCLA

Kiowa Ranch, San Cristobal, New Mexico
26 April 38

Dear Miss Herbig,[1]

I just got your letter and here I sit trying to remember about "David". The winter before he wrote it Lawrence had been very desperately ill in Oaxaca, Mexico – We went to Mexico City, he very weak and the doctor told me he had tuberculosis and was a very sick man, only a year or so to live (but he lived another seven years.) "Take him to your ranch, that is the place for him," the doctor said. At Laredo we had a ghastly struggle with the health officials who would not let him enter the U.S.A. But finally we arrived at the ranch, Lawrence very sick. But it was spring and he lay on a canvas bed on the small porch outside the cabin and slowly, day by day his strength came back, he could hardly believe it. It seemed a miracle. It made him deeply, almost religiously happy to feel better again. Slowly he could walk again a little way, then take a real walk, then actually plan and do things again.

As he lay on his bed, getting stronger, he wrote "David". I had been reading the old testament again in German and the puzzling figure of "David" with his so personal relationship to the Lord would send me to Lawrence asking him "How was it?"

The poignancy of "David" is partly a result of Lawrence's own escape from the valley of death. He freed himself in writing this play in voicing Saul's madness and despair, and Samuel's struggle to transfer his allegiance from Saul, whom he had loved to David at the Lord's command.

Lawrence was these people while he wrote, and writing he escaped his own shadows and wrote himself back to health.

The outer form of the life of these old testament people Lawrence believed to have been much like the near Taos Indians.

Later on he did not care so much for the play, maybe it had cost him too much.

They wanted the play in Munich, we translated it together into German, but I never knew whether it was performed.

The play has been acted by the stage society in England, we neither of us saw it; it was winter and Lawrence could not risk the journey from Italy. I don't know how much of a success it was, but have an impression, that it was a bit of a muddle, as if the actors hadn't known what it was all about.[2]

I hope this is of some use to you – I am *very* much looking forward to the play –

Very sincerely,   Frieda Lawrence

Notes

1. Kathryn Shirley Herbig (1916–60) was in 1938 a junior music major at Occidental College, Los Angeles. She assisted with the outdoor performance of Lawrence's biblical play *David*, directed by Kurt Baer von Weisslingen and produced 12 May 1938 in the Hillside Theater at Occidental. Both Frieda Lawrence and Aldous Huxley attended. The manuscript of the play was exhibited in the Occidental College library.
2. The play was produced by Robert Atkins for the 300 Club and Stage Society, 22–3 May 1927, at the Regent Theatre, London, and reviewed in *The Times* (24 May) and in the *Nation and Athenaeum* (28 May). In October 1927 Max Mohr (1891–1934) attempted to stage the play in Berlin.

201. Jake Zeitlin to Flora Belle Ludington, 6 May 1938

Text (abridged): TSCC UCLA

May 6, 1938

Miss Flora Belle Ludington
Librarian
Mount Holyoke College
South Hadley, Mass.

Dear Flora Belle:

Thanks for taking so much trouble with the Lawrence manuscripts. I am writing Mr. Rugg[1] today and sending him a copy of the inventory list with a bill for the insurance and a memo for the thirteen copies of the Lawrence catalogue.

It takes a while for things like this to germinate, but I hope that there will be some sales as a result of the exhibition. Maybe Mr. Collamore will have an inspiration. . . .

Frieda Lawrence will be here about the tenth when Occidental College presents a performance of *David*. This will be the first American performance of Lawrence's play. Occidental is very much interested in Lawrence and I think will do a good job on the play. Frieda is a great woman and I am glad to know her.

You will be interested to hear that I am moving my shop to a great big brick barn covered with ivy out of the down-town district. There are five rooms upstairs in which I shall make my living quarters and the whole thing is being remodeled into a very beautiful place. I think I shall at last live with more quietness. When are you coming back here; I wish you could see the new place.

With best regards,

Sincerely,   Jake Zeitlin

Note
1.   Harold G. Rugg was a librarian at Dartmouth College.

202. Jake Zeitlin to H. B. Collamore, 13 May 1938
Text: TSCC UCLA

May 13, 1938

Mr. H. B. Collamore
95 Pearl St.
Hartford, Conn.

Dear Mr. Collamore:

Thanks for your kind note. I do hope that finances improve soon since it would be a shame for you not to get the two manuscripts you so much want.

David was performed last night in an out-door theater here. A very impressive group of celebrities including Aldous Huxley, Gerald Heard, Dudley Nichols, John Spewack, Helen Gahagan and Melvin Douglas were present. Frieda Lawrence was there and was quite moved. *David* is not a great play, but there are some magnificently poetic lines in it. Some of them are like pure scripture. The theme, as you may know, is of the conflicting love and hate in the heart of Saul for David. I shall send you a copy of the program, since it is a rather nice Lawrence item and was printed by Ward Ritchie, about whose work you may be hearing back there.

Thanks for the invitation to call if I should ever come east. The chances are slim, but I shall certainly remember you are there if I do.

With kindest regards, I am

Yours sincerely,   Jake Zeitlin

203. Jake Zeitlin to R. J. Barry, 13 May 1938
Text: TSCC UCLA

May 13, 1938

Mr. R. J. Barry
C. A. Stonehill, Inc.
262 York St.
New Haven, Conn.

Dear Mr. Barry:

I am very glad to have your inquiry regarding the Lawrence manuscripts. A good many of the most important ones are still available. However I do not know how long they will remain unsold. At present a good part of the collection is on tour and it is being shown at Dartmouth College just now. After that it comes back here. I don't know distances in New England, but if it is not too far, I think you would do well to run over to Dartmouth and see the collection.

Since I am acting as agent for Mrs. Lawrence and I am being allowed a very small discount, I cannot, unfortunately, allow a discount on individual items. The prices are very low, however, as you can see from the enclosed price list. Of course if you could buy a group of the manuscripts, I think I could get Mrs. Lawrence to allow a discount, but that would depend on the quantity of material bought. The entire collection, as it stands, could be purchased for $20,000.00.

I shall be glad to hear from you regarding your further interest.

Yours sincerely,   Jake Zeitlin

204. Frieda Lawrence to Jake Zeitlin, June [1938]

Text: MS UCLA

Kiowa
June

Dear Jake Zeitlin,

I feel our business relations are'nt businesslike enough – For instance that man who promised to pay in February has'nt sent any money yet and now it is June. I dont know what is happening – and would like to know –

I hope you like your new place[1] and are happy –

Rachel[2] says she would like to have your little girl [Judith] but could not look after her properly for less than 10 dollars a week –

Have not heard from the Huxleys and am worried –

Yours ever sincerely   Frieda L –

Angelino is making pots at his wheel!

Notes
1. Jake Zeitlin moved to 624 Carondelet Street in 1938.
2. Rachel Hawk (b. 1898).

205. Jake Zeitlin to Frieda Lawrence, 26 August 1938
Text: TSCC UCLA

August 26, 1938

Mrs. Frieda Lawrence
Rancho Los Pinos
Taos, New Mexico

Dear Frieda:

Enclosed is my check for $295.38, being your portion of payments received from Mr. Hanley on the manuscripts.[1] I expect to be able to send another check shortly and at that time I hope to be able to give you another detailed statement.

I hope that all goes well with you and that Angie is progressing with his pottery. Aldous, as you know, is busily at work writing for M. G. M. and I think is enjoying the job. We talk over the telephone frequently but have had only about two visits in the last two months.

I shall be glad to hear how you are getting along.

With kind regards,   Jake Zeitlin

Note
1.   Jake Zeitlin's commission was 15 per cent.

206. Lawrence Clark Powell to Frieda Lawrence, 1 September 1938
Text (abridged): TS HRC

14052 Davana Terrace, Van Nuys, California
Sept. 1, 1938

Dear Mrs Lawrence –

Many months ago Jake Zeitlin told me that you wanted me to have one of Lawrence's shorter mss. for my part in doing the catalog and arranging the exhibit and opening at the Los Angeles Public Library; but now he is indifferent about it.

I want to tell you frankly that I am not an autograph or ms. collector, and am not interested in having just a specimen of Lawrence's handwriting. If I had anything at all of his, I should like it to be something which was close to him. Thus of all the shorter mss. the one which has the most meaning to me is the original version of the Foreword to the Collected Poems, eight pages in all.[1] I trust you will appreciate my frankness. I would of course never have presumed to have asked you for anything of Lawrence's, and am writing only because of what J. Z. told me you said. . . .

with all good wishes,   Lawrence Clark Powell

Note

1. No. 58 in the Powell catalogue, priced at $200.

207. Bertram Rota to Jake Zeitlin, 1 October 1938

Text: TS UCLA

Bodley House, Vigo Street, London, W.1
October 1st 1938.

Dear Mr. Zeitlin,

If you have any copies of your catalogue of the Lawrence manuscripts left I will be obliged if you would send me one or two. I have thought of two more customers who are possible buyers for some of the less expensive manuscripts.

I never received the group of catalogues which you proposed sending and so did not insert the suggested advertisement in the *Times Literary Supplement*. What is the position now? I imagine you have sold a good deal and feel that you have nearly exhausted the possibilities.

Yours sincerely,   Bertram Rota

208. Jake Zeitlin to Frieda Lawrence, 7 October 1938

Text: TSCC UCLA

October 7, 1938.

Mrs. Frieda Lawrence
Rancho Los Pinos
Taos, New Mexico

Dear Frieda:

The man[1] who bought the group of manuscripts last year was here for several days. He has promised another payment in a couple of weeks. While he is sometimes slow I can assure you that he is entirely reliable and that his financial standing is such that the full amount of any debt he contracts could be paid without any delay in case something should happen to him.

He wishes to buy another group of the manuscripts including the following items from the Catalogue:

No. 3   Sons and Lovers
No. 9   Apropos of Lady Chatterley's Lover
No. 10   Pornography and Obscenity
No. 5   Women in Love
No. 54   Love Poems and Others
No. 64   Last Poems
No. 77   Sea and Sardinia

He's willing to pay three thousand dollars[2] for the group on an installment basis, payment to commence for these as soon as he has completed paying for the last group, everything is to be paid in full by the end of 1939 or at the latest the Spring of 1940. He is anxious to have your decision on this as soon as possible as he would like to include the above group in an exhibition of his Lawrence material which is to be held next month in Buffalo. I recommend your accepting his offer since I really think that, considering the fact of *Sons and Lovers* being an incomplete manuscript of which several versions exist and *Sea and Sardinia* being a typescript with very few autograph notes, the offer is very fair.

I am enclosing an authorization for you to sign and I hope that you will return it as soon as possible with your favorable answer since I think it would be very nice to have as much Lawrence material included in the exhibition. I am sure there will be a great deal of publicity.

Last Wednesday I lunched with Maria and Aldous. They have taken a house and planned to stay here for six months longer. Aldous is resting a great deal and seems to be doing well although he is still very delicate.

Please give my best regards to Angelo,

Cordially,   [JZ]

Notes
1. T. E. Hanley.
2. Separate prices totalled $3650.

209. Frieda Lawrence to Lawrence Clark Powell, 12 October 1938
Text: MS Occidental College

TAOS, NEW MEXICO
12. Oct 38

Dear Mr Powell,

I am sorry you did not come to see me this summer – Please stay a little while if ever you can come –

I am writing to Jake Zeitlin to give you that Mss –

Poor Una! You see I have nothing to do with Mabel anymore – But this is the story: Mabel invited a Hildegard who was "after" Jeffers[1] and one evening Una came from a party and found Robin and H talking and Una went and took poison and shot herself – you know how excitable Una is – and I know how Mabel can make one feel – Una left a note saying: "As I am no longer any use I'd better go" –

Now I *do* hope they know what Mabel is – I also liked Merrild's book[2] very much – They are coming back to Hollywood. Do you know them?

I am very glad to give you that Mss – I always liked it too –

With my best wishes and thanking you for the work you did with such interest –

Sincerely yours   Frieda Lawrence

Notes
1. Lawrence Clark Powell had written a book on Jeffers, *Robinson Jeffers: The Man and His Work*, published in 1934 in Los Angeles by Jake Zeitlin's Primavera Press.
2. *A Poet and Two Painters* (London: Routledge & Kegan Paul, 1938).

210. Frieda Lawrence to Jake Zeitlin, 12 October 1938
Text: MS UCLA

TAOS, NEW MEXICO
12. Oct. 38

Dear Jake Zeitlin,

I should have written before and acknowledged your last cheque – But you know how busy my summer is.

As you advise I will accept that offer. Personally I think that *Sons and Lovers* terribly interesting with Miriam's comments –

I hope all is well and flourishing with you – We are all well, horses and cows and chickens and pigs –

We want to stay here this winter, Angelino wants to stay with his kiln, he works very hard and has made some handsome things –

I hear often from the Huxleys, I think they are very happy with their friends there –

Perhaps Aldous will write another film –

All good luck to you and you will see that that man pays. Those cheques come in very handy –

Our best to you both

Yours ever   Frieda

Powell wanted an Mss –

Powell wants the *Foreword* to Coll. Poems. He deserves it, dont you think?

211. Jake Zeitlin to Bertram Rota, 14 October 1938
Text (abridged): TSCC UCLA

October 14, 1938

Bertram Rota
Bodley House
Vigo Street, London W1

Dear Mr. Rota:

I am surprised to learn that the ten copies of the Lawrence Catalogues were not sent to you sometime ago, and I am therefore forwarding you this number in the hope that they will still prove useful. While a number of the items have been sold, quite a few of the inexpensive ones as well as the more important ones are still available, and I shall be glad to have your cooperation. . . .

Yours sincerely,   [JZ]

212. Jake Zeitlin to Frieda Lawrence, 17 October 1938
Text: TSCC UCLA

October 17, 1938

Dear Frieda,

Your letter and agreement arrived this morning. Hanley will be delighted. I am sending the manuscripts off to him today.

I am glad to hear that you are all so happily occupied at the ranch. My place is getting fixed up beautifully, and I am in a very good state of spirit.

I think Powell does deserve the manuscript Foreword to *Collected Poems*, and I hope you give it to him.

By the way, be careful whom you let edit the Chatterley manuscript. An unscholarly worker might botch things up. You are as always, too generous.

I hope you will remember that I would like to have the manuscript of "We Need One Another." If you feel I deserve it I should appreciate it very much.

Best regards to you and Angelo from all of us.

Most sincerely,   [JZ]

213. Jake Zeitlin to T. E. Hanley, 29 March 1939

Text: Telegram UCLA

MARCH 29, 1939

T. E. HANLEY

BRADFORD, PA.

MRS. LAWRENCE INSISTS ON SUBSTANTIAL PAYMENT ON MSS THIS MONTH. WOULD APPRECIATE BEST YOU CAN DO. REGARDS JAKE

214. Frieda Lawrence to Jake Zeitlin, 22 April 1939

Text: MS UCLA

Kiowa Ranch
22. April 39

Dear Jake,

We arrived in a snow-storm, but now it is spring and we are working very hard, carrying manure and all is well –

Your fine catalogue came – thank you –

Just a line to wish you luck –

Best greetings from both –   Frieda –

215. Frieda Lawrence to Jake Zeitlin, 13 July 1939
Text: MS UCLA

13 July 39

Dear Jake,

Would'nt it be a good job for both of us to sell those Mss!

New brooms you know –

Never a word from Henrietta Martin![1]

Are you getting on with [the film version of] St Mawr? or not begun?

Are you passing through here?

We are so dry, no rain for 3 months.

We are in trouble with the emmigration people. Angelino I suppose for living together – Moral turpitude –

I was so touched, both Dudley Nichols[2] and Aldous [Huxley] offered to fly here –

Would you ask Dudley if he knows a *good* New York lawyer who would defend Angelino, Maurice Ernst perhaps, if there is a case? But it may be too damned expensive. I have'nt Dudley's address.

Dont say anything to others, better be quiet about it –

Yours ever   Frieda

Notes
1. Henrietta Martin, originally from San Francisco, was the wife of Fletcher Martin, a Los Angeles artist who was part of an artists' group that met regularly at Ward Ritchie's home; the advent of the Second World War scattered the group.
2. See Letter 241n.1.

216. Frieda Lawrence to Jake Zeitlin, [early August 1939]
Text: MS UCLA

Dear Jake,

Thank you ever so much for wanting to help –

I wrote all the details to Dudley, who wrote like an angel of a friend, that he would go to Washington if necessary – even –

He can tell you – I hope now that the Perkins is strong enough to manage it – Fortunately she came just at the time of this upset and friends talked to her –

It would be wonderful if you made a film of St Mawr with Aldous. Yes, I think he is just finishing his new book –

I get lots of visitors. We need rain, rain terribly –

I shall be *60* on the 11th of August! Was'nt I right not to sell the Mss to stingy Harvard –

We need not be in such a hurry to sell them –

I told you that the tiny Mss we sent to that refugee thing was a sensation.[1] You had marked it at 15 – it sold for 150 –

Yours ever   Frieda

Note
1. See Letter 164.

217. Frieda Lawrence to Lawrence Clark Powell, 22 August 1939
Text: MS UCLA

22. Aug 39

Dear Mr Powell,

I am glad you reminded me of the book – I will climb up in the garage where they are and get one right now!

I hope I shall see your essay and wish I could have talked to you – the beastly Kingsmill, so smug and the Ford, are there really 53 – Have you Rebecca West? Have you this one I am sending with mine? Richard Goodman I dont know –

I also send you the "Letters" – I have another in this edition –

I would *adore it*, if those Lawrence letters to me were done – People are scared of them, I think – They are so much Lawrence, I feel –

I wish you could come – it's so lovely, really –

Make an effort!

I am so bad at writing letters and books! They are always only in my head!

I had my son[1] here from England and he loved it –

Angelino works away –

With many greetings to you and your wife –

I have a house for you if you can come –

Yours affectionately   Frieda Lawrence

Note
1. C. Montague Weekley (1900–82).

218. Frieda Lawrence to Jake Zeitlin, 9 October 1939
Text: MS UCLA

9. Oct. 39

Dear Jake,

Your letter and cheque and proposition were very welcome. I was a little worried about the money, because England wont let any money go out of the country, unless you have special permits.

We need a new car, so now we wait till you send the rest of the money.

Yes, this war seems the height of stupidity – I still hope for peace.[1] I also hope like you do, that even I shall live to see a better world. My daughter Elsa has got a husband in the british navy, a nice man.[2]

Here it just seems incredible. Still, peaceful autumn, the mountains all gold.

I have not heard from the Huxleys for some time. I know they will be unhappy.

What about Washington and the Mss? I have not heard from Dieterle and the Plumed Serpent.[3]

With kindest regards from both of us   Frieda

Notes
1. So did Angelo Ravagli, whose son, according to Dorothy Brett (MS UCBerkeley), was serving in the Italian army (Brett to Una Jeffers, 4 September 1939).
2. Bernal Edward de Martelly Seaman (1899–1990). His mother, Eileen Seaman (1873–1957), was a friend of the family.
3. William Dieterle (1893–1972), German director who emigrated to Hollywood in 1930. His biographical films of the late 1930s were his best, including *The Story of Louis Pasteur* (1936) and *The Life of Emile Zola* (1937). He returned to Europe in 1958.

219. Frieda Lawrence to Jake Zeitlin, 21 November 1939
Text: MS UCLA

Kiowa Ranch, San Cristobal, N.M.
21. Nov 39

Dear Jake,

Would you send this letter to Ward Ritchie – please?

We are at the lower ranch and I have'nt got their adress –

Hope you and Josephine[1] are fine –

Yours   Frieda

Note
1. Jake Zeitlin married Josephine Ver Brugge in October 1939.

220. Frieda Lawrence to Jake Zeitlin, 8 May 1940
Text: MS UCLA

Kiowa Ranch
8 May 40

Dear Jake,

Thank you for your letter – We are struggling with adobe and planting – Good news about Sons and Lovers, alas, Selznick[1] has a contract with me, so you must arrange with him –

If your director would like a treatment by me and John Becket talk to John Becket adress 326 San Vincente Santa Monica phone S. M. 52167 I made a very good treatment of Plumed Serpent with him –

Zoe Aken[2] is also making a play of Virgin and the Gipsy –

We can do with the money from your client[3] at the moment –

Perhaps you can have half of the comission with Selznick – I hope so –

Glad you are all well –

All the best from us, sorry we did not see you again before leaving.

Frieda

Becket's M. G. M. A. S. 43311 Extension 1158 –

Notes

1. David O. Selznick (1902–65), successful Hollywood producer of such films as *David Copperfield* (1935), *Anna Karenina* (1935), *A Star is Born* (1937), the triumphant *Gone with the Wind* (1939), and *I'll Be Seeing You* (1944, directed by Frieda Lawrence's friend William Dieterle).
2. Zoë Akins (1886–1958), well-known American dramatist and screenwriter, author of *Déclassé* (1919) and other plays. Her 1935 dramatization of Edith Wharton's *The Old Maid* won a Pulitzer Prize.
3. T. E. Hanley.

221. Frieda Lawrence to Lawrence Clark Powell, 15 September 1940
Text: MS UCLA

Kiowa Ranch, San Cristobal, N. M.
15. Sept. 40

Dear Larry,

You could not have sent me anything nicer than the Rilke book –[1]

I like him, his german is like music, but when you compare him to Lawrence, he is not so satisfying and hopeful.

The english is *bad* – did you read the introduction? awful –

You are working hard again –

It has rained, I wish you could see the place, the mountains turning yellow and the sage in bloom.

I am sorry the Huxleys wont come. Averardi[2] stayed for a week in your little cabin.

I hope you all flourish and the infant and Fay – [3]

The war goes on and how one wishes it would end! If it is no bother for you who have so much to do with books if you come across a second hand Hölderlin,[4] send it to me, would you? If it is no trouble.

Many greetings to you all –

Ever yours   Frieda Lawrence

Tell Jake that the small Lawrence Mss he sent to Prince Löwenstein sold again for another 150 d[ollars] – that makes 300 –

The Löwenstein came yesterday.

Thank you for the photos. I liked them very much!

Notes
1. Perhaps Rainer Maria Rilke, *Fifty Selected Poems*, with English Translation by C. F. MacIntyre (Berkeley: University of California Press, 1940).
2. Francis Bruno Averardi, Lecturer in Italian, UCLA, 1935–42.
3. Fay (1911–90) was Larry Powell's wife.
4. Johann Christian Friedrich Hölderlin (1770–1843), German poet.

222. Frieda Lawrence to Jake Zeitlin, 9 December 1940
Text: MS UCLA

Kiowa Ranch, San Cristobal, N.M.
9. Dec 40

Dear Jake,

Are you better? Your last handwriting looked shaky.

Thank you very much for the cheques. They were welcome.

We are at the lower ranch[1] and are cosy, but the war gets us down, occasionally – it gets worse and worse –

Love to you and Josephine –

Yours   Frieda

Note
1. Los Pinos. According to Dorothy Brett (MS UCBerkeley), Frieda Lawrence left for Hollywood about a month later (Brett to Una Jeffers, 5 January 1941).

223. Frieda Lawrence to Lawrence Clark Powell, 1 May 1941

Text: MS UCLA

Kiowa Ranch, San Cristobal, N.M.
1. May 41

Dear Larry,

When we left neither you nor Fay were very well –

I hope by now you are allright both of you –

It's the first of May, but it looks like *snow* again –

I am going to bother you, Larry –

By accident I heard over the radio Lawrence's "Rocking-horse winner." It was good and unusual –

Now there are many short stories that I think might do for radio, so I wrote to a Mr Jerome Schwartz Columbia Broadcasting System, Columbia Square, Los Angeles –

I had a nice letter from him, he wanted a complete list of the novels and stories and plays –

It would be so helpful if you got in touch with him and advised him – I have got nothing here, as we are still at the lower ranch –

I will tell Mr Schwartz about you –

We are looking forward to seeing you at the ranch this summer – I told you Richard Aldington[1] will be there – We can put you up just the same –

With kindest regards and we want to know how you are –

Yours ever   Frieda

Note

1. Richard Aldington (1892–1962) first met the Lawrences in 1914. His novel *Death of a Hero*, which Lawrence read in manuscript in 1929, is a disillusioned account of World War I. Later he edited two volumes by Lawrence, *Last Poems* (1932) and *Selected Poems* (1934), and in 1950 published *Portrait of a Genius, But . . .* , his biography of Lawrence.

224. Knud Merrild to Frieda Lawrence, 21 August 1941

Text: MS HRC

2610 South Robertson Blvd., Los Angeles, Calif.
Aug. 21 – 1941

Dear Frieda.

I had your telegram today, and tomorrow I plan to go to the bank[1] with Zeitlin and take over the manuscripts – which I imagine will be very simple. The MSS are in a bank box, and Zeitlin will give the box over in my name and so I get the keys to the box. The MSS themselves wont have to be removed. I already have received the *blue Lady Chatterley*[2] which I have here at home, but I will take that to the bank and place it in the Box with the MSS.

Nothing has yet happened to Zeitlin, but he fears they will make him go into receivership in which case he will be out. When he got wind of what was probably coming he called me up and I went down to him to get the "Blue Lady" – but his lawyer told him not to turn over the MSS til we had your consent.

Now that we have that, the receivers can't lay hand on your things. – I asked Zeitlin if you had any money coming from the business *to see to it* that you would get it. He said that the money you had coming would be given priority. I stressed the possibility that you might need the money, since your Income from England has been curtailed. – I am glad to say that I think Zeitlin thought of you first, and that he is doing what he can to serve your interest. – I feel sorry for him if he is forced out of his business. – He doesn't yet know what he will do.

Now you must instruct me regards the MSS – I am not letting any body get near them, after I get the keys, not even Zeitlin unless you give me permission. The whole thing might yet blow over, and Zeitlin continue – in which case he would probably want to have access to the MSS – *you must definitely tell me* what to do regards Zeitlin as I dont know your agreement concerning the MSS.

Now we will wait and see what happens and I shall write you again. Zeitlin I am sure will write you too.[3] – I am writing this in haste – hope you are well – best greetings to you and Angie – I will let Else tell our news.

Merrild

Notes
1. Security National Bank.
2. One of two copies specially printed for Lawrence by the Tipografia Giuntina, the shop that printed the Florence edition of *Lady Chatterley's Lover* (1928). Both special copies are now at the Humanities Research Center.
3. Jake Zeitlin's letter, if written, has not survived.

225. Frieda Lawrence to Knud Merrild, 28 August 1941
Text (abridged): MS HRC

Aug. 28. 1941

Dear Merrild,

What a wonderful thing it is to have such friends as you and Else! I can rely on you and that is a rare thing in this world.

I think Zeitlin tries to be fair with me and I feel sorry for him, that he cant make a go of his business.

So I feel quite safe with you having an eye on things – . . .

Zeitlin writes he would like in any case to be allowed to sell the Mss – So we will let him; but for the time being and if Zeitlin wants to get any Mss out, he will have to ask you and that is perfect as far as I am concerned.

I am *very* grateful to you for taking all this trouble –

Ever your old   Frieda

226. Frieda Lawrence to Jake Zeitlin, [September 1941]

Text: MS UCLA

Dear Jake,

I am very sorry you have all these [financial] difficulties – I hope it is not as bad as you feared – and that you can weather it –

Yes, I want you to go on handling the Mss and what else you can – Merrild having them now is allright –

I hope you are well and Josephine, it is hard on her too –

Thank you for the cheque – We had a fine summer, but the war gets one down occasionally –

All good wishes to you from Angelino too –

Yours   Frieda

227. Knud Merrild to Frieda Lawrence, 6 September 1941

Text: MS HRC

2610 South Robertson Blvd., Los Angeles, Calif.
Sept 6 – 1941

Dear Frieda:

Thank you for letter the other day and for the nice words you say about us, we only hope we may deserve them, and are very happy if we can be of any help to you.

We have been worried about you getting means to live from, and were very glad to hear you had gotten money from England.

I have just talked with Gordon who has been fired from the Studios but now has a short Job with Orson Welles – he said Welles was interested in some short stories by Lawrence for the radio – Gordon will write you about it – Now dont expect too much – it cant be hardly anything in money but it will help to revive Lawrence in this country – so more might follow later on.

There is nothing new in the Zeitlin case, but it is due to come up soon. I have taken over the box with the MSS and am the only one who has the keys to the bank box, so when ever Zeitlin wants any body to look at the MSS I or Else will be there with the keys. I dare say the "General" will be as good as I! – We are glad you are coming to California this winter, Ojai is not too far for visits.

How is Angie getting along with the ranch these days, I hope well. Best wishes to you both.

Merrild.

Else asks me to send her love to Frieda and Angie with best wishes.

228. Frieda Lawrence to Knud Merrild, 12 September 1941

Text (abridged): MS HRC

12 Sept 41

Dear Merrild,

Thank you for your letter. . . .

Angie is working at his pottery, he has not so much time as there is the cow and the pig and the chickens and little chickens and the alfalfa and the horses.

Your letter came yesterday on Lorenzo's birthday. He would have been 56 –

Can you imagine him being older? I cant. . . .

It has been a beautiful summer, much rain – and many flowers –

Now it is already autumn and beautiful – . . .

Ever with best greetings   Frieda

229. Knud Merrild to Frieda Lawrence, 28 December 1941

Text (abridged): MS HRC

2610 South Robertson Blvd., Los Angeles, Calif.
Dec. 28 – 1941

Dear Frieda:

Thank you for the Xmas greetings[1] and amusing drawing. I am glad you have not lost your sence of humor. Vi saw Josephine Zeitlin the other day and she told us that Jake is sick again from the ulcer in his stomack. At my earliest moment I shall go and see him and also find out about the business. I shall then let you know. . . .

from yours *truly*   Merrild.

Note
1. Frieda Lawrence had written him on 24 December 1941 (MS HRC), saying, "Dear Merrild, please look after the Zeitlin business for me."

230. Frieda Lawrence to Willard Hougland, [*c.* 1944]
Text (abridged): MS UCLA

Friday

Dear Willard,[1]

Your letter was good medicine – At first I was sad, now I am mad – I look on this as a challenge – This is my say:

Lawrence was a great man and where books are read he is known all over the world. Being his wife I am known too and I believe mostly with respect – When Lawrence died, there was much to be done, there was much material, that had not been published – I needed somebody with sense to help and advise me – Angelino had a great respect for Lawrence he helped me faithfully in this important job, Not only in my personal life. Hundreds of people from all over the world have been to see me and they must have seen that our[2] way of living was simple and wholesome – – I *wont* be pulled down and made cheap. . . .

It has snowed again, but lovely in between –

Love to you   F
Burnt the letter –

Notes
1. Willard Hougland (1906–58) was a writer, publisher, and for a time director of the Laboratory of Anthropology in Santa Fe, New Mexico. During the 1940s he helped Frieda manage the Lawrence estate. Later, in the South Bay area of Los Angeles, he operated a rare books store and art gallery located on the Coast Highway. He arranged with Lawrence Clark Powell to turn over his manuscript collection, rich in D. H. Lawrence and Norman Douglas, to the UCLA Library. An obituary by Kirk McDonald appeared in the Redondo Beach (CA.) *Daily Breeze*, 5 December 1958, p. 6.
2. our] my

231. Frieda Lawrence to Lawrence Clark Powell, 26 May 1944
Text: MS UCLA

El Prado, New Mexico
26 May 44

Dear Larry,

I am delighted at your ship coming in, but the Lord knows that ship was due a long time ago – and you worked so hard.

The Harwood Foundation here in Taos with the University of New Mexico want to make a Lawrence memorial – But it's all very much at the beginning – [1]

I wish I could talk to you about it – I know so little about that kind of a job –

I am glad you liked Lady C – She has been attacked by Sumner[2] – He found 92 "spots", he must be very pure – But it's the publisher's responsibility –

Esther[3] is very New England – She said: "Does Frieda Lawrence think she is the only one who knows anything about sex?" That made me laugh –

I am glad to think of your activity, *not* destructive –

Angie sends his best – to you both –

                              Affectionately   Frieda L –

I hope Fay and the children are well and happy –

Notes

1. The Foundation, sponsored by the University of New Mexico, hoped to build a library room for Lawrence materials and to secure a curator and bibliographer. Frieda Lawrence planned to give twelve manuscripts and five paintings.
2. In 1944 Frieda Lawrence authorized the Dial Press (New York) to publish *The First Lady Chatterley*. Appearing on 10 April, the novel roused the ire of the New York Society for the Suppression of Vice, whose secretary, John S. Sumner, bearing a search warrant, seized 398 copies on 27 April. On 29 May, New York Magistrate Charles G. Keutgen found the book "clearly obscene". But after a brief trial in October, a special sessions court declared the novel "not obscene" on 1 November 1944.
3. Esther Forbes wrote a Manuscript Report for the Dial Press edition.

232. Frieda Lawrence to Lawrence Clark Powell, 17 June 1944

Text: MS UCLA

                              El Prado, New Mexico
                              17. June 44

Dear Larry,

I am so glad you are interested in Movements in European History – It was written in Cornwall, I dont remember what waryear 15 or 16.

That winter he read "Decline and Fall" of the Roman Empire by Gibbon – It is a big book – and he did'nt skip it – Other books too, but I dont remember.

"The Rainbow" had just been banned[1] therefore the pseudonym – I remember his saying how few historians had a historical sense, he admired Gibbon very much – I am not sure that it was not the same winter that he also read all Fennimore Cooper with great relish and the books that resulted in Essays in classic American Literature.

The writing of "Movements" I think were a relief to him from the actual agony of the war –

I have a copy with blue pencilmarks. The book was printed by the Irish Freestate and where Lawrence writes: "The pope's mistress["], the Irish Freestate altered it to "The pope's Friend" etc –

I will send it you, if you like – As to the Harwood's Lawrence memorial, I wish it could be connected in some way with your university, and that this might be a more lively centre of interest; Especially as you so truly understand Lawrence.

I cant think of any more, except that we were very poor at the time – Lawrence was worried about how we were going to live – *Nobody* wanted his writing after the banning of the Rainbow – Nobody wanted "Women in Love." He suffered much at the time about the state of things in England – Aldous wrote me how awful it is *now* – All honesty gone, all morals, all civic liberty – So that's *that* – great men in the long run dont fight in vain – I hope –

My love to you all –   Frieda

Note
1. In November 1915, after Lawrence's *The Rainbow* had received hostile reviews, the Scotland Yard police came to Methuen, the publisher, and impounded all copies in stock; these were soon destroyed by court order.

233. Frieda Lawrence to Willard Hougland, [mid-June 1944]
Text (abridged): MS UCLA

Saturday

Dear Willard,

Yes, we will go to the ranch, only we cant stay without a car – . . .

Powell just wrote he wants to write on L[awrence]'s "Movements in European history" – I wrote if he would be interested in a connection with his university –

I am jittery about the war – Worse and worse and God help us – I think we might have a good time, they painting and you writing and I cooking –

I do hope Lady C is *safe* – But nothing is safe – . . .

Love to you and Georgine   F –
from me too   Angie

234. Frieda Lawrence to Willard Hougland, [Summer 1944]

Text (abridged): MS UCLA

Dear Willard,

. . . I am up at the ranch and Tedlock and family are here – He and I work and there is quite a lot of understanding in him and thorough hard work – [1]

But now I have another grief – I am reading the second Lady C [in manuscript] and find her *more* wonderful than ours[2] – – Why did'nt I read her?

I will point out some great parts to you, when I see you!

At a party Dukes says: *"We're only an experiment in* mechanisation, that will be properly used in the next phase."

A sense of fear fell on the room. This soldier seemed to see all his own world so definitely swept away, to replace something else.

"I belong to the mechanistic experiment" he said. "But I wish I could have crossed over, to the democracy of touch". We ought to send this version to Esther Forbes –

Maybe Houghton Mifflin if all goes well would publish the 3 – . . .

Love to Georgine and yourself –   F –

Notes

1. E. W. Tedlock, Jr (b. 1910) spent the year 1944–5 as a Rockefeller research fellow working on Lawrence's manuscripts. In 1948 his *The Frieda Lawrence Collection of D. H. Lawrence Manuscripts: A Descriptive Bibliography* was published by the University of New Mexico Press.
2. *The First Lady Chatterley*, published by the Dial Press in 1944. Willard Hougland had acted as Frieda Lawrence's agent.

235. Frieda Lawrence to Willard Hougland, 28 February 1945

Text (abridged): MS UCLA

Route I, Box 558, Brownsville, Texas
28 Febr 45

Dear Willard,

. . . Tedlock wrote the University people came and were *impressed* with all the Mss! I will think about the agent business,[1] it ought to be simple that part, till we tackle the publishers! And then it will be allright when I am dead. . . .

Fortunately, it is so beautiful here, we go to the sea and Angelino caught *8 big* fish yesterday! He goes nuts then – Oranges in bloom, easterlilies, and lots of flowers in the garden and fields; we dont see many people and I am glad, I *have* my friends, but never have people taken less notice of me than here and it is a treat – Had a letter from Henry Miller, he says: "You are a legend, but a living one." Funny!...

Love from us both – F –

Note

1. In a letter to Willard Hougland of 16 February 1945 (MS UCLA), Frieda Lawrence had written: "Now we will arrange that you are the american agent for L –".

236. Frieda Lawrence to Ben Abramson, 16 July 1945

Text: MS UCLA

El Prado, New Mexico
16. July 45

Dear Mr Abramson,

Your catalogue always interests me particularly and also scares me a bit – You are interested in Lawrence – You have so many Lawrence letters and you know he just wrote what he felt like at the moment and was by no means cautious – Somebody might be hurt – It may interest you to know that Giulia Pini was our young peasant maid at the Villa Mirenda near Florence –

I am sorry about the Miriam corrections, he had asked her if she would have anything altered –

Pino Orioli sold many of these things, that I had left with him in a trunk[1] – I dont mind so much that he sold them, I only wish that people dont get hurt –

Also I have a letter of Norman Douglas where he answers Lawrence's question: do you want to publish Magnus's "Foreign Legion" and Douglas says, "go right ahead old boy" – and Douglas had forgotten – A young man here[2] has just spent a year in going over Lawrence's Mss – paid by Rockefeller for the Harwood Foundation here – There will be a Lawrence memorial and I give some Mss and the little chapel on Kiowa Ranch where his ashes are –

I thought all this might interest you –

Sincerely yours   Frieda Lawrence

Notes

1. See Letter 126.
2. E. W. Tedlock, Jr.

237. Frieda Lawrence to Knud Merrild, [8 August 1945]

Text (abridged): MS HRC

[postmarked] TAOS N. MEX
AUG 8 1945

Dear Merrild,

... You wrote me so beautifully about the Mss, you know it was a pleasure to give it to you and you *do* deserve it – [1]

Your old friend   Frieda

Note

1. Frieda Lawrence had given Merrild the manuscripts of *Apocalypse*.

238. Frieda Lawrence to Willard Hougland, 30 November 1945

Text (abridged): MS UCLA

30 Nov 45

Dear Willard,

... Had one of those Tedlock letters saying Matt [Pearce][1] had *not* got the Mss, sort of hurt – Why dont they say straight: Willard you forgot? Also you had done nothing about the bibliography Tedlock says – So I'll calm him down – ...

Then why dont we *all* go to Big Sur? Georgine too? The soaking will do us all good – ...

It seems such an opportunity! I am looking forward to it! ...

Love to you both   F –

Note

1. T. M. Pearce (1902–86) was head of the English Department at the University of New Mexico in Albuquerque.

239. Frieda Lawrence to T. M. Pearce, 2 January 1946

Text: TS copy New Mexico

River Inn, Big Sur, California
January 2, 1946

Dear Matt,

I am more sorry than I can say about the Mss. business.

I was so pleased to give you that particular Mss. that you wanted. You have had such a genuine interest in Lawrence and did all you could to publish him! O dear! And the Mss. lost! I still have a faint hope it will turn up.

Willard, as you see, says in this letter that he will get the insurance, but we wanted the Mss. I will give you another one! Think what you would like! It is very beautiful here. The sea is a joy. We have seen the Jeffers and Henry Miller, and all sorts of people one knows. Sally Bok, you remember her.

This is just a word to tell you how sorry I am.

All the best of wishes to you and Helen.

Bynner liked Helen's picture of me so much. He *took* it!

Frieda

Greetings from Angie

240. Frieda Lawrence to Willard Hougland, 2 January 1946

Text (abridged): MS UCLA

River Inn, Big Sur, California
2 Jan 46

Dear Willard,

That is a stupid business about the Mss! Maybe it still turns up. Matt Pearce wanted it so much – I shall have to give him another one – Let's forget about it!

It is very, very beautiful here! To see the sea and such a sea! We saw Henry Miller and the Jeffers and a number of people have turned up already –

We have done something a bit wild – On the 15th we move into a *mansion* with private beach, a ballroom, a library etc 4 elegant bathrooms, it is a dreamplace, but there is *hardly* any furniture – – We share it with 2 young couples[1] – Houses are terribly scarce – We move in on the 15th – But it's done me good already to be here – One needs to change one's pattern occasionally – Henry Miller lives up a terrific hill, it scares one to drive up it! . . .

Angie sends you greetings –

Yours   Frieda

Note

1. In the Los Angeles *Calendar* of 8 November 1981, Cecil Smith wrote: "For a while, she and her last lover, Angelo Ravagli, the handsome *maggiore* in the Italian army, lived in a house I leased in Carmel. It was a huge manor house, and a lot of us lived there in a kind of early commune." In a letter of 18 February 1946 (MS UCLA), Frieda Lawrence wrote to Willard Hougland: "This is to say that with Cecil Smith . . . and John Ney we made a moviescript of Lady C – Good I think and it was fun."

241. Dudley Nichols to Frieda Lawrence, 6 May 1946

Text (abridged): MS HRC

RKO Radio Pictures, Inc., 780 Gower Street, Los Angeles 38, Calif.

May 6, 1946

Dear Frieda:

I am overwhelmed. Really you shouldn't have done it. One manuscript would have been the most generous of gifts. To receive two – well, I'm speechless. . . . Reading a manuscript by Lawrence is a peculiar excitement, for one can follow the changes and movements of his mind. On the printed page you see and feel what he finally wanted you to see and feel – the single finished movement. But in manuscript you sense its ruminations, its pauses and series of insights and growing feelings and the search for clarity. I remember what pleasure you gave me when you let me read the manuscript of the first *Lady Chatterley*. . . .

Sincerely,   Dudley[1]

Note

1. Dudley Nichols (1895–1960), a journalist who came to Hollywood in 1929 and became a distinguished screenwriter of the 1930s and 1940s. He won an Academy Award for his screenplay of *The Informer* (1935); in 1946 he produced and directed *Sister Kenny* (see Letter 242).

242. Frieda Lawrence to Una Jeffers, 21 May 1946

Text: MS UCBerkeley

Taos, New Mexico

21. May 46

Dear Una,

It made our months in Carmel so friendly having you there – I want to thank you for all you did for us – It was very nice to see Garth [Jeffers] – Is he with you still? –

One of the young man Cecil Smith at the Highlands was asked to do a profile of Robin, he wrote me and said: "my admiration for him is so great that I would babble like a highschool girl writing about Frank Sinatra". I want to send you and Robin an Mss of Lawrence's – That will be a pleasure for me –

Una, do you remember Hildegard? She came here, very sick and she died and we buried her in that cemetry on the way to the pueblo – Her husband and her nice girl came and it was a forlorn, moving sort of a funeral. She had been ill for years –

Taos is very alert and we are busy – Brett is happy in her new house[1] and Mabel has the Vanderbilts in the big house; they stayed in mine and it was terribly spotless when we arrived.

It was wonderful to stay with the Huxleys, then we spent a few days with the Dudley Nichols in their very swanky house –

I am going up with Tennessee Williams to the ranch with a friend of his.[2] We were going last week, when he got appendicitis and had an operation. Now he is practically well – I like him very much –

Mabel goes to Embudo for weekends, down by the river – It is not warm yet – I often think of your lovely corner – I hope all is well with you – Wolfgang Reinhardt[3] is interested in the script we did of Lady Chatterley, I would be so pleased especially for those two young men –

Dudley was full of schemes and he thinks his latest movie "Sister Kenny" will be a great success –

My best wishes for you and Robin and Garth – –

affectionately   Frieda

Greetings from Angelino

Notes
1. Located near Frieda Lawrence's Los Pinos ranch.
2. Williams's friend was a Mexican youth, Poncho Rodriguez y Gonsalez, nicknamed "Santo", at one time a desk clerk at the La Fonda Hotel in Taos.
3. Wolfgang Reinhardt, Hollywood writer and producer, joined Warner Brothers in 1943.

243. Frieda Lawrence to Willard Hougland, 10 February 1947

Text (abridged): MS UCLA

Laguna Vista, Port Isabel, Texas
10. Febr 47

Dear Willard,

... I bought a small house here and it's fascinating, the greatest contrast to "our" country imaginable. By the way it's supposed to be the best climate for hearttrouble in the U.S.A. – ...

Yours ever   F –

If I explained to you about Lady C selling in *Cairo* and Australia and Mondadori in Milan is bringing out in italian all 3 Lady Cs it would take me a week – I am so *fed up* – –

244. Frieda Lawrence to Rebecca S. James, [Summer 1947]

Text: MS New Mexico

Kiowa Ranch

Dear Becky,[1]

I am writing this letter to you to explain to the committee, if you will –
I have come to the conclusion, that giving the Lawrence Mss to the
Harwood [Foundation], would really be giving them to the University of
New Mexico and there is no point to that, as far as I can see – lent many
Mss to the University for an exhibition and they never held the exhibition – So I withdraw my offer and am very sorry to have given you
and Winnie a lot of trouble – but I hope you can see my point – It is all so
complicated too – I have also had some offers for the Mss and I could use
the money to help in Europe –

Affectionately   Frieda Lawrence

Note

1. Rebecca S. James (1891–1968) was Secretary of the Governing Board of the Harwood
    Foundation in Taos, NM. Directed by Spud Johnson, the Harwood had hoped to
    house some of Lawrence's manuscripts.

245. Frieda Lawrence to Lawrence Clark Powell, 17 March 1950

Text: MS UCLA

Port Isabel Texas
17. March 50

Dear Lawrence Powell,

I was very pleased to get your book and be reminded of you and the
work you and Jake did, such good work! Lawrence is having another
boost, a million cheap books[1] – A very good play of Lady C in french is
in the making – [2]

Please remember me to your wife and Jake and all best wishes to you –
It is a charming little book!

Greetings   Frieda Lawrence

Notes

1. Published by Penguin Books. To Willard Hougland on 26 March 1949 (MS UCLA),
    Frieda Lawrence wrote: "They are (the Penguin) printing a million cheap Lawrence
    books."
2. To Richard Aldington on 13 April 1950, Frieda Lawrence wrote that the play was
    "excellent, I thought, delicate and alive – done by Gaston Bonhuer and Philippe de
    Rothschild!" (*Frieda Lawrence and Her Circle*, p. 98).

246. Lawrence Clark Powell to Frieda Lawrence, 23 March 1950

Text: TSCC UCLA

March 23, 1950

Mrs. Frieda Lawrence
P. O. Box 314
Port Isabel, Texas

Dear Frieda:

How good to have your note about the Recollections which Jake and I sent you.[1] It has been a long while since we have met. When do you come this way again?

Fay and I and the boys are all thriving. We hope to be on sabbatical leave in Europe next year. I have kept closely in touch with Richard Aldington ever since he left Los Angeles and have learned from him of the wonderful revival of interest in Lawrence which is taking place in England and also on the Continent.

I have had news of you from Willard Hougland who comes through this way fairly often. Not long ago he brought me an issue of the Taos paper containing a beautiful picture of you and your sister. You look younger every year.

Please accept my affectionate wishes for your good health and long life.

Yours cordially,   Lawrence Clark Powell, Librarian

Note

1. Lawrence Clark Powell, "Recollections of an Ex-bookseller" (Los Angeles, 1950), a pamphlet printed to mark the anniversary of the new bookshop of Zeitlin and Ver Brugge.

247. Laurence Pollinger to Frieda Lawrence, 31 August 1951
Text (abridged): TS HRC

Pearn, Pollinger and Higham, Ltd.
39–40, Bedford Street, Strand, London, W.C.2.
31st August, 1951

Mrs. Frieda Lawrence,
El Prado,
Taos,
New Mexico,
U.S.A.

Dear Frieda,

. . . Yes, of course, I shall be delighted to help you sell D.H.L.'s manuscripts. Send me a *complete list* of all of those that are in your actual possession and I will then see what can be done. . . .

As ever,   Laurence

248. Frieda Lawrence to Lawrence Clark Powell, 12 April 1952
Text: MS UCLA

El Prado, Taos, New Mexico
12. April 52

Dear Larry,

Thank you very much for sending the photographs of the "forum",[1] I am very glad to have them – It was real fun, all due to your efficiency!

I am afraid Prof Ewing[2] was shocked at the sum I asked for Lady Chatterley, but I dont really want to sell the Mss, and I think it is a most significant Mss.

I hope you dont work too hard but I know how you love it. Now I am looking forward to the records of the Forum, that you said you would send.

Angelino has departed for Italy, I wonder what his reactions will be –

I so enjoyed seeing you, it is such a pleasure to see people "come off" and you are surely one of those who have.

With all best wishes to you both

most sincerely   Frieda

Notes
1. A reference to a panel discussion held on 7 March 1952 at the UCLA Library. The panel consisted of Frieda Lawrence, Aldous Huxley, Lawrence Clark Powell, Majl Ewing, and Dorothy Mitchell Conway.
2. Majl Ewing, a wealthy collector, taught English at the University of California at Los Angeles for many years. On 15 April 1952 Frieda wrote to Angelo Ravagli (MS HRC): "Prof Ewing bought the *one* Mss 400 dollars."

249. Frieda Lawrence to Jake Zeitlin, 1 September [1953?]
Text: MS UCLA

El Prado, New Mexico
1. September

Dear Jake,

It was nice to hear from you and that all goes well with you and Josephine and the babies –

I have so few of Lawrence's pictures left, I dont want to sell any – It is strange how the interest in Lawrence goes on, they wanted to have an exhibition in Paris – And all over the world his books are translated – It is a great pleasure for me!

And you knew his value always!

With love to you both   Frieda

250. Frieda Lawrence to Warren Roberts, 15 April 1954
Text: MS Roberts

El Prado, Taos, New Mexico
15. April 54

Dear Mr Francis Roberts,

Of course I am deeply pleased with your enterprise. It sounds wonderful. No, I do not know much about your university, except that it is a great one.

I have been thinking that you really ought to come here, I have so many odds and ends, here at this place and at the upper ranch where L[awrence] lived. Also I have some of the pictures and Mss and typescripts. I think Lawrence would come very alive to you if you could come here and go to the upper ranch and see the small chapel where he is buried.

I am going to write to my good english agent

Lawrence Pollinger
39–40 Bedford Street
Strand London WC2 England

about your plan. You might write to him about Peter Stockham and what he is doing.[1]

Also Professor Harry T. Moore

9 Woodland Hill
Wellesley Hills Mass

knows a great deal about Lawrence material. He might know of a collection. I have not got a proper collection, but all kinds of things.

I live a very simple life and have no secretary.

In the winter we go to a little house I have in Port Isabel Texas, when we go to it next autumn, I would like to see your university on the way. A young painterfriend Joe Glacco[2] was arranging an exhibition of L's pictures in New York this spring, but he went to Rome and the exhibition has been postponed.

You have a big job before you, but one that makes me happy and I wish you the best of luck!

Sincerely yours   Frieda Lawrence

Notes
1. Peter Stockham may have been planning to compile a bibliography of D. H. Lawrence's works.
2. Joe Glasco was Frieda Lawrence's neighbour.

251. Frieda Lawrence to Warren Roberts, 12 May 1954
Text: MS Roberts

El Prado, Taos, New Mexico
12. May 54

Dear Mr Roberts,

That is good news, that you are coming soon. Yes, you will find accomodation, we might get it for you, but maybe it is better if you choose for yourself. I know you will be interested in the Lawrence material I have. I will show you all I have got.

My agent in London, Lawrence Pollinger will give you much information, he has been a wonderful agent and friend. Lawrence Pollinger 39–40 Bedford Street, Strand, London WC2 England. You have a big list; there are many spanish translations, I have some japanese too.

I am glad it is the first time you are coming here, I hope you will like it you and your family.

No, the tourists come later.

I am very pleased your great University takes an interest in Lawrence; it is also intelligent, because his significance in the world grows and grows.

So let us know when you come.

Sincerely   Frieda Lawrence Ravagli

252. Angelo Ravagli to Jake Zeitlin, 31 August 1954

Text: TS UCLA

P.O. Box 15 – El Prado – Taos – New Mexico

August, 31, 1954

TO MR. JAKE ZEITLIN

815 N. La Cienega Blvd
Hollywood, California

Dear Jake,

Remembering your valuable contribution and cooperation in handling the Manuscripts of D. H. L. in the past, and knowing how competent you are in apprisals of any kind of leterary work, I need your help.

You may know that the Texas University is interested in purchasing what we let them have of D. H. L. material, but, in order to do so we need your apprisal of each items. (A fair price Market to date)

Are you willing to do *it right away, and for how much*?

Please let me know as soon as possible.

To give you an idea about what you have to do, here are the lists:

1)   List of D. H. L. Holograph MM.SS.
2)   ʺ   ʺ   ʺ   corrected typescripts
3)   ʺ   ʺ   ʺ   First and special Editions Books
4)   ʺ   ʺ   ʺ   Articles and stories printed in Magazine or books
5)   ʺ   ʺ   ʺ   Uncorrected Typescripts – ARTICLES
6)   ʺ   ʺ   ʺ   ʺ   ʺ   – SHORT STORIES
7)   ʺ   ʺ   ʺ   ʺ   ʺ   – POEMS
8)   ʺ   ʺ   ʺ   ʺ   ʺ   – PLAYS
9)   Recent Editions of D. H. Lawrence's Books

Hoping that you and family are all well as is the case with us at present.

Sincerely Yours   (Angelo Ravagli)   [signed] Angie –

P.S.   Please if you are going to handle the job, please do not copy my lists, put just a price in margine of each item and sen them back.

PPs.   We have also lots of books of Lawrence translated in many different languages. If I send you a list, could you appraise them too?

253. Angelo Ravagli to Jake Zeitlin, [10 September 1954]

Text: MS (of reported telegram) UCLA

9/10/54

Western Union –

Taos New Mexico

Agree. Do come Sept 21 will fetch you Santa Fe airport. Let me know time of arrival.[1]

Note

1. Among Jake Zeitlin's papers is a pencilled draft, like this one, of a telegram to Angelo Ravagli that reads: "Must postpone trip / Will arrive via T.W.A. Albuquerque Sunday 6:29 P.M. Jake."

254. A. Fredric Leopold to Frieda Lawrence, 1 October 1954

Text (abridged): TS HRC

Youngman and Leopold
6363 Wilshire Boulevard, Los Angeles 48, California
October 1, 1954

Mrs. Freda Ravelli
Ranchos de Taos
New Mexico

Dear Mrs. Ravelli:

Mr. Hans de Schulthess, a good friend and client of mine, asked me to write you concerning a possible sale by you of various manuscripts . . . now in your possession having to do with your deceased husband, D. H. Lawrence.[1]

I told Mr. de Schulthess that prior to any sale, I would like to know the exact nature of the property which was to be sold. . . . I do not believe that I can overstress the importance of putting a sale such as you contemplate in the correct form for tax purposes. . . .

In the event you desire us to take any further steps in the premises I would appreciate it if you would let us know and also authorize Mr. Zeitlin to give us any information which he has and which we request concerning the value of the items you propose to sell. . . .

Very truly yours,   A. Fredric Leopold

Note

1. A. Fredric Leopold recalls that, "As a member of an old and prominent Swiss family, and as a successful businessman, [Hans de Schulthess] was in a position not only to enjoy, but to acquire objects which interested him" (letter to the editor, 22 January 1990).

255. Jake Zeitlin to Angelo Ravagli, 6 October 1954

Text: Telegram UCLA

OCTOBER 6, 1954

ANGELO RAVAGLI
EL PRADO
TAOS, NEW MEXICO

EXPECT TO ARRIVE SANTA FE SATURDAY OCTOBER 9, 2:31 P.M. PIONEER
AIRLINES, FLIGHT 64

JAKE

256. Frieda Lawrence to Alan C. Collins, 12 October 1954

Text (abridged): MS HRC

El Prado, New Mexico
12. Oct 54

Dear Mr Collins,[1]
  . . . The University of Texas, the richest in the world is making a
Lawrence centre in Austin, they want to make it the biggest in the world
and are buying everything they can connected with Lawrence. It is
pleasant to deal with such decent people. They want to buy the upper
ranch too, a place for study! We go to Austin on our way to Port Isabel. . . .

Sincerely yours   Frieda Lawrence Ravagli

Note
1.   Alan C. Collins was President of the New York office of Curtis Brown, a literary agency.

257. Frieda Lawrence to A. Fredric Leopold, 12 October 1954

Text: MS HRC

12. Oct 54

Dear Mr Leopold,
  Thank you very much for your letter with all its information. You will
hear from us, when we have been to the University of Texas – In about a
month's time. Then we can let you know something definite. We shall
be glad if you can help us! Please thank Mr de Shulthess for getting you
in touch with us.

Sincerely yours   Frieda L. Ravagli

258. Jake Zeitlin to Frieda Lawrence, 15 October 1954

Text: TS UCBerkeley

October 15, 1954

Mrs. Frieda Lawrence Ravagli
El Prado, Taos, New Mexico

Dear Mrs. Ravagli:

Attached is a listing[1] of the D. H. Lawrence Manuscripts, Corrected Typescripts and Books which I have personally examined and appraised at your home in Taos on October 10, 1954.

In 1937 I catalogued and offered for sale a number of D. H. Lawrence Manuscripts, some of them were sold at the prices I then placed upon them and I have since had inquiries which indicate that my valuations were such that the others could be sold at similar prices.

Further, in considering the valuation I have been guided by, 1) relative literary importance, 2) amount of holograph material, 3) whether the item is unpublished or published.

With my previous prices and selling experience as a basis I feel confident the present values I have placed on your manuscripts and books are not unrealistic.

Totaled as separate items the value of the manuscripts, corrected typescripts and books, comes to $24,251.75. If, however, you have a prospective purchaser for the collection as a whole, I would consider that a lot price of $20,000.00 would be a fair figure.

Yours cordially,   Jacob Zeitlin

Note
1. See Appendix C.

259. Angelo Ravagli to Jake Zeitlin, 18 October 1954

Text: MS UCLA

El Prado, New Mexico
October 18, 1954

To Zeitlin and Ver Bruce
815 No. La Cienega Blvd
Los Angeles, 46. Calif.

Dear, dear Jake –

You are a real lamb – You did a wonderful job, and whats more, in record time – Bravo – and thanks so much also for a pretty shirt you sent me –

I will never regret of been frendly to you during your short – too short visit, because you give us so much work and kindness in return –

We enjoyed your visit very much –

Frieda joines me in sending you best regards for you and Josephine –

With all my appreciation I am very

Sincerely yours   Angelino.

P.S.   I will keep you informed how the things goes in Austin – we are leaving Taos the third of November – your folders looks very impressive!! – AR.

260. Frieda Lawrence to Warren and Pat Roberts, 25 November 1954
Text: MS Roberts

Box 201, Port Isabel, Texas
Thanksgiving Day.[1]

Dear Warren and Pat,

It's hateful we feel as we do. But for us there is no point in leaving the manuscripts with you. There is nothing definite about their sale and the ranch seems a castle in Spain. – So many young men come to Taos to see me and like to see the Mss – and we can sell them, when we like and what we like. –

It is too bad. We enjoyed our Austin visit so much and you did such a lot for us and so did Dean [Harry] Ransom. But then we have to think of our children too.

I do hope it wont make any difference to our personal relationship. Anyhow, I think you said, Warren, that Macdonald[2] (was it) had a very complete set of books, so you wont want ours too.

Thank you for your nice letter, Pat.

Yours, disturbed about this,   Frieda –

Notes
1.   Postmarked "Nov 26, 1954".
2.   Edward D. McDonald, early bibliographer of Lawrence.

261. Frieda Lawrence to Warren Roberts, 30 November 1954
Text (abridged): MS Roberts

Box 201, Port Isabel
30. Nov 54

Dear Warren,

First I want to say, *that you must keep the Mss* till spring anyhow that you can go on with your work, not only for your sake but also for Lawrence's. Also that we will send you the copyright information from *Brylawski* when we get it so that Dr Ransom can use it.

Now we never in the world suspected your integrity. But we had had our own ideas and they were not the same as yours. That's all. We thought we would hand the material over to you and you would pay it gradually and we would be rid of any further responsability for it all. But it was not so. You still would choose what you wanted and you might never have wanted all of it. We paid Zeitlin 300 dollars besides all the work A[ngelino] did. So it would be to our disadvantage to leave the things with you. Angelino got worked up and wrote more harshly than he ever meant to. So now, I know you feel the same (thank goodness) we want to make peace all around. I respect and admire Dr Ransom for his enthusiasm and you too. Also we thought there were limitless funds at the University's command, that led us on the wrong track too. We did not realise what difficulties Dr Ransom is up against. It looked as if you were stingy with us. Then I had seen in my mind's eye, the ranch alive with young people working there in peace on anything they were anxious to do and now it seemed so far away. So always one only sees one's own point of view. It was so easy with Hanley, he choose what he wanted and pays us so much a month.

I would be awfully sorry to diminish any triumph Dr Ransom had and deserves.

·   ·   ·

Yes, we also feel you are our friends. How could we feel otherwise? You made us at home with you. All the critici[s]m of Dr Ransom I would make is that in his enthusiasm he bites of[f] more than he can chew. (off the record) –

So I write with a goodwill towards you.

My best to the Pat (I see her at the party, making it a success!)

Frieda

You see Angelino wants to be businesslike and American!

262. Warren Roberts to Frieda Lawrence and Angelo Ravagli, 31 December 1954

Text (abridged): TS HRC

Friday Morning
Dec. 31 – 1954.

Dear Frieda and Angie:

... I have been thinking that you might get the Zeitlin money back at least (also I'm afraid you will sell all these things to someone else) by selling the University an option for six months or for some period for two hundred dollars or so – I've forgotten what you said you paid him. Would you be willing to let us have an option[1] for a time. If so let me know for how long and for how much. Jake Zeitlin hasn't answered my letter, but I had a nice one from Bertram Rota and a Mr. George Lazarus in England who told me all about the manuscripts they bought from Zeitlin at the time of the 1937 sale. . . .

Dr. Ransom told me the other day that he is attempting to have enough money to secure the purchase of all the material we are after – yours included – by spring. I hope so. . . .

Best to you both from all of us,   Warren

Note
1. option]   option for six months or

263. Frieda Lawrence to Warren and Pat Roberts, 1 January 1955

Text (abridged): MS Roberts

Box 201, Port Isabel, Texas
Already the 1.1.55

Dear Warren and Pat,

We had a fine Xmas and New Year! Had a party and the people devoured some of the good things you sent! Please thank Pat for her nice letter and tell her that I have invited my children's old german nurse to stay with me while Angie is away – . . .

Now I have come to the conclusion that it is too soon for Lawrence's work to be in one place – Not fluid enough – too final – It intrigues people to be able to buy an Mss. You dont need an option, you have time till the first of April. Any time you or the University wants one you can buy it. You did not want the whole lot anyway – Also I can give one now and then to a friend, I enjoy that – I should have thought of that before, but in my enthusiasm I did'nt. Also from our point of view it seems best to get the money when we sell anything. I for one cant live so very much longer.

I am glad for your own work that you have all that stuff to go into. I know it will help you.

No, we dont want to be paid for Zeitlin, we would have done that anyway –

The best of wishes to all of you

and greetings   Frieda

264. Frieda Lawrence to Jake Zeitlin, 30 January 1955
Text: MS UCLA

Box 201, Port Isabel, Texas
January 30. 55

Dear Jake,

Thank you for proposing to negotiate for us with the Austin people, but we want the Mss back. We will leave them with the Austin people till spring. There at Austin it was all so vague. I know we can always sell the Mss if we want to. You also said you might like some. We are both too old to wait for an uncertain hand-out – Next time we want hard cash – It is simpler, at the present we dont want to sell.

The photographs you took were so good. – We enjoyed your visit and I wish you could come with Josephine one day.

I am sorry to tell you that that good Knud Merrild died on New Year's Eve. He died quietly without pain, of heart trouble. –

That's how it goes. –

We are having a wonderful winter. The Frenchies paid us a visit and now the Andersons are here –

Affectionately   Frieda

265. Angelo Ravagli to Jake Zeitlin, 31 January 1955
Text: TS UCLA

P. O. Box 201 – Port Isabel – Texas
January, 31, 1955

TO Zeitlin and Ver Bruce
815 No. La Cienega Blvd
Los Angeles, California.

Dear Jake,

Thank you for your prompt reply. I am going to ansuer to the first part and Frieda will do the rest.

It is obvious that in the last analysis what the seller wants and what the buyer will pay is what will determine the value of the property.

But my case is quite different. What I am asking you is for the income tax purpose.

As you know, for the tax one must use figures and not words. So, in order to pay no more, no less of what we should, we must extablish an approximate quota of the increase in the value of D. H. L. manuscripts, from 1930 to date.

To give you an example it will work like this: To start with, my Accountant will consider the D. H. L. materials, sold or for sale, as a Real Estate and make us pay taxes only on the profit made after this property was inherited. Is that clear?

So will you please help me in fixing a percent of what you think approximately the property increase value? If you dont want commit yorself, then let me know, i will think of onoter way. To may judgement a 15% should be fair, do you think is more or less?

Please reply by return mail. I must file the income-tax return right away, in order to be able to start for my trip to Argentina to pay a short visit to my sister that I dont se for the last 22 years.

Hope you understand and you will give a hand. Your suggestion, as usual, is very valuable for my purpose.

Hasta la vista

Sincerely yours   Angie   (Angelo Ravagli)

266. Jake Zeitlin to Frieda Lawrence, 8 February 1955
Text: TSCC UCLA

February 8, 1955

Mrs. Frieda Lawrence Ravagli
P.O. Box 201
Port Isabel, Texas

Dear Frieda and Angie:

For tax purposes I think it would [be] quite fair to place a 15 per cent increase in value on the manuscripts.

I am sorry to hear that the University of Texas deal is not going through. If on your return from Argentina you wish me to help in any way I shall be glad to do so. I hope you have a good trip and return soon well and happy.

We were very unhappy to hear about Knud Merrild. He was a good honest man in the truest sense. The world could spare him less than it could a few of the liars and troublemakers that are running around loose these days. It is hard to see old friends go. We never replace them.

Love from everyone.

Cordially,   [JZ]

267. Lawrence Clark Powell to Frieda Lawrence, 22 June 1955
Text: TSCC UCLA

June 22, 1955

Mrs. Frieda Lawrence Ravagli
Kiowa Ranch
San Cristobal, New Mexico

Dear Frieda:

We have just acquired eight letters Lawrence wrote to Rachel Annand Taylor and would like to publish them privately as a keepsake for the Friends of the UCLA Library.[1] May we have your permission? They came from Mrs. Taylor via our London agent, and were written mostly in 1910 and 1911. They are beautiful and important letters, all unpublished and hitherto unknown.

How are you and Angie? Fay and I have moved to Malibu and love it. We send our faithful and affectionate greetings to you both.

Yours cordially,   Lawrence Clark Powell, Librarian

P.S.   I think Harry Moore did a wonderful job in the biography.[2] Has Texas now acquired the manuscripts?

Notes
1. Published as *Eight Letters by D. H. Lawrence to Rachel Annand Taylor*, with a Foreword by Majl Ewing (Pasadena, CA: Castle Press, 1956).
2. Harry T. Moore, *The Intelligent Heart: The Story of D. H. Lawrence* (New York: Farrar, Strauss, and Young, 1954).

268. Frieda Lawrence to Lawrence Clark Powell, 27 June 1955
Text: MS UCLA

El Prado, Taos, New Mexico
27. June 55

Dear Larry,

Yes, you have my permission to publish the Rachel Annand Taylor letters. I never knew her, but she must have been charming. Lawrence imitated her voice to me, reciting "Where are the knights of yesteryear?" We are, I am thankful to say, very well. You know that Merrild died. Else, his wife wrote to me, she would like to have his book on L[awrence] published again. It was a good, sincere book – Would you have an idea about this? Her address: Else Merrild, Sönderdalen 22, Söborg, Denmark. – There is such a fierce L. revival.

No, Texas has not acquired the manuscripts. We have them again. All was so vague. Berkeley wants an exhibition there at the university. I am glad to have them back. Harry Moore worked very hard on that book, but for me there was something of L's "not there." There is a man called Mark Spilka who has written about L with a deep insight.[1]

I am glad you moved to Malibu, it must be nice there now.

Poor Aldous came to see us, I was very fond of Maria, a loyal friend – But he has a steady fund of acceptance. He had written some pages after she was dead, how he had helped her to die, very moving. – I am sure you are always busy.

With all good wishes to you and the family.

Always sincerely yours   Frieda L. Ravagli

P.S.   Dont forget to clear the letters with the Viking –

Note
1. In 1955 Mark Spilka published *The Love Ethic of D. H. Lawrence* (Bloomington: Indiana University Press) to which Frieda Lawrence contributed a foreword.

269. Frieda Lawrence to Angelo Ravagli, 7 July 1956

Text (abridged): MS HRC

7. July 56

My dear Angie,

    ... Larry Powell came to see me, he sort of hides in Santa Fe from his tough work. He has 200 librarians under him. He wanted "Rainbow" but Hanley does too.[1] ...

Love to you, see you soon   F –

Note

1. T. E. Hanley purchased the manuscript of *The Rainbow* for $3500 – what Jake Zeitlin had appraised it for in 1954. See Appendix C, List I, No. 39.

270. Angelo Ravagli to Warren Roberts, 11 August 1956

Text: Telegram Roberts

TAOS NMEX
1956 AUG 11
1103 AM

WARREN ROBERTS
3015 WEST AVE AUSTIN TEX

FRIEDA PASSED AWAY TODAY

ANGIE

271. Jake Zeitlin to Angelo Ravagli, [12 August 1956]

Text: Telegram HRC

1220 PM

ANGELINO RAVAGLI
TAOS NMEX

FRIEDA LIVED A FINE LIFE TO A RIPE AGE. YOU DID MUCH TO KEEP HER HAPPY. SINCERE SYMPATHY AND LOVE

JAKE AND JOSEPHINE

LETTERS ABOUT THE MANUSCRIPTS OF
APOCALYPSE

272. Jake Zeitlin to Else Merrild, 25 October 1960
Text (abridged): TSCC UCLA

October 25, 1960

Mrs. Else Merrild
c/o Mrs. William Dietrick
Shelton Hotel
525 Lexington Avenue
New York, New York

Dear Else:

The man that you want to talk to about getting out a paperback reprint of Merrild's book is Victor Weybright, New American Library. . . .

It was good to see you and to have the pleasant visit. I shall not forget about the Apocalypse Ms., the Hugh Walpole letters and the Lawrence water color. Also, I shall not forget to see you when next I come to Denmark.

Yours sincerely,   [JZ]

273. Else Merrild to Jake and Josephine Zeitlin, 18 November 1960
Text: MS UCLA

Nov. 18, 60.

Mr. and Mrs. J. Zeitlin
815. N. La Cienega Blvd.
Los Angeles 46. Calif.
U.S.A.

Dear Josephine and Jake:

Thank you for a very pleasent visit and lunch – it was really very nice seeing you again.

Thanks also, Jake, for your letter to New York – unfortunately Mr. Weybright did not want Merrilds book. I might try England –

I have three [*illegible*]'s wonder if that is something you would be interested in – –

Hope you come over, and that I am here at the time.
With my very best wishes

Yours Sincerely   Else.

274. Jake Zeitlin to Else Merrild, 22 November 1960
Text: Telegram copy UCLA

1960 NOV 22 PM 2 38

LT ELSE MERRILD
SONDERDALEN 22
SOBORG, DENMARK

HAVE INTERESTED CUSTOMER FOR LAWRENCE APOCALYPSE MANUSCRIPTS
WOULD YOU CONSIDER 15,000 CASH PLEASE CABLE DECISION

ZEITLIN

275. Else Merrild to Jake Zeitlin, 23 November 1960
Text: Telegram copy UCLA

1960 NOV 23 AM 8 01

JABBERWOCK
LOS ANGELES CALIF

15000 DOLL TO INTEREST ME

ELSE

276. Else Merrild to Jake Zeitlin, 23 November [1960]
Text: MS UCLA

Nov. 23,

Dear Jake:

I just got your telegram. I presume you mean 15,000 Doll. cash to me –
that interest me – Write me an Air Mail it only takes three days –
Have send you a Telegram

in haste   Else Merrild

277. Lew D. Feldman to Jake Zeitlin, 23 November 1960
Text: Telegram UCLA

1960 NOV 23 PM 4 08

J ZEITLIN
815 NORTH LA CIENEGA BLVD LOSA

WILL MEET ANY REASONABLE FIGURE FOR APOCALYPSE SUBJECT TO EXAMINA-
TION PAYMENT 30 DAYS AFTER ACCEPTANCE YOU HAVE ENOUGH INFORMATION
TO ARRIVE AT PRICE ACCEPTABLE TO ALL PARTIES

LEW.

278. Jake Zeitlin to Lew D. Feldman, 23 November 1960
Text: TSCC UCLA

November 23, 1960

Mr. Lew D. Feldman
House of El Dieff, Inc.
30 East 62nd Street
New York 21, New York

Dear Lew:

I cabled the lady about the Lawrence Apocalpyse manuscript. Her answer stopped me cold. She wants $15,000.00. I think we had better let her relax a while unless you think that the boys in Austin would pay that kind of money.

Yours cordially,   [JZ]

279. Jake Zeitlin to Else Merrild, 28 November 1960
Text: TSCC UCLA

November 28, 1960

Mrs. Else Merrild
22, Sönderdalen 22
Söborg, Denmark

Dear Else:

My customer is completely overwhelmed by your reaction and suggestion of a price of $15,000.00 for the Lawrence manuscript. There is no basis for such a figure that I know of.

I might possibly get him to come up to $3,000.00 but this would be a great deal. I want to sell the manuscript for you and get the best possible price, but you will have to be reasonable if you want to sell it.

I hope you will think it over and let me know.

Yours cordially,   [JZ]

280. Else Merrild to Jake Zeitlin, 1 December 1960
Text: MS UCLA

Dec. 1, 60.

Dear Jacob:

Believe me I was just as overwhelmed by your telegram with the offer of 15,000. thats why I repeated the price.

Shall send you the telegram so you can se it was not I who was unreasonable.

As I told you when I was in L.A. I am not at present in need of money, and not too anxious to sell it – have keept it to a rainy day or a very temting offer. 3000 might be a very good price, but I feel, perhaps wrongly, that that I can get later too – it does not really temt me.

The price is that – your cut or clear.

I like to sell the letters and the picture, will send a loose sketch and can send the picture after xmas if you like.

With my best regard also to Josephine

Yours very truly   Else.

281. Jake Zeitlin to Else Merrild, 5 December 1960
Text: TSCC UCLA

December 5, 1960

Mrs. Else Merrild
Sönderdalen 22
Söborg, Denmark

Dear Else:

The cable company made a mistake and I am very much embarrassed. It happens that I have an actively buying customer for Lawrence manuscripts. He has considerable money and is particularly keen on getting the Apocalypse manuscript. Customers like this do not come along every day. One has to strike while the iron is hot. Since last writing you I have had another conversation with him and he has authorized me to offer you $4,000.00 for your Apocalypse manuscript. This is a net price to you. It is frankly much more than I had guessed he would pay and I hope that you will not hesitate. I also think that if he buys this he will also be in the market for the letters and the picture. I suggest that you send me a photograph of the painting. If you are agreeable to selling the Apocalypse manuscript for $4,000.00 net to you please cable. I can arrange to have payment made to you in Denmark or paid into your account in the United States, whichever you prefer.

Josephine joins me in sending best greetings.

Yours cordially,   [JZ]

282. Else Merrild to Jake Zeitlin, 9 December 1960
Text: MS UCLA

Dec. 9, 60.

Dear Jake:

Thank you for letter also for writing Laughlin[1] that was very kind of you. I meet him years ago, but don't really know him.

I have never opened the packed with Man[uscript] before to-day – am very exited and facinated now I shall want to read it before selling.

When I was in L.A. you said it was probably the hologr. Man[uscript] 105 pages I had – Yes I have that, but also fragment of earlier vision, in pink cahier, on the cover of wich is written Apocalysis II and then there is a green notebook insribed for uncle david e.t.c. wich is jumping in the number of the pages.[2]

Now that seems to be *two* Man[uscripts] and then the green notebook – am not familiar with it yet. –

As I just opened it, have never asked anybody what it is worth, I feel it is stupid of me not to know a bit more about it – a friend who has connections in England feels I should get a reaction from there and I hope you will forgive me for being curious, and naturly I like to get the best price too, I am not rich.

I hope you don't feel hurt, I would hate that, and I do believe you will only treat me right, but after all L[awrence] was English and they naturly have a greater interest in keeping it over here.

I suppose it should be sold to-gether or could the first be sold alone and the rest by itself?

Like to have your reaction to that So I can't give an answer to your offer of 4000 just now – will let you know when I know more, it might take a little time.

friendly Greeting   Else

Notes
1. At the New Directions Press.
2. Powell catalogue, Nos 110.A. and 110.B. The corrected typescript is No. 110.C.

283. Jake Zeitlin to Else Merrild, 14 December 1960
Text: TSCC UCLA

December 14, 1960

Mrs. Else Merrild
Sönderdalen 22
Söborg, Denmark

Dear Else:

I see no reason why you should not investigate prices on the Lawrence manuscript in England, but I can assure you that the British are not paying prices for such things that Americans are. After you have informed yourself concerning British prices I would appreciate your giving me a chance to buy the manuscript at whatever final figure you set before selling it elsewhere. As you may understand, I am acting on behalf of a customer and he is the one who is setting the offered prices. He is much disappointed that you have delayed in deciding but I agree that you should make every effort to get the best price you can. My customer had hoped to buy the manuscript within the present tax year since he spends out of income and does not know what his next year's income will be.

You should not break up the group of manuscripts. They belong together and it would be a disservice to scholarship if they were separated.

Please let me know as soon as you can when you have made a decision and again I beg you to please not sell it elsewhere without giving me a chance.

Josephine joins me in sending best wishes for the holiday season.

Yours sincerely,   [JZ]

284. Else Merrild to Jake Zeitlin, 30 December 1960
Text: TS UCLA

Dec. 30, 60.

Dear Jake:

Please excuse the delay i feel rotten at present.

My niece who is a Librarian, has written one place in England, and after that, i am not so sure prices are so much lower there. We know for a fact that Etruscan Places was sold for a few months ago for 2000 english £, and that as fare as the blue book [Powell catalogue] goes must be a corrected Typescript, and don't you think Apocalypse is more importen?

I agree with you the Manuscripts should be keept to-gether – if possible. They run about the same length, but the last is broken up a bit more sketchily, but perhaps more interesting.

I do like to have you sell it, but it might be difficult to give a price, or to know what is the best price. Etruscan Places was sold at an auction. If your customer wanted to pay me 4000 for the first what can i get for the other?

Jan. 9, 61.

Sorry i did not get this of, but am not at all well at present just got out of bed.

Had a letter from England. They want me to send the Mann. for inspection, they also want a price. I have not decided what to do yet – Can you give me a price.

Best regard also to Josephine

Sincerely yours   Else Merrild

285. Jake Zeitlin to Else Merrild, 12 January 1961
Text: TSCC UCLA

January 12, 1961

Mrs. Else Merrild
Sönderdalen 22
Söborg, Denmark

Dear Else:

I am very sorry to hear that you have not been feeling well.

It is true that the manuscript of *Etruscan Places* was sold at auction for 2000 English pounds. It was purchased by an agent of the University of Texas, who have been spending money recklessly, and that price is not likely to be repeated now that they have spent their money for this manuscript. I have discussed your manuscript of the *Apocalypse* with my customer and have told him that you have made inquiries in England. He feels that he might pay $5000.00 for the entire group, manuscript and corrected typescript of *Apocalypse*, provided you would care to send it to me for examination. He has seen the description of the group, as described in the [Powell] catalogue of the Exhibition of the manuscripts which was held here, and wants all the material together. If you would send it to me by Air Parcel Post, insured, I am almost certain that I can get you the $5000.00.

I have received the drawing of the Lawrence water color but I am unable to suggest a price. If you have some idea of what you want for it I will speak to my customer about it. He is a very difficult man and does not like to make offers.

Do be careful of your health. Maybe if we sell the *Apocalypse* you can come to California for a while. I think you will be more comfortable here than in the trying winter weather there.

Josephine sends her kind regards.

Yours cordially,   [JZ]

286. Else Merrild to Jake Zeitlin, 31 January 1961
Text: TS UCLA

Jan. 31, 61.

Dear Jake:

You misunderstand, I do not have any typed Mann. look in the blue book.[1] What I have is A and B. A is the one you offered 4000 for, and B is the part your costumer wants to pay 1000 for, and that I can't see.

I have a much better guranty from England than his offer, and then it might bring more.

The Mann. is in England, but only for inspection and I just had the offer to-day.

I like to have you sell it, but I can't sell it for less. If you think he want's to pay the same for B as for A, I can send it over otherwise I feel I must sell it in England. I feel sure you understand that.

I understand you must see it, but I do not want to send it if you feel it is unlikely you can sell it for that.

Kind regards

Sincerely yours   Else.

Let me hear as soon as possible, as I am thinking of going South – I need some sun.

Note
1. The "blue book" is the Powell catalogue, which had blue paper covers. The typescript of *Apocalypse* had been purchased by T. E. Hanley.

287. Jake Zeitlin to Lew D. Feldman, 7 February 1961

Text (abridged): TSCC UCLA

February 7, 1961

Mr. Lew D. Feldman
House of El Dieff, Inc.
30 East 62nd Street
New York 21, New York

Dear Lew:

The lady in Europe, who owns the Lawrence manuscripts, has just written me about them. She wants $4,000.00 each for the A and B manuscripts of the *Apocalypse*. She says she has an offer for this much from England but wants to give me first refusal. I would be willing to take a profit of $1,500.00 each. What can we do about it? . . .

Yours cordially,   [JZ]

288. Jake Zeitlin to Else Merrild, 9 February 1961

Text: Telegram copy UCLA

FEB. 9. 1961

MRS. ELSE MERRILD
SONDERDALEN 22
SOBORG, DENMARK

ABSOLUTE LAST OFFER FOR BOTH APOCALYPSE MANUSCRIPTS FIVE THOUSAND DOLLARS. REMEMBER AUCTION HOUSES DO NOT MAKE GUARANTEES. PLEASE ADVISE.

REGARDS,   ZEITLIN

289. Else Merrild to Jake Zeitlin, 22 February 1961

Text: TS UCLA

Feb. 22, 61.

Dear Jake:

Please forgive me for not answering sooner, under normal condition it is really not like me. It has been a very difficult winter for me with bad health, and on top of that other unpleasant difficulty.

As i have said before, i like to have you sell it but i olsa think to offer 4 for one and 1 for the other is too fare apart, they are not completely alike, not at all.

I will take 6 for them both, and that is my lowest, if the del is made while the Dollar exchange is as to-day (everybody over here expect the $ to be lowered)   If your customer wants to pay 6 (to me) i can send the Mann. and olsa the painting, and the letters, and you can tell me what you can do with the rest, if he does not want to pay that, lets just forget about it, i will put it back in the box or perhaps send it to England, where they have an auction of that kind in marts.

There is no hard feeling, and i hope it is the same with you.

best regard to you both

Sincerely yours   Else.

290. Jake Zeitlin to Else Merrild, 27 February 1961
Text: Telegram copy UCLA

FEB. 27, 1961

ELSE MERRILD
SONDERDALEN 22
SOBORG, DENMARK

AGREE TO SIX THOUSAND DOLLARS FOR THE APOCALYPSE MANUSCRIPTS SUBJECT TO CUSTOMER'S EXAMINATION. PLEASE SEND VIA AIR PARCEL POST INSURED. ALSO SEND SEPARATELY LETTERS AND PAINTING.

REGARDS,   ZEITLIN

291. Jake Zeitlin to Lew D. Feldman, 27 February 1961
Text: TSCC UCLA

February 27, 1961

Mr. Lew D. Feldman
House of El Dieff, Inc.
30 East 62nd Street
New York 21, New York

Dear Lew:

I have finally gotten a firm price from the owner of the D. H. Lawrence Apocalypse manuscripts. This consists of items A and B, as listed under No. 110 in the Manuscript Catalogue published by the Los Angeles Public Library, 1937. Item C, the corrected typescript, is apparently not there. The owner has agreed to accept $6000.00 net from me for the two. Before having them sent over I should like to have a clear confirmation from you that you will pay $7,500, as discussed by us in previous conversations, provided the manuscripts are as described. Please write me as soon as possible confirming our understanding so that I can instruct the owner to send them on. I should also like to know when payment can be expected after the manuscripts have been received and accepted since I shall have to pay the owner promptly. The owner requests that she be advised promptly since she has been asked to put the manuscripts up for auction in March.

With kindest regards, I am

Yours cordially,   [JZ]

292. Lew D. Feldman to Jake Zeitlin, 1 March 1961
Text: TS UCLA

House of El Dieff, Inc.
March 1, 1961

Zietlin & Ver Brugge
815 No. La Cienega Blvd
Los Angeles 46, California

My dear Jake:

We are in receipt of your letter of February 27.

This is our understanding of the situation: since the net price to the University of Texas will come to at least $7,500, we have offered waiving any commission in this matter since any figure beyond a net of $7,500 makes the going distinctly rough. We would like to see the Austin collection get it, but your insistence on a profit of $1,500 makes us pretty much a fifth wheel in the matter. On the other hand, after examination Dr. Roberts[1] will be in a better position to determine what to do. At this moment we cannot guarantee purchase at the stipulated price of $7,500. However, he has authorized the request that the manuscript material be forwarded to him for examination. We cannot foresee what his wishes will be in the matter. We can only repeat that he is aware of the three sections of the manuscript as discussed with you over the phone the other day, together with the fact that he wants a week from receipt of the material, before he concludes what has to be done. If the material is particularly desirable we are quite sure that a specific date for payment will be allocated although, at this moment, we can give you no assurance on this score either. It is our considered opinion that at $7,500 it is still priced too high for us to arrange purchasing and financing.

Your only practical outlook is simply to advise your client that you have an interested and serious buyer who would like to see the manuscript, with the proviso that he requires a week for examination. Beyond that we are neither authorized to go nor do we care to venture.

We hope this is perfectly clear now, without any possibility of a misunderstanding.

Cordially,   Lew David Feldman

Note
1. Warren Roberts, Director of the Humanities Research Center.

293. Jake Zeitlin to Lew D. Feldman, 2 March 1961
Text: TSCC UCLA

March 2, 1961

Mr. Lew D. Feldman
House of El Dieff, Inc.
30 East 62nd Street
New York 21, New York

Dear Lew:

Thank you for your very clear statement of our understanding concerning the Lawrence Apocalypse manuscripts. I have cabled the owner to send them, subject to examination, on approval and I don't think we will have any difficulty in arranging for Mr. Roberts to have a week in which to examine the manuscripts. I do not want to take advantage of you or to see you go uncompensated and I therefore offer to pay you $500.00 out of my $1500.00 profit in case the University of Texas purchased the manuscripts for no more than $7,500.00. I assume that if they buy it they will issue a post-dated purchase order on the basis of which I can arrange a loan. Under these conditions I assume that I will have to pay the owner the $6,000.00 immediately and carry the account myself.

I hope this deal goes through without any hitches. It's time that we closed one.

With kindest regards, I am

Yours sincerely,   [JZ]

294. Else Merrild to Jake Zeitlin, 7 March 1961

Text: TS UCLA

Mar. 7, 61.

Dear Jake:

I send the MANN. mar. the 1' you have it or should have it in a few days.

Am sending the picture to-day, and the letters in a few days.

Let me know if you can sell picture and letters and what you can get for it.[1]

If you sell the MANN. i would like you to send me the money as soon as possible becauce we expect the Dollar to be devaluaded, and that would be very unfortunate for me, and not only just now.

The best to both of you

Sincerely yours   Else.

Note

1. The "picture" was D. H. Lawrence's watercolour "Yawning". In a letter to Mervyn Levy dated 16 September 1963, Jake Zeitlin wrote: "This painting came to me from Mrs. Knud Merrild whose husband did the book about Lawrence called *A Poet and Two Painters*. It was given to them by Mrs. Lawrence some time between 1937 and 1945. I purchased it from Mrs. Merrild about a year ago." Levy edited the *Paintings of D. H. Lawrence* (New York: Viking, 1964).

295. Jake Zeitlin to Else Merrild, 9 March 1961

Text: TSCC UCLA

March 9, 1961

Mrs. Else Merrild
Sönderdalen 22
Söborg, Denmark

Dear Else:

Your letter of March 7th has just arrived. So far the Lawrence manuscripts did not reach us. Did you send the m by air as requested? If not, then I assume that they will be a little while getting here.

I shall look forward to seeing the picture and the letters. As soon as they arrive I will report to you.

Yours cordially,   [JZ]

296. Jake Zeitlin to Else Merrild, 21 March 1961
Text: TSCC UCLA

March 21, 1961

Mrs. Else Merrild
Sönderdalen 22
Söborg, Denmark

Dear Else:

The Lawrence manuscript of the Apocalypse arrived this morning. I am calling my customer by long distance immediately and making arrangements to send it to him for inspection. As you will understand, things like this take a little time to put through, but I am confident that we should have an answer within ten days to two weeks.

Here's hoping the customer is as enthusiastic about the manuscript when he sees it as when we corresponded about it.

I look forward to receiving the painting and letters in the near future.

Kindest regards,   [JZ]

297. Bill of Sale from Zeitlin & Ver Brugge to the Humanities Research Center, University of Texas at Austin, 21 March 1961
Text: TSCC UCLA

815 North La Cienega Boulevard
Los Angeles 46, California
3/21/61

SOLD TO: University of Texas
            Humanities Research Center
            Box 7594
            Austin 12, Texas
            Attn: Dr. F. W. Roberts

            Quantity: 1
            Author: Lawrence, D. H.
            Title of Publication: APOCALYPSE. Holograph Manuscript.
            Fragments and Holograph manuscript in green note-
                book.
            Amount: $7,500.00

298. Jake Zeitlin to Else Merrild, 30 March 1961
Text: TSCC UCLA

March 30, 1961

Mrs. Else Merrild
Sönderdalen 22
Söborg, Denmark

Dear Else:

I have just received word that the D. H. Lawrence manuscript of *Apocalypse* has been accepted by my customer. Payment should be forthcoming within the next 30 days. Please advise me whether you want the money transmitted to you in Denmark or deposited to your account in the United States.

I hope your health is improved and that the weather in Denmark has also become more agreeable.

Josephine joins me in sending affectionate greetings.

Yours cordially,   [JZ]

LETTERS ABOUT THE MANUSCRIPTS OF
LADY CHATTERLEY'S LOVER

299. Jake Zeitlin to Lew D. Feldman, 27 March 1963
Text: TSCC UCLA

27 March 1963

Mr. Lew D. Feldman
House of El Dieff, Inc.
30 East 62nd Street
New York 21, N.Y.

Dear Lew:

Yesterday I had lunch with the glamorous Mrs. de Schulthess.[1] She told me that the only thing she would consider selling is the group of three manuscripts of *Lady Chatterley's Lover*. She does not want to sell the presentation copy of the book itself, nor any other of the materials that belonged to the late Hans de Schulthess. Actually, the estate is still in probate and a proposal has to be made and the materials have not yet legally become her property. She is therefore not able to make any firm commitments or enter into a transaction until these matters have been closed.

Tentatively, and in principle only, she is agreeable to considering a price of $20,000. net to her for the manuscripts, and has promised me that she will not make any disposal of them without advising me. She plans to consult her attorney and tax advisers this week, but does not think that she can give me any conclusive decision until after her return from Europe which will be some time in August. She is a wealthy woman and does not need money. The argument that bears any weight with her concerning the sale of the manuscripts, is that they should be placed where students of Lawrence can make proper use of them.

I will let you know if there is more to report. In the meantime I would be glad to have your reaction to the above.

Yours cordially,   [JZ]

Note
1. See Introduction, p. 24, for details.

300. A. Fredric Leopold to Jake Zeitlin, 23 May 1963

Text: TS UCLA

6505 Wilshire Boulevard, Los Angeles 48, California
May 23, 1963

Mr. Jacob Zeitlin
Zeitlin & Ver Brugge
815 North La Cienega Boulevard
Los Angeles 69, California

Dear Mr. Zeitlin:

I have tried to get in touch with you several times, but we seem to have missed connections.

I thank you for your appraisal of the D. H. Lawrence manuscripts of *Lady Chatterley's Lover*. By way of background, the three manuscripts of *Lady Chatterley's Lover* are as follows: the first is 420 pages, the second (in 2 volumes) is a total of 570 pages (the first of such volumes being 265 pages) and the third (also in 2 volumes) is a total of 707 pages (the first volume being 408 pages).

If this in any way affects your appraisal, would you please let me know.

Kindest regards.

Sincerely,   A. Fredric Leopold, Co-Executor
Estate of Hans G. M. de Schulthess

301. Jake Zeitlin to Lew D. Feldman, 24 May 1963

Text (abridged): TSCC UCLA

24 May 1963

Mr. Lew D. Feldman
House of El Dieff, Inc.
39 East 62nd Street
New York 21, New York

Dear Lew:

The co-executor of the estate of Hans de Schulthess advises me that the three manuscripts of *Lady Chatterley's Lover* are as follows:

1. 420 pp.
2. 2 vols. – 570 pp.
3. 2 vols. – 707 pp.

Mrs. de Schulthess is still abroad and no action is contemplated until after her return. I will keep you advised. . . .

Kindest regards,   [JZ]

302. Jake Zeitlin to A. Fredric Leopold, 24 May 1963
Text: TSCC UCLA

May 24, 1963

Mr. A. Fredric Leopold
6505 Wilshire Boulevard
Los Angeles 48, California

Dear Mr. Leopold:

Thank you for your letter concerning the D. H. Lawrence manuscripts of *Lady Chatterley's Lover*. I appreciate the information you have supplied.

For the present I see no reason to change the appraisal.

Should Mrs. de Schulthess be interested in disposing of this manuscript at any time I would appreciate being advised.

Yours cordially,   [JZ]

303. Jake Zeitlin to A. Fredric Leopold, 1 October 1963
Text: TSCC UCLA

1 October 1963

Mr. A. Fredric Leopold
6505 Wilshire Boulevard
Los Angeles 48, California

Dear Mr. Leopold:

This is merely to remind you that we are very seriously interested in the de Schulthess D. H. Lawrence manuscripts of *Lady Chatterley's Lover*, and are very eager to have an opportunity to negotiate their purchase if and when a disposal might be made.

I am leaving for a month in Europe and expect to be back on October 29. If in the meantime there is anything to report, please get in touch with my secretary, Miss Sylvia Meller, who will know where I am to be reached.

Yours sincerely,   [JZ]

304. Jake Zeitlin to Lew D. Feldman, 4 February 1964
Text: TSCC UCLA

4 February 1964

Mr. Lew D. Feldman
House of El Dieff, Inc.
30 East 62nd St.
N.Y. 22, N.Y.

Dear Lew:

I have just come back from a conversation with Amalia de Schulthess. She tells me that she cannot sell the *Lady Chatterley* manuscripts until after the closing of the estate which should be some time early in 1965, probably before April 1st. She is, however, willing to enter into a written contract to sell as soon as the estate is closed, subject to the following terms:

1.   Total price for the three *Lady Chatterley* manuscripts (this does not include the special copy of the book on blue paper, which she has determined to keep for herself) $25,000.00

2.   Payment to be made as follows:

　　$ 1,000 upon signing of the agreement

　　11,500 upon delivery of the manuscripts in 1965

　　12,500 payable in one year after the delivery of the manuscripts – some time in 1966.

She wishes to specify that there shall be no public announcement of the sale within two years.

If these terms are satisfactory, I suggest that you write me spelling out our understanding and specifying the basis upon which we are to participate in the purchase and sale; that we are [each][1] to receive 50 percent of the price at which the manuscript is sold.

I should like it also understood that I am to be named to the purchasers, as one of the sellers, and that if and when public announcement is made of the sale, our name is to be included in any publicity concerning the sale.

I shall await your response at your early convenience.

Yours cordially,　　[JZ]

Note
1.   *each* has been cancelled.

305. Lew D. Feldman to Jake Zeitlin, 7 February 1964
Text: TS UCLA

House of El Dieff, Inc.
February 7, 1964

Zietlin & Ver Brugge, Booksellers
815 No. La Cienega Blvd.
Los Angeles 69, Calif.

Dear Jake:

In reference to yours of 4th of February concerning the good Lady, as discussed previously, we had no other idea but to go 50/50 down the line with you in this matter. We would agree to all the stipulations indicated in your letter, and we will send you our half payment of $500 immediately upon our mutual agreement as to the language of any contract that her attorneys might draft.

Similarly, our half payment upon delivery of the manuscripts in 1965. Naturally, the statement 1965 in itself, is utterly too vague, and if you are agreeable, we would like very much for it to be in January, 1965; similarly, the balance, still on a 50/50 basis, payable in January, 1966.

What constitutes two years after sale? We take it that this would be two years after signing of the agreement; therefore, as quickly as we come to an understanding about the agreement in 1963, the two years should date from the signing of such agreement. It is entirely possible, of course, that there may be no announcement whatsoever.

The agreement, of course, should be made out both in your firm name and in ours as the buyers, and likewise in the matter of any public announcement, both our firms shall be noted as co-owners.

If all the above is satisfactory, we would be willing to get this off the ground as quickly as it fits in your plans.

Best,

    As ever, HOUSE OF EL DIEFF, INC., Lew D. Feldman, Pres.

306. Jake Zeitlin to Lew D. Feldman, 10 February 1964
Text: TSCC UCLA

10 February 1964

Mr. Lew Feldman
House of El Dieff, Inc.
30 East 62nd Street
New York 21, N.Y.

Dear Lew:

This is in response to your letter of February 7, 1964. I should like to point out that it may not be possible to effect the actual sale and delivery of the manuscripts until after the closing of the estate. This probably cannot take place until some time between January 1 and April 1, 1965, due to the length of time which must transpire until the closing of the probate. I therefore doubt if we could get an agreement to deliver in January, 1965, as you wish.

Naturally, I shall try my best but I feel that I should make it clear to you that this is doubtful. According to the verbal understanding that Mrs. de Schulthess and I have, she cannot actually consummate the sale until after probate is closed, but what she can do is sign an agreement to sell after closing of probate and she is willing to do this upon payment to her of $1,000. which is to be considered a deposit, returnable to us if the sale cannot be consummated.

I am requesting Mrs. de Schulthess to have her attorney draft an agreement spelling out the understanding. As soon as I have received this, I will forward a copy to you for [your] okay.

I hope I will be able to get this done very soon.

Yours cordially,　　[JZ]

307. Jake Zeitlin to Amalia de Schulthess, 10 February 1964
Text: TSCC UCLA

10 February 1964

Mrs. Amalia de Schulthess
12938 Evanston Boulevard
West Los Angeles, California

Dear Mrs. de Schulthess:

In accordance with our recent conversation, I hereby offer to enter into a contract to purchase the three manuscripts of D. H. Lawrence's *Lady Chatterley's Lover*, now in the estate of Hans de Schulthess, subject to the following terms:

a. $1,000. to be paid to you as a deposit upon the signing of an agreement between you as the seller and the following as the joint purchasers:

Zeitlin & Ver Brugge, 815 No. La Cienega Blvd., Los Angeles, Calif.
House of El Dieff, Inc., 30 East 62nd Street, New York 21, N.Y.

b. $11,500. upon delivery of the manuscripts after the closing of the estate, which we understand is to take place some time early in 1965, probably before April 1st.

c. $12,500. to be paid to you one year after the delivery of the manuscripts.

d. We understand that there is to be no public announcement of the sale of the manuscripts within two years after the signing of the agreement to sell.

If you will have your attorneys make up an agreement based on the above terms, I will arrange to have it signed by ourselves and the House of El Dieff, Inc. The latter firm is acting jointly with us and it is our intent that the manuscripts go into the collection of a university library. I would suggest that you have your attorneys present the agreement in draft form.

I hope that you will be able to arrange this as soon as possible. As you know, one must strike while the iron is hot, and too great a delay might affect the consummation of our sale to the university.

Yours cordially,   [JZ]

308. Lew D. Feldman to Jake Zeitlin, 12 February 1964
Text: TS UCLA

House of El Dieff, Inc.
February 12, 1964

Zeitlin & Ver Brugge
815 No. La Cienega Blvd.
Los Angeles 69, Calif.

Dear Jake:
   Your proposed letter to Mrs. de Schulthess is O.K.
   We will look forward to the draft of the agreement.
   Best.
             As ever,   HOUSE OF EL DIEFF, INC., Lew D. Feldman, Pres.

309. Harry Ransom to Jake Zeitlin, 7 August 1964
Text: TS UCLA

Office of the Chancellor
The University of Texas, Austin, Texas 78712
August 7, 1964

Mr. Jacob Zeitlin
815 No. La Cienega Boulevard
Los Angeles 69, California

Dear Mr. Zeitlin:
   As you know, The University of Texas has been building for some years a distinguished D. H. Lawrence Collection.

The origins of this collection were made possible by D. H. Lawrence's widow in the last years of her life. On those foundations, we have built the most extensive collection of Lawrence manuscripts in existence – including not only the Frieda Lawrence manuscripts acquired by [T. E.] Hanley, but also major collections of Lawrence's early works, both literary and artistic, large files of Lawrence's correspondence, and the most extensive collection of Lawrence criticism in this country.

If it might be possible to acquire from the family of Hans Deschultess the manuscripts of *Lady Chatterley's Lover*, The University of Texas would combine all present Lawrence collections into a permanent library to bear the permanent name, the Deschultess–Lawrence Collection, housed separately and maintained in perpetuity. We would plan, of course, to see that this collection continued to grow and to guarantee both its accessibility to Lawrence scholars and its wise utilization by all institutions of higher education.

I have just received approval of the Executive Committee of The University of Texas Board of Regents for this plan. I hope that you will be willing to make this suggestion to the representatives of the Deschultess family.

Sincerely yours,   Harry Ransom, Chancellor

310. Jake Zeitlin to Harry Ransom, 10 August 1964
Text: TSCC UCLA

10 August 1964

Dr. Harry Ransom
Chancellor
The University of Texas
Austin 12, Texas

Dear Dr. Ransom:

I have received your letter concerning the interest of the University of Texas in acquiring the manuscripts of *Lady Chatterley's Lover*.

Enclosed are copies of two letters I have just written – one to Mrs. de Schulthess and the other to Mr. Leopold, who is the co-executor of the estate.

I hope that this wonderful offer will receive the response that it deserves. As soon as I have any further information, I shall communicate with you.

Yours cordially,   [JZ]

311. Jake Zeitlin to Amalia de Schulthess, 10 August 1964
Text: TSCC UCLA

10 August 1964

Mrs. Amalia de Schulthess
c/o American Express
Florence, Italy

Dear Amalia:

Some days ago I had a telephone communication from one of the attorneys handling the estate of Hans de Schulthess. He advised me that Hans had left the manuscripts of *Lady Chatterley's Lover* to be placed in a university collection where they would be with other Lawrence material and would serve the greatest use, and asked my advice.

Following this conversation, I discussed the matter with Dr. Harry Ransom, Chancellor of the University of Texas. Enclosed is a copy of the letter from Dr. Ransom indicating the great interest they have in D. H. Lawrence and stating that if it were possible for the manuscripts of *Lady Chatterley's Lover* to be placed with them, they would combine all present Lawrence collections into a permanent library to bear the name of the de Schulthess–Lawrence Collection.

I should think that this would be a wonderful way to memorialize Hans as well as to see that the manuscripts go to the best place. I hope that you feel the same way and will do what you can to see that they are placed there. I plan to leave here the end of this month and to be in Florence September 13–16. If you have not left there by then, I shall look forward to seeing you. I shall be giving a lecture at the Galileo Celebration, under the auspices of the Institute and Museum of the History of Science in Florence. In case you have returned before I get there, I shall look forward to hearing from you after my return.

I hope all goes well with you. With warmest regards, I am

Yours cordially,   [JZ]

312. Jake Zeitlin to A. Fredric Leopold, 10 August 1964
Text: TSCC UCLA

10 August 1964

Mr. A. Fredric Leopold
6505 Wilshire Boulevard
Los Angeles, Calif. 90048

Dear Mr. Leopold:

Some days ago I had a telephone conversation with an attorney whose name I cannot recollect. He was associated with the firm handling the legal affairs of the estate of Hans de Schulthess. He inquired of me concerning the possible interest of the University of Texas in receiving the D. H. Lawrence manuscripts of *Lady Chatterley's Lover*, which is part of the de Schulthess estate and requested my suggestion concerning the proper institution with which it should be placed.

Following this conversation I had a talk with Dr. Harry Ransom, Chancellor of the University of Texas. Enclosed is a copy of a letter from Dr. Ransom in which he states that the University of Texas would be most eager to acquire these manuscripts and if they can be placed with them, they would combine all present Lawrence collections into a permanent library to bear the name of the de Schulthess–Lawrence collection, housed separately and maintained in perpetuity.

I hope that you will see fit to consider this proposal and to transmit it to Mrs. Amalia de Schulthess. I plan to leave here the latter part of this month for a visit to Europe. I intend to be in Florence from the 13–16 September. If Mrs. de Schulthess is still in Florence, I should like to discuss it with her there. If not, I should appreciate your advising me of the inclination of the executors, at your convenience.

Yours cordially,   [JZ]

cc: Mrs. de Schulthess

313. Jake Zeitlin to Harry Ransom, 24 August 1964
Text (abridged): TSCC UCLA

24 August 1964

Dr. Harry Ransom
Chancellor
The University of Texas
Austin, Texas 78712

Dear Harry:

I had a visit today with Mrs. Amalia de Schulthess and I find that the attorney who spoke to me was a bit precipitous. Mrs. de Schulthess tells me that the estate is involved in litigation due to claims by the second Mrs. de Schulthess. She advises me, however, that the manuscripts of *Lady Chatterley's Lover* were willed to her. Due to the legal involvements nothing can be done concerning the manuscripts until the close of probate and the settlement of conflicting claims. Also there is the problem of the appraisal for tax purposes[1] which was, as you can understand, considerably less than the value which might be placed upon them if offered for sale.

Mrs. de Schulthess also told me that because of the heavy strain upon the estate she will probably have to sell the manuscripts rather than make a present of them. She did say that she would present a very fine painting by Lawrence as soon as she was free to do so. I have advised her that failing the possibility of a gift of the manuscripts, the University of Texas would in all likelihood be interested in purchasing them and she has promised to come in later this week to discuss the drawing up of an option which would give me the exclusive right to dispose of the manuscripts whenever they can be freed from any possible legal involvements. At the moment this is the sum of what I can report. If something more of significance should emerge during our conversation later this week, I will report it to you. . . .

Yours sincerely,   [JZ]

Note
1. See Letter 300.

314. Jake Zeitlin to Amalia de Schulthess, 12 November 1964
Text (abridged): TSCC UCLA

12 November 1964

Mrs. Amalia de Schulthess
12938 Evanston Boulevard
West Los Angeles, Calif.

Dear Amalia:
. . . Can you tell me what if anything is happening concerning the *Lady Chatterley* manuscripts? I plan to go to the University of Texas on the 20th of this month and would like to report to them on what the possibilities of purchase are.
With kindest regards, I am

Yours cordially,   [JZ]

315. Lupe Amador to Jake Zeitlin, 17 November 1964

Text (abridged): TS UCLA

12938 Evanston, Los Angeles 49, Calif.

17 November 1964

Mr. J. Zeitlin
Zeitlin & Ver Brugge
815 North La Cienega Blvd.
Los Angeles 69, Calif.

Dear Mr. Zeitlin:

Mrs. Amalia de Schulthess has asked me to communicate with you. . . .

She is unable to write to you herself, since she is immobilized at the present time at the Santa Monica Hospital, as a result of a recent accident.[1] She will be in the hospital for at least another three weeks.

Very truly yours,   Lupe Amador, for Amalia de Schulthess

Note

1. See Introduction, pp. 23–4.

316. Jake Zeitlin to Lew D. Feldman, 3 March 1965

Text: TSCC UCLA

March 3, 1965

Mr. Lew David Feldman
The House of El Dieff, Inc.
30 East 62nd Street
New York 21, New York

Dear Lew:

Herewith enclosed is the form of agreement that I have drawn up in connection with the three *Lady Chatterley's Lover* manuscripts and the book. I am signing this and paying Mrs. de Schulthess immediately since, as I told you, I do not believe it is wise to court the possibility of anything happening through a delay. I am taking over the manuscripts and book and paying Mrs. de Schulthess on Friday.

My understanding with you is that the manuscripts and book are to be sold for $50,000.00[1] and that we are to share equally in the costs and in all profits derived from the sale.

I will be talking to you on the telephone as soon as I have received the manuscripts and book and will await your instructions.

If you feel that we should have a further agreement of a different nature please let me know. In the meantime I shall proceed upon the understanding as discussed in our telephone conversation today.

Yours cordially,   [JZ]

Note
1. To the University of Texas at Austin.

317. Jake Zeitlin to Lew D. Feldman, 5 March 1965
Text: TSCC UCLA

5 March 1965

Mr. Lew D. Feldman
The House of El Dieff, Inc.
30 East 62nd Street
New York, N. Y. 10021

Dear Lew:

I placed a telephone call for you this morning but your secretary told me that you are in Washington and not likely to be back until tonight. Just in case we do not communicate by phone in the meantime, I wish to report that Mrs. de Schulthess and her lawyer had another conference and decided that she would rather have the entire sum in cash without postponement of any partial payments.

I have explained to them that it will take a few days for the transfer of funds and that I would again get in touch with her as soon as arrangements have been completed. I have to go to Santa Barbara this Sunday to give an address on Monday, and will not be back here until Tuesday. I hope that you will, by that time, be able to complete arrangements for forwarding to me your check for one-half of the $30,000. As soon as this is received, I will add my half and pay her and receive the manuscripts and book which have now been taken out of the bank and are at her home.

I have prepared a new bill of sale which I intend to have her sign and of which I herewith enclose a copy. If you feel it needs changing, please let me know.

I also should like to have some kind of a formal agreement with you concerning our joint purchase and sale of the manuscripts and book. Do you mean to include the book with the manuscripts in the sale to Ransom? If it is not included we should be able to get a good price for this separately.

I may be talking to you in the meantime but this is being sent off just in case we do not reach each other by telephone.

Yours cordially,   [JZ]

318. Jake Zeitlin to Amalia de Schulthess, 5 March 1965
Text: TSCC UCLA

815 No. La Cienega Blvd., Los Angeles, California 90069

March 5, 1965

Mrs. Amalia de Schulthess
12938 Evanston Boulevard
West Los Angeles, California

Dear Mrs. de Schulthess:

This is to constitute our agreement covering the purchase of the three versions of D. H. Lawrence's manuscripts of *Lady Chatterley's Lover*, as described on the attached sheet, together with a volume of the book printed on blue paper and inscribed by D. H. Lawrence.

It is agreed that the full price for the three manuscripts and the book is $30,000. Herewith attached is our check for the full amount.

This letter constitutes a receipt of the three above-mentioned manuscripts and the book.

Yours sincerely,   Zeitlin & Ver Brugge, by Jacob Zeitlin

I, Amalia de Schulthess, hereby warrant that I am the sole, equitable and legal owner of the aforesaid manuscripts and book and do herewith transfer full title to Zeitlin & Ver Brugge.

319. Lew D. Feldman to Jake Zeitlin, 9 March 1965
Text: MS UCLA

3–9–65, 8:30 PM

Dear Jake –

Check enclosed as per phone conversation. Call or wire when you have the mss. and book in your possession – we will draw up a simple agreement for us both –

Best   Lew

320. Lew D. Feldman to Jake Zeitlin, 12 March 1965
Text: TS UCLA

House of El Dieff, Inc.
March 12, 1965

Mr. Jacob Zeitlin
Zeitlin & Ver Brugge
815 No. La Cienega Blvd.
Los Angeles, Calif. 90069

Dear Jake:

We are glad that the matter of the LADY has been closed, as per our agreement. We are in receipt of your telegram containing your note "Await instructions." As per our prior agreement, we have agreed to your request that if there be any publicity regarding acquisition and sale it should be our responsibility in every case to indicate that your firm and ours are acting in this matter in full concert as co-partners.

We have, as per our recent conversation with Dr. Ransom, his consent to our cataloguing the manuscripts and the book and at the moment we are tentatively considering presenting this as one of the items in our currently projected catalogue SIXTY FIVE, which is next in the series of de luxe catalogues such as the copy of SIXTY FOUR you acknowledged receiving.

We repeat again that all descriptive matter, if we go through with the cataloguing project, will indicate in a very obvious way that we are offering the items jointly.

If you will send the three manuscripts and the book on to us by way of Railway Express, insured for $50,000. we shall appreciate same.

As we told you on the phone the other day we follow the rigid practice of not sending material on to Austin before we receive the official order of confirmation. This case will prove no exception.

Based on current experience, if the present payment practice is maintained at Austin for current purchases doubtless we shall be paid within the year 1965. But, please do not hold me to this as a positive date since we are stating it based on personal conviction without a specific announced payment date from Austin.

In the meantime, permit us to congratulate you most sincerely for having surpassed the difficulties of negotiation and actual acquisition. Even though we have been pushed up so strongly from our beginning price of $20,000. to the accepted figure of $30,000.

At the moment, we are inclined to completely forget the outline of publication that we made to you and unless something along such publication lines occur[s] to you we shall probably pass it by.

We hope all the above is completely clear and satisfactory.

Kindest regards to Jo and yourself.

As ever,   Lew D. Feldman

321. Jake Zeitlin to Lew D. Feldman, 15 March 1965
Text: TSCC UCLA

15 March 1965

Mr. Lew D. Feldman
House of El Dieff, Inc.
30 East 62nd Street
New York, N. Y. 10021

Dear Lew:

Your letter of March 12 has just been received. Mrs. de Schulthess has requested that there not be any immediate publicity regarding the acquisition and sale of the manuscripts. She has various reasons for wishing them to not be publicized for at least six months. I know that it takes quite a while for a new catalogue to be issued and I have no doubt that should you decide to put them in your catalogue 65, it will probably take several months to get it out.

I assure you that I shall not make any announcement of the acquisition of these manuscripts for the time being and that any announcements made later will be in the name of both your firm and ourselves as purchasers. I also understand that should you make any announcement or listing of the material it will be done as a joint offering.

Your practice of not sending material on to Austin before receiving an official order of confirmation is entirely agreeable with me. I understand that we can hope to be paid within the present year, 1965, but of course we will be agreeable to whatever final payment date is set.

We are packing the manuscripts this afternoon and will send them off by railway express insured for $50,000. as soon as this can be done.

I assure you that it was no easy matter to persuade Mrs. de Schulthess to come to a conclusion on the transaction and that I made every possible effort to keep the price down. She was not altogether inclined to sell but I finally convinced her that it is better to have the cash than to postpone the sale, since the future is always indefinite.

We are very happy to have been able to carry this collaboration forward with you. It is the kind of thing that takes good team work on the part of all of us and you have certainly done yourself well to date.

Josephine joins me in sending kind regards to Sally and yourself.

Yours cordially,   [JZ]

P.S.   Your copy of purchase contract is enclosed. J. Z.

322. Jake Zeitlin to Amalia de Schulthess, 16 May 1966
Text: TSCC UCLA

16 May 1966

Mrs. Amalia de Schulthess
30, Lungarno A. Vespucci
Florence, ITALY

Dear Amalia:

A long time ago I promised that I would write you a note acknowledging that I have in my possession the following:

    1.   Corrected Typescript, *Lady Chatterley's Lover*, 3 pp.   Value $500.[1]

    2.   Doves Press. Wm. Shakespeare's *Hamlet*, bound in full white pigskin, enclosed in fleece-lined blue buckram case. Value $100.

This constitutes my acknowledgement that these are in my possession and that I will remit the prices indicated when they are sold.

I have not so far disposed of them but have hopes of placing the L. C. Ms. within the next month.[2]

I have not heard from you for a very long time and I hope that all is well. I would welcome news from you. It is possible that I will be coming to Florence this summer, but I have not as yet been able to fix a definite date.

With much affection, I am

Yours sincerely,   [JZ]

Notes

1.   This is a fragment of chapter xii typed by Maria Huxley in February 1928 while the Lawrences and the Huxleys were on holiday in Les Diablerets, Switzerland.
2.   Jake Zeitlin sold it to the University of Texas on 24 May 1966.

323. Jake Zeitlin to Amalia de Schulthess, 1 November 1966
Text: TSCC UCLA

1 November 1966

Mrs. Amalia de Schulthess
30, Lungarno A. Vespucci
Florence, Italy

Dear Amalia:

Enclosed you will find our check for $500. covering the three page D. H. Lawrence autograph which I have sold for you. I think I have done very well on it and I hope that you are pleased.

I keep hoping that you will have some reason to be coming back to Los

Angeles for a visit. This year I did not get to go abroad but I will be going next May, if not sooner.

In the meantime I hope that you are in good health and life is serving you well. I think of you often.

With much affection   [JZ]

324. Amalia de Schulthess to Jake Zeitlin, 9 November 1966
Text: MS UCLA

Firenze
November 9th '66

Dear Jake:

If you could see our city now![1] Words are completely inadequate to describe the damage, the mountains of mud and debris, the shops completely wrecked, one after another all along too many streets; the loss of homes, very often the homes of people of little means, where each piece of furniture meant scraping for so many months if not years. –

I'm writing by candle light in the midst of the afternoon of a gray and foggy day. The candle next to me in the shape of an orange, given to me by a man near the place where I'm working these days.

Your check was gratefully received, as I'm without much money for the past months or so, thanks to having to fight my own attorney as well, who has proven totally incapable! But I can't complain. My feet are dry, I'm not hungry, and my work has gone well till this catastrophe hit us – now I'm doing work of a different sort; but hope to return to my little foundry before too long. Have done some more animals, little ones (which I can always sell –) but also some larger ones; – please, make some more money (or is it necessary?) so you can buy one of them –

Don't forget yours affectionately   Amalia in Firenze

Note

1. In 1989 Amalia de Schulthess recalled: "This was the time of the Great Flood that hit Florence in the fall of 1966. I lived right on the Arno, on the top floor of one of the many large palazzos that line the river, which meant doing close to 100 steps in near total darkness, coming and going, due to the lack of electricity. Going to work, at the other end of town, was impossible, so I started to help out in the neighborhood. One day at the optometrist's washing countless eyeglasses, another at the restaurant where I ate frequently cleaning muddy chairs, etc."

Appendix A

Appraisal of D. H. Lawrence Manuscripts Belonging to Mrs. D. H. Lawrence

Based on a Descriptive Inventory
Compiled by D. J. Wells and H. K. Wells

and Examination of Originals at the Harvard College Library
Treasure Room (January 1937)

HOLOGRAPH MANUSCRIPTS

NOVELS

1. Fragment of 4 pages numbering 7–10. Presumably from an early version of *Sons and Lovers*. $15.00

2. Part of an early version of *The White Peacock*. About 75 pages. $75.00

3. *The Trespasser*. Incomplete early version. Quite different from published version. About 160 pp. $175.00

4. *Paul Morel* (Sons and Lovers). Early draft. Undoubtedly written before he met Frieda Weekley, i.e., before February 1912. Incomplete. About 300 pages. $600.00

5. Manuscript of *Kangaroo* (539 pp.) Novel published 1923. Complete save for lost chapter "Adieu". $350.00

6. Holograph manuscript of *The Rainbow* (707 pp.) Previously *The Wedding Ring*; complete as first published in 1915. Only slightly altered upon second publication, 1926. $400.00

7. *The Virgin and the Gypsy* (160 pp.) $200.00

8. Holograph manuscript of *The Trespasser* (487 pp.) Complete as published in 1912. $350.00

Note: *D. J. Wells (Deborah Jeannette Wells) was the wife of Harry K. Wells.*

SHORT STORIES

9. *Two Blue Birds* (30 pp.) Short story published in *The Woman Who Rode Away*. $45.00

10. *Smile* (9 pp.) Short story published in *The Woman Who Rode Away*. $20.00

11. *More Modern Love* (20 pp.) Early version of story published under the title of "In Love", included in *The Woman Who Rode Away*. Pages numbered 1–20. $35.00

12. Early version of *The Blue Moccasins*. Pages numbered 1–9 (7 and 8 missing). $10.00

13. Early version of part of *Glad Ghosts*. Pages numbered 52–62 (58–9 missing). $10.00

14. *The Undying Man* (8 pp.) A Jewish folk tale, one of several sent to Lawrence by Koteliansky. This was the only one he began to work on. Published in *Phoenix*, 1936. Also fragment of 8 lines in quotation marks. $15.00

15. *"Patent Leather" black notebook* contains an incomplete untitled story (short) of a hermit. Unpublished. Begins: "There was a man not long ago . . .". Ten pages, ending: "And made himself bread, and cooked pies, and mended his clothes." Note on last page: "Tombs at Volterra penitentiary." $35.00

16. *Mother and Daughter* (44 pp.) Story published in *The Lovely Lady*. $60.00

17. *Daughters of the Vicar* (24 pp.) Slightly different from that story published in *The Prussian Officer*. Probably the published version is from a corrected typescript of this manuscript. $35.00

18. *Rawdon's Roof* (22 pp.) Story published in *The Lovely Lady*. $35.00

19. *New Eve and Old Adam* (14 pp.) Short story published in *A Modern Lover*. $25.00

20. *The Last Laugh* (25 pp.) Short story published in *The Woman Who Rode Away*. $35.00

21. *The Old Adam* (27 pp.) Short story published in *A Modern Lover*. $40.00

22. *All There* (4 pp.) Published in *Phoenix*, 1936. $15.00

23. *The Fox* (part typescript) (67 pp.) Published in *The Ladybird*. $50.00

24. *The Witch à la Mode.* Short story published in *A Modern Lover.* Two earlier versions of the same story:
     a. Intimacy (36 pp.)
     b. The White Woman (56 pp.) $100.00

25. Incomplete early version of *Daughters of the Vicar* (pp. 19–54 with 27–28 missing). $20.00

26. *The Rocking Horse Winner* (30 pp.) Short story published in *The Lovely Lady*. $40.00

27. *Things* (19 pp.) Short story published in *The Lovely Lady*. $30.00

28. *Untitled short story* (6½ pp.) Incomplete; unpublished; begins: "There were, three years back, two schools in the mining village of High Park: a National and a British." $20.00

29. *Untitled and unpublished* short story somewhat similar to his play *The Widowing of Mrs. Holroyd.* Incomplete. Begins: "When Elizabeth came down she found her mother alone . . ." (30 pp.). $35.00

30. *Untitled short story*, incomplete and unpublished. Probably belongs to early period of Lawrence's career. Begins: "Then come into the kitchen," said Mrs. Bercumshaw . . . (11 pp.). $20.00

31. *First chapter and a half* of a projected novel or novelette. Untitled and unpublished. It belongs to the Croydon teaching period of Lawrence's life, 1910–11. Begins: "There is a cottage off the Adiscombe Road . . .". $25.00

32. *Two Marriages* (33 pp.) Early version of *Daughters of the Vicar* published in *The Prussian Officer*. $40.00

33. *Odour of Chrysanthemums* (32 pp.) Story, first published in *English Review*, June 1911. Published later in *The Prussian Officer*. $40.00

34. *Strike-Pay* (15 pp.) Short story published in *A Modern Lover*. $25.00

35. *A Sick Collier* (11 pp.) Story published in *The Prussian Officer*. $25.00

36. *Her Turn* (10 pp.) Short story published in *A Modern Lover*. Manuscript was called *The Collier's Wife Scores*, but that was crossed out and the new title put over it. $25.00

37. *The Christening* (9 pp.) Very early story, published in *The Prussian Officer*, 1914. $20.00

38. *Goose Fair* (13 pp.) Short story. Original version. Story published in *The Prussian Officer*, probably copied from corrected typescript of this early version. $25.00

39. *Glad Ghosts* (69 pp.) Story published in *The Woman Who Rode Away*. The chief characters are Sir Herbert and Lady Cynthia Asquith. First published: Ernest Benn Limited, Bouverie House, London, 1926. $100.00

40. *Jimmy and the Desperate Woman* (31 pp.) Short story complete as published in *The Woman Who Rode Away*. $85.00

41. *A Chapel among the Mountains* (16 pp.) Story published in *Love among the Haystacks*. Written in 1912 but not published until after Lawrence's death in 1930. $25.00

42. *Honour and Arms* (17 pp.) Story published as *The Prussian Officer*, 1914, in the book by that title. $25.00

43. *The Captain's Doll* (78 pp.) Complete manuscript of the novelette published in *The Ladybird*, 1923. $150.00

44. *The Woman Who Rode Away* (48 pp.) Story published in book of stories by the same title. The chief character is undoubtedly Mabel Dodge Luhan. $85.00

45. *St. Mawr* (129 pp.) Novelette published as the title story along with *The Princess*. (In addition to the 129 pp. there are six pages numbered 17–22 and one page numbered 58, perhaps of an earlier version.) $175.00

46. *The Escaped Cock*. Part II (32 pp.) Incomplete, entirely different from published version. $45.00

47. *The Border Line* (25 pp.) Early version. Beginning is quite akin to beginning of published version, but the bulk of the manuscript is absolutely unique and important. Along with *Jimmy and the Desperate Woman*, it forms an attempt to draw a picture of John Middleton Murry. There are at least three versions of

	The Border Line, only one of which is published and that in *The Woman Who Rode Away.*	$50.00
48.	*The Vicar's Garden* (7 pp.) Short story; possibly an early, but quite different version of *Shadow in the Rose Garden,* published in *The Prussian Officer.*	$15.00
49.	*Unfinished short story,* untitled (20 pp.) Begins: "My mother made a failure of her life...".	$35.00
50.	*Legend* – short story (8 pp.) Unpublished early version of the story *A Fragment of Stained Glass,* published in *The Prussian Officer.*	$15.00

POEMS

51.	Seven holograph poems:	$150.00
	a. *Restlessness* – published in *Amores* in somewhat altered form. (First verse of manuscript omitted in published version.)	
	b. *Fire* – longer and entirely different from version published in *Pansies.*	
	c. *Traitors oh Liars* – unpublished.	
	d. *Softly, then Softly* – unpublished.	
	e. *And What Do I Care* – unpublished.	
	f. *Change of Life* – unpublished.	
	g. *O Americans.*	
52.	*Eagle in New Mexico.* Unpublished and entirely unique version (similar to poem included in *Birds, Beasts and Flowers* only as to subject matter).	$25.00
53.	Unpublished pansies:	$75.00
	a. "Reach over, then reach over."	
	b. "Traitors, oh Liars, you Judas lot!"	
	c. "Are you pining to be superior? Then go to hell!"	
	d. "Softly, then, softly."	
54.	*Pansies*:	$75.00
	Finding your level – different mostly in form from published version.	
	Altercation – differs only in a few words or phrases from published version – *Pansies.*	
	What Is Man Without an Income? – differs slightly from published version.	

Climbing Up – quite different from published version. Not in very general content, but in number of stanzas and wording.

Canvassing for the Election – not like the one published in *Pansies*.

A Rise in the World.

55. Four holograph poems (all published in *Last Poems*): $35.00
    a. *Bells*
    b. *Triumph of the Machine*
    c. *Father Neptune's Little Affair with Freedom*
    d. *The Man in the Street*

56. Twenty-five holograph poems: $250.00
    a. *Kisses in the Train – Love Poems and Others*, exactly as published.
    b. *Cruelty and Love*
    c. *Cherry-Robbers*
    d. *Lilies in the Fire*
    e. *Coldness in Love*
    f. *Reminder* (first page or so missing).
    g. *Bli Hennef*
    h. *Lightning* – printed specimen copy.
    i. *Song-Day in Autumn*
    j. *Aware*
    k. *A Pang of Reminiscence*
    l. *A White Blossom*
    m. *Red Moon-Rise*
    n. *Return*
    o. *The Appeal*
    p. *Repulsed*
    q. *Reminder*
    r. *Dream Confused*
    s. *Corot*
    t. *Morning Work*
    u. *Transformations*
    v. *Renascence*
    w. *Dog-Tired*
    x. *End of Another Home Holiday*
    y. *Wedding Morn*

57. Nine Holograph Poems: $150.00
    a. *The End of Another Home Holiday*. Slightly different version of that published in *Collected Poems*, vol. I, and *Love Poems and Others*. Differs mostly

in matter of form and style, not content. (2 versions in ms.)

    b. *Restlessness* – ms. quite different from published version in *Amores*.

    c. Part of *Turned Down* – published in *Collected Poems*, vol. I – different version of 5th stanza – called *Perfidy* in *Amores*.

    d. Part of *Violets* – differing slightly from that published in *Love Poems and Others* and *Collected Poems*, vol. I.

    e. 2 stanzas of *Cherry-Robbers* – different from version published in *Love Poems and Others*.

    f. *Restlessness* – *Amores* slightly different.

    g. *Violets for the Dead* – *Love Poems and Others*, slightly different.

    h. *Song* – under title of *Flapper* in *New Poems*, quite different.

    i. *Wind Among the Cherries*.

58. *Cherry-stealers* – published as *Cherry-Robbers*, differs slightly from published version. $35.00

59. *A Letter from Town – The Almond Tree* – differs considerably from *New Poems* version. $35.00

60. *Perfidy* – almost exactly like *Amores* version, substitutes "her" for "your". $25.00

61. *A Bell* – published in *Collected Poems* as *A Passing Bell* – almost the same. $25.00

62. *Dreams Old and Nascent* (1st three stanzas missing). Almost exactly like published version in *Amores*. 1st verse of *Nascent* precedes Nascent in the manuscript. Manuscript *Nascent* poems slightly different from *Amores* version. $15.00

63. *Discipline*. Vastly different from published version in *Amores*. $25.00

64. *Baby-Movements:* $35.00

    a. *Running Barefoot – Amores – Baby Running Barefoot* – differs slightly.

    b. *Trailing Clouds* (*A Baby Asleep after Pain*) differs slightly.

PLAYS

65. *David*. Ms. of play written at Kiowa Ranch during Lawrence's convalescence from his Mexican illness, 1925. *David* had been produced in England (178 pp.). $150.00

66. *Altitude* (28 pp.) Two scenes of a play centering around breakfast at Mabel Dodge Luhan's Ranch near Taos, NM. The character names are fictitious. $50.00

67. *The Merry-Go-Round* (148 pp.) Complete unpublished play, probably written in 1912. It was found in the attic of Mrs. Lawrence's sister's house in Heidelberg, after Lawrence's death. $250.00

68. Untitled unpublished play (72 pp.) Complete with the exception of the first 5 pages which are missing. It is variously known as *The Married Man, The Daughter in Law, The Mother in Law*. It was staged in England in the summer of 1936. Found after Lawrence's death, in an attic in Heidelberg, along with *The Fight for Barbara* and *The Merry-Go-Round*. $100.00

69. *The Fight for Barbara* (154 pp.) Complete unpublished play written in Germany probably in 1912. It was discovered in Frau Doktor Else Jaffe von Richthofen's attic in Heidelberg after Lawrence's death. It dramatizes the first meeting between Lawrence and the Baronin von Richthofen, Frieda Lawrence's mother, in Bavaria, 1912. $150.00

NOTEBOOKS

70. *Notebook – Pheasant*. $10.00
    a. Practice Lessons in Spanish, Frieda.
    b. *See Mexico After* by Louis Q. (1 page). One page attempt at rewriting.

71. *Brown-Pink-Yellow-Red Notebook* $50.00
    a. *Reflections on the Death of a Porcupine* (15 pp.) trans. into German by Frieda L.   Unfinished.
    b. *The Jeune Fille Wants to Know*. Same as published except lacking last paragraphs.
    c. Page of Accounts.

    d. *Man is a Hunter* (5 pp.) Published in *Phoenix*.

    e. Notes for *Scrutiny* on John Galsworthy.

72. *Notebook*: Red-black with green back contains: $75.00
    a. *The Blue Moccasins* (32 pp.) Short story published in *The Lovely Lady*.
    b. Translation from the Italian of *Il Lasca: The Story of Doctor Manente* (69 pp.)
    c. *Introduction to Pictures* (17 pp.) Pub. in *Phoenix*, 1936.
    d. Accounts on inside cover and fly-leaf.

73. *Notebook*: Green-black (on cover: D. H. Lawrence, 1920). $150.00
    a. Notes in Diary Form (12 pp.) Feb. 6, 1920 to Nov. 17, 1924.
    b. Poems included in *Birds, Beasts, and Flowers*.
    c. Figures on one page.
    d. Note on inside of cover – Dec. 1, 1921 – list of mss. sent off.

74. *Small Black Notebook* $75.00
    a. *Cavalleria Rusticana* (9 pp.)
    b. *La Lupa* (The She-Wolf) (7 pp.)
    c. *Fantasticalities* (10 pp.)
    d. *Jeli the Shepherd* (32 pp.)
    e. Spanish lesson – 2 practice pages.
    f. Fragment – *Journey to Southwest* – unfinished (7 pp.)

75. *Black Notebook* (white record on cover). Fly-leaf: signature, D. H. Lawrence Kiowa Ranch near *Taos*, NM – 26 August, 1924, containing: $300.00
    a. *Hopi Snake Dance* (18 pp.)
    b. *Introduction to Bibliography* (McDonald's) of D. H. L.'s works (4 pp.)
    c. *The Princess* (53 pp.)
    d. *Mornings in Mexico*
        1. *Friday Morning* (later published as *Corasmin and the Parrots*) (8 pp.)
        2. *Saturday Morning* (later published as *Market Day*) (9 pp.)
        3. *Sunday Morning* (later published as *Walk to Huayapa*) (14 pp.)
        4. *Monday Morning* (later published as *The Mozo*) (13 pp.)

e.   *Resurrection* (published in *Phoenix*) (4 pp.)
f.   *See Mexico After* by Louis Q. (11 pp.). Final
     version. Erroneously included in *Phoenix*. It
     was not written by Lawrence, but by a young
     Mexican. Lawrence made a few corrections in it.
g.   *Suggestions for Stories* (never carried out!)
     D. H. L.
     1.   *The Weather Vane* (*The Flying Fish* first part
          only was written and recently published in
          Phoenix) (1 p.)
     2.   *The Wedding Ring* (½ p.)
     3.   *The Dog* (¼ p.)
     4.   *The Woman out of the Water* (¼ p.)
h.   *Philosophical Fragment* (3 pp.)
i.   *Noah's Flood* (4½ pp. longer than blue notebook
     version. Introduces Noah.)
j.   *Two Poems: Mediterranean in January* and *Beyond
     the Rockies*, both pub. in *Laughing Horse*, April,
     1926 (2 pp.)
k.   *Preface to Black Swans* by M. L. Skinner (3 pp.)
     (Unpub.)
l.   *Climbing Down Pisgah* (6 pp.) Published in
     Phoenix.

76. Green Notebook inscribed: "For uncle David with
     best wishes for a happy birthday from Harwood"
     (daughter of Earl and Achsah Brewster) Sept. 11 1929.
     Included are: $75.00
     a.   *Fire*, a fragment – really an invocation to *Fire* –
          unpub. (2 pp.)
     b.   Unpub. version of *Apocalypse*. Quite different
          from the pub. text (pp. 11–35, 23–58, 27–32, 43–
          56, 13–14).
     c.   Notes for *Apocalypse*.
     d.   *The Elephants of Dionysos*. Written on back of
          first part of fragment called *Fire*, published in
          Phoenix, 1936.

77. *Brown-White Notebook* $75.00
     a.   *Last Poems*, Aldington's ms. "A". All published.
     b.   One page of accounts.
     c.   Two poems trans. into German by Frieda
          L[awrence]: *Leda* and *Ein Beruf*.

d. Two of three notes by L[awrence] on inside cover.

78. Notebook – dark blue – light blue – white and black $50.00
a. *Nettles.*
b. *Last Poems* (ms. "B"; more *Pansies*).
c. *Pansies.*

79. *Dull blue notebook* (L'Ancora–Firenze) $75.00
a. Contains *Noah's Flood* – pub. in *Phoenix*. Shorter version than one in black notebook.
b. List of letters written March 13, 1928 (32 letters in one day).

80. *Yellow-black notebook*. Bought in Oaxaca. L[awrence]'s name on fly-leaf. Contains: $250.00
a. *The Flying Fish* (unfinished). Written on board ship en route from the Gulf to England while he was still quite ill from his Mexican illness. The first nine pages are (dictated to Frieda) in Frieda's hand.
b. *Review for Vogue* – different from the version published.
c. *Poems: Pansies.*
1. *The Old Orchard* – altered and longer version pub. in *The Calendar*, April, 1927.
2. *I Know a Noble Englishman* – one of *Nature's Gentlemen*, etc. Last line: "Taking it out in spite on women." Unpublished.
3. *How Beastly the Bourgeois Is* – different version than one in *Pansies*.
4. *If You Live among the Middle Classes* – unpub.
5. *Natural Complexion* – last verse different from one published in *Pansies*.
6. *The English Voice* – pub. as *Oxford Voices* in *Pansies* – quite different.
7. *The Gentleman.*
8. *What Matters* – quite different from one in *Pansies*.
9. *The Young Are Not Mean in Material Things.*
10. *The Young Want to be Just*, etc.
d. *Introduction to Pansies* – dated Christmas, 1928. The one pub. is dated Jan. 1929, and is quite a different version – longer, too.

    e. *Sex Appeal* – later pub. in *Assorted Articles* as *Sex versus Loveliness*.

    f. *Do Women Change?* – incomplete – longer version pub. in *Assorted Articles*.

    g. Contents of *Pansies* – list of contents.

81. Six Holograph Manuscripts – Descriptive Pieces: $125.00

    a. *Untitled Manuscript* (6 pp.) Pub. as *A Little Moonshine with Lemon* in *Mornings in Mexico*, also in *Laughing Horse*, April, 1926 (D. H. Lawrence number).

    b. *Letter from Germany* (6 pp.) Written in March, 1924, first pub. after Lawrence's death in *The New Statesman and Nation*, October 13, 1934, and in *Phoenix*, 1936.

    c. *The Dance of the Sprouting Corn* (16 pp.) Pub. in *Mornings in Mexico*.

    d. *Mercury* – descriptive sketch (9 pp.) Pub. in *Phoenix*.

    e. *Fireworks* (8 pp.) Pub. in *Phoenix* as *Fireworks in Florence*.

    f. *Christs in the Tirol* (6 pp.) First version of "Christs in the Tirol" was published in *Phoenix*. Both versions differ considerably from "The Crucifix across the Mountains" included as first chapter of *Twilight in Italy*.

82. *A Scrutiny of John Galsworthy* (15 pp.) Pub. in a collection of essays by various authors, entitled *Scrutinies*. Also published in *Phoenix*. $50.00

83. *Pornography and Obscenity* (22 pp.) Pub. as last half of article by same title in *Phoenix* and original pamphlet – "Pornography and Obscenity". Contained in *This Quarter*. $75.00

84. Three Essays: $35.00

    a. *We Need One Another* (11 pp.)

    b. *The Real Thing* (7 pp.) These two essays were pub. together in a little booklet under the title *We Need One Another*. They were also pub. in *Phoenix*, 1936.

    c. *Nobody Loves Me* (12 pp.) Pub. in *Phoenix*.

85. *Apocalypse* (105 pp.) Written at Bandol on the French Riviera not long before his death, it was published posthumously. It is a study of St. John of Patmos. $150.00

86. *Education of the People* (116 pp.) Written in 1918, but not published until 1936 in *Phoenix*. It was intended for *The Times Education Supplement*, but was rejected as not being "just what we wanted". $150.00

87. *Pornography and Obscenity* (9 pp.) First part of pub. version, up to paragraph beginning "The whole question of Pornography...". $35.00

88. *Studies in Classic American Literature: Nathaniel Hawthorne* (10 pp.) Early version pub. in *The English Review*, May, 1919. In addition, there are some 15 pp. continuing discussion on *Scarlet Letter* and going on to *Blithedale Romance*. Quite different from essays published in book form. $75.00

89. *Morality and the Novel*. Two versions: $50.00
    a.   Pub. version (in *Phoenix*) (9 pp.)
    b.   Unpub. version quite different (9 pp.), beginning on p. 107 of notebook paging.

90. *Art and Morality*. Two versions of one article: $50.00
    a.   Beginning "Art is immoral". Unpub. version (9 pp.).
    b.   Beginning "It is part of the common claptrap..." (10 pp.). Version pub. in *Phoenix*.

ARTICLES

91. Continuation of the Introduction to the Titus Edition of *Lady Chatterley's Lover*, Paris, 1929; "My Skirmish with Jolly Roger". Pub. together with "My Skirmish with Jolly Roger" as *A Propos of "Lady Chatterley's Lover"*. $50.00

92. Autobiographical sketch in the form of a story. Unfinished. Pub. in *Phoenix*, 1936. $100.00

93. Twenty-nine short articles: $350.00
    a.   Manuscript entitled *The Duc de Lauzun*, but crossed out. Pub. as *The Good Man* in *Phoenix*, 1936.
    b.   Ms. entitled *The Duc de Lauzun* pub. under that title in *Phoenix*, 1936.
    c.   *Is England Still a Man's Country?*: article published in *Assorted Articles*.

d. *Red Trousers* (4 pp.) Article pub. in *Assorted Articles*, also pub. in *Evening News* (London) as *Oh! For a New Crusade*.

e. *The State of Funk* (6 pp.) Article, pub. in *Assorted Articles*.

f. *Insouciance* (4 pp.) Article.

g. *Enslaved by Civilization* (4 pp.) Article, pub. in *Assorted Articles*.

h. *Men Must Rule* (4 pp.) Article, pub. in *Assorted Articles*, under title of *Master in His Own House*.

i. *Why I Don't Like Living in London* (4 pp.) Article, pub. as *Dull London* in *Assorted Articles*.

j. *Thinking about Oneself* (4 pp.) Article, pub. in *Phoenix*, 1936, for first time.

k. *Oh, These Women* (6 pp.) Article, pub. in *Assorted Articles* as *Give Her a Pattern*.

l. *Matriarchy* (6 pp.) Article, pub. in *Assorted Articles*.

m. Untitled article variously called *Summer in Tuscany* and *Germans and Latins*. It was published under the latter title in *Phoenix*, 1936 (10 pp.).

n. *Why the Novel Matters* (14 pp.) Article, pub. in *Phoenix*, 1936.

o. *Books* (8 pp.) Article, pub. in *Phoenix*, 1936, for first time, but written in 1924.

p. *The Novel and the Feelings* (12 pp.) Article, pub. for first time in *Phoenix*, 1936.

q. *Men and Women* (12 pp.) Article, published in *Assorted Articles* under title: *Men Must Work and Women Too*.

r. *Indians and Entertainment* (14 pp.) Article, published in *Mornings in Mexico*. (This ms. contains an added paragraph at the end.)

s. *Ownership* (4 pp.) Article, pub. in *Assorted Articles*.

t. *Laura Phillipine* (4 pp.) Article, pub. in *Assorted Articles*.

u. *The Risen Lord* (6 pp.) Pub. in *Assorted Articles*.

v. *The Modern Novel* (13 pp.) Being an earlier and shorter version of the essay pub. as *The Novel* in *Reflections on the Death of a Porcupine*.

w. *New Mexico* (8 pp.) Article, pub. in *Phoenix*.

      x.   *Aristocracy* (16 pp.) Ms. of essay pub. in *Reflections on the Death of a Porcupine*.

      y.   *Making Pictures* (6 pp.) Article, pub. in *Assorted Articles*.

      z.   *Cocksure Women and Hensure Men* (2½ pp.) Pub. in *Assorted Articles*.

   aa.   Short note to Nancy Pearn about placing this article.

   bb.   *Making Love to Music* (13 pp.) Article, pub. in *Phoenix*, 1936. At the end of the ms. is a letter undoubtedly to Nancy Pearn, dated Florence, April 26, 1929.

   cc.   *Pictures on the Wall* (9 pp.) Pub. in *Assorted Articles*.

94.   *Four Reviews* in one (10 pp.): $50.00
      a.   *Nigger Heaven*, by Carl Van Vechten.
      b.   *Flight*, by Walter White.
      c.   *Manhattan Transfer*, by John Dos Passos.
      d.   *In Our Time*, by Ernest Hemingway.
Published first in *The Calendar of Modern Letters*, April 1927, later in *Phoenix*.

95.   Review of *Art Nonsense* by Eric Gill (7 pp.) Pub. in *Phoenix*, 1936. This is the last thing Lawrence wrote. It was written two or three days before he died, March 2, 1930 at Vence in the South of France. $100.00

96.   Review of *Peep Show* by Walter Wilkinson (8 pp.) Incomplete and quite another version from that pub. in *Phoenix*. $10.00

97.   Review of *Heat* by Isa Glenn (8 pp.) Pub. in *Phoenix*. $15.00

98.   Review of *Gifts of Fortune* by H. M. Tomlinson (8 pp.) Pub. in *Phoenix*. $25.00

99.   Review: *The Station*: *Athos, Treasures and Men* (8 pp.) *England and the Octopus, Comfortless Memory, Ashenden*. Pub. in *Phoenix*. $20.00

100.   Review of *The Social Basis of Consciousness* by Trigant Burrow (12 pp.) Pub. in *Phoenix*. $20.00

101.   Review of *Fallen Leaves* by V. V. Rozanov (8 pp.) Pub. in *Phoenix*. $15.00

102. Review of *The Origins of Prohibition* by J. A. Krout
(8 pp.) Pub. in *Phoenix*, 1936. On the last page is a
letter from D. H. Lawrence to Miss Pearn, dated Villa
Bernarda, Spotorno, Nov. 21, 1925. $40.00

103. *Introduction to Paintings* (37 pp.) Pub. as "Introduction
to These Paintings" in *The Paintings of D. H. Lawrence*
and in *Phoenix*. $50.00

104. Foreword to *The Collected Poems of D. H. Lawrence*
(8 pp.) Entirely different from the pub. version. $50.00

105. *Seven Short Manuscripts*: $100.00
     a. *Introduction to "Bottom Dogs"* by Edward Dahl-
        berg (8 pp.) Pub. in *Phoenix*. Ms. signed and
        dated Bandol, 1929.
     b. *Introduction to "Dragon of the Apocalypse"*
        (21 pp.) Pub. in *Phoenix*.
     c. *Introduction to "The Mother"* by Grazia Deledda
        (7 pp.) Pub. in *Phoenix*.
     d. Addition to Introduction to Verga's *Cavalleria
        Rusticana* (21 pp.) Trans. by D. H. Lawrence.
     e. *Introduction to "The Grand Inquisitor"* (14 pp.)
        Pub. in *Phoenix*.
     f. *Introduction* to his translation of Verga's *Mastro-
        Don Gesualdo* (17 pp.) Quite different from pub-
        lished version.
     g. *Little Novels of Sicily*. Mss. of translation of
        Verga's work. Page missing from translation of
        Across the Sea.

106. Holograph manuscript of translation of Giovanni
Verga's novel *Mastro Don-Gesualdo* (550 pp.). $150.00

CORRECTED TYPESCRIPTS

NOVELS

107. Corrected typescript of *My Lady's Keeper* (*Lady Chatterley's Lover*) (423 pp.) Complete and as published. $500.00

108. Corrected typescript of *The Plumed Serpent*. Complete and as published. Numbering is by chapters. Last page marked "The End". $175.00

MISCELLANEOUS

109. Corrected typescript of *Rawdon's Roof* included in the posthumous volume of short stories entitled *The Lovely Lady* (20 pp.). $15.00

110. Corrected typescript of Nathaniel Hawthorne's *Blithedale Romance* (13 pp.) Pub. in the *English Review*, 1918. (Unpub. in book form. A completely different version was included in *Studies in Classic American Literature*.) $35.00

111. Corrected typescript of *The Escaped Cock*, Part I. (24 pp.) Pub. Paris, 1929. Later by Martin Secker as *The Man Who Died*. $25.00

112. Twenty-seven corrected typescripts of *Assorted Articles* (short): $250.00
    a. *Do Women Change?* (7 pp.) Addition in holograph of 1½ pages.
    b. *Give Her a Pattern* (7 pp.)
    c. *Ownership* (5 pp.)
    d. *Master in His Own House* (5 pp.)
    e. *Insouciance* (5 pp.)
    f. *Matriarchy* (7 pp.)
    g. *Cocksure Women and Hensure Men* (5 pp.)
    h. *Is England Still a Man's Country?* (4 pp.)
    i. *Dull London* (5 pp.) (Previously *Why I Don't Like Living in London*.)
    j. *Red Trousers* (5 pp.)
    k. *The State of Funk* (9 pp.)
    l. *The Risen Lord* (12 pp.)

    m. *Enslaved by Civilization* (8 pp.)
    n. *Men Must Work and Women as Well* (18 pp.)
        (previously *Men and Women*)
    o. *Making Pictures* (9 pp.)
    p. *Pictures on the Wall* (14 pp.)
    q. *On Being a Man* (7 pp.)
    r. *On Human Destiny* (8 pp.)
    s. *Chaos in Poetry* (10 pp.)
    t. *The Mozo* (14 pp.)
    u. *Corasmin and the Parrots* (9 pp.)
    v. *Jimmy and the Desperate Woman* (25 pp.)
    w. *Wintry Peacock* (26 pp.)
    x. *Sun* (20 pp.)
    y. *The Last Laugh* (21 pp.)
    z. *David* (7 pp.) (an article)
   aa. *Democracy* (8 pp.) (4 parts)

113. Corrected typescript of *The Diary of a Trip to Sardinia* (304 pp.) Published 1923. $50.00

114. Corrected typescript of the *Collected Poems of D. H. Lawrence*, vol. I. Ms. for New York (complete). $50.00

115. Corrected typescript of *St. Mawr* (178 pp.) $75.00

116. Corrected typescript of *Etruscan Places* (160 pp.) $60.00

117. *Mr. Noon* (141 pp.) $75.00

118. *Apocalypse* (116 pp.) $50.00

119. Corrected proofs of *Women in Love* (508 pp.). Secker, London, 1920. $150.00

120. Corrected proofs of *Love Poems and Others* (64 pp.). Duckworth, London, 1912 $75.00

121. Corrected proofs (galley sheets) of *The White Peacock*. Heinemann, London, 1910. $150.00

122. *Five items*: $50.00
    a. Typescript of the play, *David* (94 pp.). Ein Schauspiel von D. H. Lawrence, Übersetzung von Frieda Lawrence und D. H. L.
    b. *Le Gai Savaire* (194 pp.) Study of Thomas Hardy. Pub. in *Phoenix*, 1936.
    c. *Studies in Classic American Literature*, XI – Herman Melville's *Typee* and *Omoo* (11 pp.). Early version quite different from pub. version.

d. *Studies in Classic American Literature*: Herman
    Melville's *Moby Dick* (20 pp.). Early and unpub-
    lished version quite unique.
e. *Two Poems*:
    1. *The Man in the Street* – pub. in *Nettles*.
    2. *Rainbow* – differs altogether from version
        included in *Last Poems*.

Appendix B

Excerpts from

The Manuscripts of D. H. Lawrence: A Descriptive Catalogue

Compiled by Lawrence Clark Powell
with a Foreword by Aldous Huxley
The Public Library, Los Angeles, 1937

Appendix B is a condensation of the Powell catalogue. It omits entirely Powell's detailed descriptions of Lawrence's manuscripts and the excerpts from published criticism of Lawrence's work, but it makes available, for each manuscript described, the prices separately printed in the four-page leaflet, "A Supplement of Prices on the Manuscripts of D. H. Lawrence Offered for Sale by Jake Zeitlin, Inc." The names of purchasers or recipients are, where known, also made available. Some of the prices that T. E. Hanley paid for his acquisitions are given in square brackets and are taken from a coded list of D. H. Lawrence materials, dated 17 November 1958, which Hanley sold to the Humanities Research Center.

PREFACE

These manuscripts are the fruit of D. H. Lawrence's twenty years of life as a writer. They range from the three poems, which were the first things he had published, to a last, death-interrupted review. During his lifetime, Lawrence gave a few manuscripts to friends, but this collection contains most of his work in the many forms he adopted. . . .

I have described the manuscripts in simple terms and sought to avoid scholarly fussiness; Lawrence detested nothing more. In my notes I have given whenever possible the circumstances of the origin of each manuscript, date and place of composition and publication, and some critical appreciations. I have used my own complete collection of Lawrence's works and the score of books about him – seventy items in all. Without the help of Edward D. McDonald's two bibliographies of Lawrence and his edition of the posthumous papers called *Phoenix*, I would have been lost. Dr. McDonald's bibliographical work is nearly unique in that it is exact, good-humored and readable. Of all the critical studies of Lawrence I believe Horace Gregory's *Pilgrim of the Apocalypse* to be the best, and I have drawn on it repeatedly. Finally to Messrs. D. J.

271

and H. K. Wells I am obliged for their work in inventorying the manuscripts upon occasion of their display in the Harvard College Library Treasure Room in January, 1937.

L.C.P.

INTRODUCTORY NOTE

Having handled many manuscripts of literary and historic interest, I am no longer easily excited. But that night when I first opened the trunk containing the manuscripts of Lawrence and as I looked through them, watched unfold the immense pattern of his vision and the tremendous product of his energy, there stirred in me an emotion similar to that I felt when first viewing the heavens with a telescope. Here was revealed the breadth and depth of the intuitive universe and through the instrument of a single man whose energies had risen and been cut off in a short span of years. Somehow there is no other way one can quite feel so near to this man who wrote *The Plumed Serpent* and *The Escaped Cock* as to read his words in his own handwriting. The force of his meaning is carried through the personal medium of the penned line as if each paragraph were meant directly for you. It is like reading a freshly opened letter. And to have leafed through the many pages of *The Rainbow* was to watch it grow and live through the writer's own eyes.

Some may maintain that the printed page is good enough for all purposes. I can only answer that they have never felt the sense of immediacy and closeness which I felt that night. Because it is my desire to share this exciting experience with as many as might wish to enjoy it, this opportunity for exhibiting the manuscripts yields me an especial satisfaction not unmixed with pride.

For their cooperation in making this exhibition possible, I wish to express the thanks of Mrs. Lawrence and myself to Dr. Remsen D. Bird, inspirer of many realized dreams, Miss Althea Warren and Dr. Lawrence Clark Powell. Also for the sponsorship and generosity in making possible the publication of this catalogue I most gratefully bow to Mrs. Richard Y. Dakin and Dr. A. Elmer Belt. And finally I wish to acknowledge Mr. Aldous Huxley's kindness in contributing so appropriate a foreword.

JAKE ZEITLIN

CONTENTS

FOREWORD
by Aldous Huxley

In China and Japan handwriting was and perhaps still is one of the fine arts. With us, even at the best of times, it was no more than a craft. In recent years it has ceased, for the great majority of Westerners, to be even a craft and has become a mere convenience, an almost negligible means to an ulterior end.

For the tenth-century Japanese, as readers of Lady Murasaki's *Tale of Genji* will remember, a good handwriting was at least as alluring as a good singing voice and almost as indispensable as a pretty face or a distinguished presence. The glimpse of a few ideographs exquisitely scrawled on a sheet of perfumed blue paper was enough to set the pulses wildly throbbing. One lost one's heart to the delicate dots on an unknown young lady's i's, to the superbly virile crosses of a gentleman's t's.

We have travelled far from Genji's more refined and happier day – so far, indeed, that many of us have altogether abandoned the pen in favour of the typewriter. Even love letters, nowadays, are often machine-made.

In the field of literature "the pen of the ready writer" has become an anachronism. Today, most books get tapped out on portables or talked into dictaphones. Fortunately, however, for the future collectors of manuscripts, there are still a few exceptions. Among those who, even in the post-war years, remained faithful to the pen, was D. H. Lawrence.

Lawrence's manuscripts, most of which, fortunately, have been preserved, furnish material for a most interesting study in the psychology of literary composition. Turning over the pages of these unpretentious exercise books, one discovers two very significant facts about the nature and the artistic methods of the man who filled them with his clear, flowing handwriting. The first is that the writing and, along with it, the whole manner and *tempo* of the composition are subject to periodical changes. There is a quiet, collected mood in which the writer works slowly and unimpetuously. Then, all at once, the regular, decorous calligraphy seems to go wild. The pen begins to hurry across the paper; the letters change their shape and character; an element of exasperated urgency comes into the handwriting; the words look somehow as though they were impatient, even furious. And furious, no doubt, is what they are – furious with the *furor poeticus* of sudden inspiration rushing up, violently and eruptively, from the depths of the creative mind.

The other significant thing one notices, as one looks through these manuscripts, is the fact that there are practically no corrections. The script runs on, page after page, with hardly a blot or an erasure. I know of only one other modern writer, whose manuscripts are freer from correction than Lawrence's, namely Arnold Bennett. Lawrence corrected very little and Bennett, to all intents, not at all. But, in spite of this common characteristic, how profoundly different in temperament and method the two men were! Bennett's handwriting was characterized by a studied perfection of form not of this age. His manuscripts are minor works of art, faultless in their uniform elegance. The script flows on as evenly as the script of a mediaeval copyist. And, indeed, in a certain sense Bennett *was* a copyist. His manuscripts were fair copies of drafts that already existed, written out and corrected down to the last detail, inside his head. Bennett, as he himself more than once explained to me in conversation, knew in advance exactly what he was going to write next. His books were there, complete, before he began to commit them to paper. He had merely to take them down. Hence the unvarying neatness, the regular beauty of his script.

Lawrence was a writer of an entirely different type. His books had no pre-existence; they came into being as he wrote. The creator did not know in advance what he was creating – was often, indeed, as his letters bear witness, extremely puzzled by the creature that emerged into existence beneath his pen; could not be certain, until the process of creation was completed, what it was all about.

Most writers, I should guess, compose in a manner that is nearer to Lawrence's than to Bennett's. They sit down to a new book without having any very exact idea what it is going to be about. A vague general notion, a guiding principle – these are all they start with. The details take form only as they write.

At this point, however, we must draw another distinction – between the writers whose work is mainly the result of first thoughts and writers whose work is mainly the result of second thoughts. Some writers have almost no thoughts that are not second thoughts. Balzac, for example, did most of his composition in the margins of his galley proofs. This is an expensive habit; and second-thinkers, as we may call them, have generally preferred to do their cutting and adding and transposing at an earlier stage in the process of book production. The final rough-draft of their manuscripts has the appearance of a patchwork quilt.

How different are the uncorrected, and, so to say, seamless manuscripts of those whose thoughts are all first thoughts, who write by inspiration and as though they were possessed by a kind of daemon! Lawrence was a writer of this type, a thinker of first thoughts who never wrote except when the indwelling daemon prompted him. For him, only first thoughts had value. He didn't believe in second thoughts, was even temperamentally incapable of superimposing a second thought upon a first. If he was dissatisfied with a story or a novel, as it emerged from the process of creation, he would not, could not, correct it; he started afresh and wrote the whole thing over again, submitting himself once more to possession by the daemon of his inspiration, allowing it to think a completely new set of first thoughts in relation to the theme of his book. Some of his long novels exist in two distinct manuscript versions. On the subject of Lady Chatterley there are actually three sets of first thoughts – three complete long-hand manuscripts of a hundred thousand words apiece. (Quite apart from any other reason, one must admire Lawrence for his extraordinary industry.) It is greatly to be hoped that one day all three versions of Lady Chatterley will be published in a single volume. By comparing and collating the texts, one would be able, I believe, to learn a great deal about the workings of the creative mind.

NOVELS

1. THE WHITE PEACOCK (1911) $1250
    A. HOLOGRAPH MANUSCRIPT, incomplete, early version, probably second draft. Five separate unstitched notebooks (5 × 8) totaling 116 pp. Differs considerably from published version. *Entirely unpublished.*
    B. CORRECTED GALLEY-SHEETS, 124 in all, complete, with many corrections and revisions in L[awrence]'s hand. Enclosed unfolded in red cardboard case.

2. THE TRESPASSER (1912) $1000
    A. HOLOGRAPH MANUSCRIPT, complete as published, 487 pp., ruled notebook paper (6½ × 8), in ink. (Pp. 477–84 missing.)

B. HOLOGRAPH MANUSCRIPT, incomplete, first version, 225 pp., unstitched ruled booklets and loose sheets (6½ × 8), in ink.

3. SONS AND LOVERS (1913)   Hanley $1500
HOLOGRAPH MANUSCRIPT, incomplete, 265 pp., ruled notebook paper (app. 7 × 9), in ink. Pagination from 1 to 353, with some pages missing. *Entirely unpublished.* [Hanley: $1150]

4. THE RAINBOW (1915)   Hanley $2500
HOLOGRAPH MANUSCRIPT, complete and unexpurgated as published in the original Methuen edition; 707 pages ruled tablet paper (8 × 10, some 8 × 12½), in ink. Pp. 1–14 are Lawrence's own typescript hand-corrected; pp. 548–614 corrected typescript. [Hanley: $3500]

5. WOMEN IN LOVE (1921)   Hanley $200
AUTHOR'S ADVANCE PROOF COPY of the English first edition. London, Martin Secker, [1920]. 508 pp. The book was not published until the following year, and first editions bear the date 1921. With numerous corrections in ink in Lawrence's hand. Full crimson morocco, blind-tooled, small tear and scratch on front cover.

6. KANGAROO (1923) $1250
HOLOGRAPH MANUSCRIPT, 539 pp., in four separate ruled notebooks, in ink. Complete as published, except for the final chapter which was removed from the fourth notebook.   [Hanley: $1500]

7. THE PLUMED SERPENT (1926) $200
CORRECTED TYPESCRIPT, 724 pp., numbered by chapters, complete as published, last page marked "The End". With frequent corrections and revisions in Lawrence's hand.   [Hanley: $200]

8. LADY CHATTERLEY'S LOVER (1928)   Hanley   Sold
CORRECTED TYPESCRIPT, 423 pp., complete as published, with extensive corrections and revisions in Lawrence's hand. This typescript was made by Mrs. Aldous Huxley. The novel was known successively as *Tenderness, My Lady's Keeper, John Thomas and Lady Jane*, and finally as *Lady Chatterley's Lover*. [Hanley: $1250]

Two Polemical Essays   Hanley $300

9. APROPOS OF LADY CHATTERLEY'S LOVER (1930)
HOLOGRAPH MANUSCRIPT, 42 pp., finely cross-ruled *cahier* paper (6¾ × 9), in ink.

10. PORNOGRAPHY AND OBSCENITY (1929)
     (Parts I and II. Part I was published originally in *This Quarter*;
     Part II is a continuation which formed, with Part I, a Faber & Faber
     pamphlet called *Pornography and Obscenity*. Collected in *Phoenix*.)
     HOLOGRAPH MANUSCRIPT, 34 pp. (6½ × 8½ and 8 × 10½), in ink.

NOVELETTES

11. THE FOX   Hanley   Sold
     MANUSCRIPT, 67 pages holograph, except for the first 29 pages
     which are corrected typescript, unruled paper (8½ × 11), in ink.
     Complete as published.   [Hanley: $400]

12. THE CAPTAIN'S DOLL $500
     HOLOGRAPH MANUSCRIPT, 78 pages, unruled paper (8½ × 11), in
     ink. Complete as published. Bound in decorated blue cardboard
     folder.

13. MR. NOON $250
     CORRECTED TYPESCRIPT, 142 pages, with numerous revisions in
     Lawrence's hand.   [Hanley: $250]

14. ST. MAWR   Huxley $1000
     A. HOLOGRAPH MANUSCRIPT, 129 pages plain and ruled notebook
     leaves (7½ × 10), in ink. Complete as published. Also 41 holograph
     pages, numbered 17–58, of an earlier version. [*Jake Zeitlin's note*:
     "destroyed in the fire at Huxley's Home 1961."]
     B. CORRECTED TYPESCRIPT, 178 pages, with frequent corrections
     and revisions in Lawrence's hand. Complete as published in 1925.

15. THE WOMAN WHO RODE AWAY $500
     HOLOGRAPH MANUSCRIPT, 48 pages, ruled notebook paper (6½ ×
     8½), in ink. Complete as published.

16. THE PRINCESS   [*Not priced separately*]
     HOLOGRAPH MANUSCRIPT, 53 pages, in ruled notebook (7¼ × 9½),
     (together with other items; see item 118); in ink.

17. THE FLYING FISH $750
     HOLOGRAPH MANUSCRIPT, 39 pages, ruled paper (6½ × 9), in ink.
     The first nine pages are in Frieda Lawrence's hand, Lawrence
     having dictated them to her when he was too ill to write. With
     extensive interlinear revisions.

18. THE VIRGIN AND THE GIPSY (1930) $650
     HOLOGRAPH MANUSCRIPT, 160 pages, in ruled notebook (7 × 8½),
     in ink. The pages are torn loose, but remain intact between the
     notebook's covers.   [Hanley: $725]

19. THE ESCAPED COCK $500
     A.   CORRECTED TYPESCRIPT, Part I, 24 pages, with corrections and
     revisions in Lawrence's hand.
     B.   HOLOGRAPH MANUSCRIPT, unfinished, Part II, 32 pages (1–32),
     ruled paper (6 × 8), in ink.

                               SHORT STORIES

20. LEGEND $75
     HOLOGRAPH MANUSCRIPT, 8 pages ruled paper (7½ × 9), in ink.
     Unpublished, early version of *A Fragment of Stained Glass*.   [Hanley:
     $85]

21. GOOSE FAIR   Medley $150
     HOLOGRAPH MANUSCRIPT, 13 pages, ruled foolscap (8 × 13), in
     ink. Bound in decorated cardboard covers.

22. ODOUR OF CHRYSANTHEMUMS $300
     HOLOGRAPH MANUSCRIPT, 39 pages, in three unstitched ruled
     booklets (6½ × 8), in ink. . . . Together with a 6 page fragment in
     pencil of an earlier version.   [Hanley: $350]

23. THE OLD ADAM   Rota   Sold
     HOLOGRAPH MANUSCRIPT, 27 pages, ruled paper (8 × 10), in ink.

24. THE WITCH À LA MODE $100
     Three progressive versions of the story published in *A Modern
     Lover* with the above title.
     A.   INTIMACY. Holograph manuscript, 36 pages, in three un-
     stitched ruled booklets (6½ × 8), in ink.
     B.   THE WHITE WOMAN. Holograph manuscript, 29 pages, ruled
     paper (8½ × 10), in ink.
     C.   THE WITCH À LA MODE. Typescript of final version, made from
     "B", 27 pages (8 × 10), with a few corrections by Lawrence.

25. STRIKE PAY   Rota $50
     HOLOGRAPH MANUSCRIPT, 15 pages, ruled paper (8 × 10), in ink.

26. HER TURN $50
    HOLOGRAPH MANUSCRIPT, 10 pages, ruled paper (8 × 10), in ink.

27. NEW EVE AND OLD ADAM $50
    HOLOGRAPH MANUSCRIPT, 14 pages, finely cross-ruled continental *cahier* paper (8½ × 10½), in ink.

28. A CHAPEL AMONG THE MOUNTAINS $250
    HOLOGRAPH MANUSCRIPT, 16 pages, ruled paper (8 × 10), in ink.

29. THE VICAR'S GARDEN $75
    HOLOGRAPH MANUSCRIPT, 7 pages, ruled paper (7½ × 9), in ink. An unpublished early, but quite different version of *The Shadow in the Rose Garden*.   [Hanley: $85]

30. HONOUR AND ARMS [THE PRUSSIAN OFFICER] $500
    HOLOGRAPH MANUSCRIPT, 17 pages, finely cross-ruled continental paper of various sizes (mostly 8½ × 13), unusually minute script, in ink.   [Hanley: $500]

31. TWO MARRIAGES $50
    HOLOGRAPH MANUSCRIPT, 33 [*Jake Zeitlin has substituted* 45] pages, ruled paper (8 × 10), in ink. *An early version of the following item.*

32. DAUGHTERS OF THE VICAR   Rota   Sold
    A.   HOLOGRAPH MANUSCRIPT, 24 pages, unruled foolscap (8½ × 13), in ink.
    B.   INCOMPLETE EARLIER VERSION, partly pencilled manuscript and corrected typescript, pages 19–54 (27–8 missing).
    C.   ANOTHER INCOMPLETE EARLY VERSION. Holograph manuscript, 23 pages, ruled paper (8 × 10), in ink.

33. THE CHRISTENING $50
    HOLOGRAPH MANUSCRIPT, 9 pages, ruled foolscap (8½ × 13), in ink.

34. A SICK COLLIER $50
    HOLOGRAPH MANUSCRIPT, 11 pages, ruled paper (8 × 10), in ink.

35. WINTRY PEACOCK   Medley $75
    CORRECTED TYPESCRIPT, 26 pages (8 × 10). Many pages completely rewritten between the lines in Lawrence's hand.

36. THE BORDER LINE   Rota   Sold
    A.   HOLOGRAPH MANUSCRIPT, 25 pages, unruled punched paper (7½ × 9½), in ink. *An early version.*

B.   ANOTHER EARLY VERSION. Holograph manuscript, 15 pages, ruled notebook paper (6½ × 8½), in ink.

37.   JIMMY AND THE DESPERATE WOMAN   Rota $100
  A.   HOLOGRAPH MANUSCRIPT, 31 pages, ruled paper (6½ × 8½), in ink.
  B.   TYPESCRIPT, 25 pages (8½ × 13), with corrections in Lawrence's hand.

38.   THE LAST LAUGH   Rota   Sold
  A.   HOLOGRAPH MANUSCRIPT, 24 pages, ruled notebook paper (6½ × 8½), in ink.
  B.   TYPESCRIPT, 21 pages (8 × 10), with corrections in Lawrence's hand.

39.   GLAD GHOSTS   Rota   Sold
  A.   HOLOGRAPH MANUSCRIPT, 69 pages, in ruled notebook (6¾ × 8¼), in ink.
  B.   An early version, incomplete, HOLOGRAPH MANUSCRIPT, pp. 52–62 (58–59 missing).

40.   SUN $50
  CORRECTED TYPESCRIPT, 20 pages (8¼ × 11¾), with many revisions and additions in Lawrence's hand.   [Hanley: $60]

41.   MORE MODERN LOVE $50
  HOLOGRAPH MANUSCRIPT, 20 pages, ruled paper (7 × 9), in ink. *An early version of "In Love".*   [Hanley: $85]

42.   TWO BLUE BIRDS $75
  HOLOGRAPH MANUSCRIPT, 30 pages, ruled paper (6 × 8), in ink. Bound at the top in marbled boards.

43.   SMILE   Sold
  HOLOGRAPH MANUSCRIPT, 9 pages, ruled paper (6¼ × 8½), in ink. Bound at the top in marbled boards.

44.   RAWDON'S ROOF   Rota   Sold
  A.   HOLOGRAPH MANUSCRIPT, 21 pages, ruled notebook paper (6½ × 8), in ink.
  B.   TYPESCRIPT, 20 pages, with a few corrections and revisions in Lawrence's hand.

45.   THE ROCKING-HORSE WINNER   Rota   Sold
  HOLOGRAPH MANUSCRIPT, 30 pages, ruled paper (6¾ × 8¼), in ink. Bound in marbled boards.

46. MOTHER AND DAUGHTER $100
    HOLOGRAPH MANUSCRIPT, 44 pages, ruled notebook paper (6 ×
    8½), in ink.   [Hanley: $175]

47. THINGS $100
    HOLOGRAPH MANUSCRIPT, 19 pages, ruled paper (6 × 7½), in ink.
    Bound in marbled boards.   [Hanley: $100]

48. THE BLUE MOCCASINS $100
    A.   HOLOGRAPH MANUSCRIPT, 32 pages, in ruled notebook (6 ×
    8¼), in ink.   [Hanley: $500 for nos 48 and 109]
    B.   An early version, incomplete, HOLOGRAPH MANUSCRIPT,
    pp. 1–9 (7, 8 missing).

49. THE UNDYING MAN $25
    HOLOGRAPH MANUSCRIPT, incomplete, 8 pages, ruled paper (6½ ×
    8), in ink.

50. [NEWTHORPE IN 2927] Autobiographical Story $250
    HOLOGRAPH MANUSCRIPT, 41 pages, in ruled notebook (6½ × 8),
    pages torn from covers but preserved intact, in ink. Unfinished.

51. SIX UNFINISHED, UNTITLED AND ENTIRELY UNPUBLISHED
    STORIES $750
    A.   "My mother made a failure of her life." Holograph manu-
    script, unfinished, 20 pages (1–20), unruled foolscap (8¼ × 13), in
    ink.
    B.   "There were, three years back, two schools in the mining
    village of High Park." Holograph manuscript, unfinished, 7 un-
    numbered pages, ruled paper (6 × 8), in pencil.
    C.   "There is a small cottage off the Addiscombe Road about a
    mile from East Croydon station." Holograph manuscript, un-
    finished, 48 pages, in four unstitched ruled booklets (6½ × 8), in
    ink.
    D.   "'Then come into the kitchen,' said Mrs. Bircumshaw."
    Holograph manuscript, incomplete, 11 pages (9–19), ruled paper
    (6 × 8), in ink.
    E.   "There was a man not long ago, who felt he was through
    with the world, so he decided to be a hermit." Holograph manu-
    script, unfinished, 10 pages, ruled paper in black patent-leather
    notebook (6 × 8), in ink.
    F.   HOLOGRAPH MANUSCRIPT, unfinished, 9 pages, ruled note-
    book paper (6½ × 8½), in ink.

POETRY

52. THREE POEMS (Dreams Old and Nascent, Discipline, Baby Movements) $300
    HOLOGRAPH MANUSCRIPT, 20 pages, unstitched ruled booklet (6½ × 8), in ink. First three stanzas of the first poem missing. [Hanley: $150]

53. LOVE POEMS (1912) $1500
    HOLOGRAPH MANUSCRIPT, 24 poems on 45 pages, ruled paper (8 × 10), in ink.

54. LOVE POEMS AND OTHERS   Hanley $150
    Love Poems and Others. London, Duckworth & Co., 1912.
    CORRECTED PAGE PROOFS, 64 pages, bound in full green morocco blind stamped (6 × 8½). With corrections in Lawrence's hand, including changes of title, etc. The published book is dated a year later.

55. NINE HOLOGRAPH POEMS $275
    The End of Another Home-Holiday (2 versions)
    Restlessness (2 versions)
    Perfidy (2 versions, 1 incomplete)
    Violets (2 versions, 1 incomplete)
    Cherry Robbers (2 versions, 1 incomplete)
    Wind among the Cherries
    Song (Flapper)
    A Bell
    A Letter from Town – The Almond Tree
    HOLOGRAPH MANUSCRIPT, 25 pages, ruled paper (6 × 8½), in ink.

56. POEMS FROM "BIRDS, BEASTS AND FLOWERS" AND A DIARY $500
    Tropic
    Peace
    Southern Night
    Sicilian Cyclamens
    Hibiscus and Salvia Flowers
    Purple Anemones
    The Ass
    Eagle in New Mexico
    The American Eagle

    HOLOGRAPH MANUSCRIPT, 22 pages, in bound ruled notebook (6½ × 8½), in ink.

57. COLLECTED POEMS. Volume I "Rhyming Poems". $125
    TYPESCRIPT, 178 pages, with corrections in Lawrence's hand.
    [Hanley: $70]

58. ORIGINAL VERSION OF THE FOREWORD TO COLLECTED
    POEMS   Powell $200
    HOLOGRAPH MANUSCRIPT, 8 pages, ruled paper (6 × 8¼), in ink.

59. A NOTEBOOK OF "PANSIES" $750
    HOLOGRAPH MANUSCRIPT, 102 pages, in ruled notebook (7 × 9½),
    bought in Oaxaca, Mexico, with Lawrence's name on fly-leaf.
    Contains 135 poems written *c.*1928. *Many unpublished and variant
    versions of "Pansies".* [Hanley: $450]

60. EARLY VERSION OF PUBLISHED "PANSIES"   Sold

    Finding your Level
    Altercation
    What Is Man Without an Income?
    Climbing Up
    Canvassing for the Election
    A Rise in the World

    HOLOGRAPH MANUSCRIPT, 10 pages, ruled paper (6 × 8½), in ink.

61. UNPUBLISHED "PANSIES"   Sold

    Reach over, then, reach over.
    Traitors, oh liars, you Judas lot!
    Are you pining to be superior?
    Softly, then softly.

    HOLOGRAPH MANUSCRIPT, 6 pages, ruled paper (6 × 8½), in ink.

62. FOUR HOLOGRAPH POEMS, AS PUBLISHED IN "LAST
    POEMS" AND "NETTLES"   Bender $50

    Bells
    The Triumph of the Machine
    Father Neptune's Little Affair with Freedom
    The Man in the Street

    HOLOGRAPH MANUSCRIPT, 4 pages, finely cross-ruled *cahier* paper
    (7 × 9), in ink. In addition there is the original and carbon
    typescript of "The Man in the Street," uncorrected, 2 pages.

63. SIX UNPUBLISHED POEMS   Bender   Sold
    A. *Eagle in New Mexico.* Holograph manuscript, 3 pages (8½ ×
11), in ink. Unpublished and unique version entirely different from
that published in *Birds, Beasts and Flowers,* except in subject matter.
    B. *Rainbow.* Typescript, 2 pages, unpublished poem, entirely
different from a single stanza of same title in *Pansies.*
    C. *And What Do I Care.* Holograph manuscript, 3 pages, ruled
notebook paper (6½ × 8), in pencil.
    D. *Fire.* Holograph manuscript, 1 page, ruled paper (6½ × 8),
in ink. Longer and different from version in *Pansies.*
    E. *O! Americans!* Holograph manuscript, 8 pages, ruled and
punched paper (8½ × 11), in ink.
    F. *Change of Life.* Holograph manuscript, 8 pages, ruled and
punched paper (8½ × 11), in ink.

64. LAST POEMS   Hanley $1000
    TWO HOLOGRAPH NOTEBOOKS, as edited and published in 1933 as
"Last Poems," by Richard Aldington.   [Hanley: $100, $450]

PLAYS

65. THE MERRY-GO-ROUND $500
    HOLOGRAPH MANUSCRIPT, 148 pages, in 13 unstitched ruled book-
lets, in ink.

66. THE MARRIED MAN $500
    HOLOGRAPH MANUSCRIPT, 72 pages (complete for the first five
pages), ruled paper (8 × 10), in ink.

67. THE FIGHT FOR BARBARA $500
    HOLOGRAPH MANUSCRIPT, 55 pages, ruled foolscap (8½ × 12¼), in
ink.   [Hanley: $550]

68. ALTITUDE ["Chaos in Taos"] $300
    HOLOGRAPH MANUSCRIPT, unfinished, 28 pages, in notebook (7 ×
8½), in pencil.

69. DAVID $750
    A. HOLOGRAPH MANUSCRIPT, 178 pages, in red notebook (7 × 9),
in pencil.
    B. TYPESCRIPT of *David,* translated into German by Frieda and
D. H. Lawrence. 94 pages.

TRAVEL SKETCHES

70. CHRISTS IN THE TIROL $100

   HOLOGRAPH MANUSCRIPT, 6 pages, unruled foolscap (8¼ × 13), in ink. *Original version.*

71. NEW MEXICO Hughes $250

   HOLOGRAPH MANUSCRIPT, 8 pages (8 × 10½), in ink. In decorated green and black boards.

72. THE HOPI SNAKE DANCE $200

   HOLOGRAPH MANUSCRIPT, 18 pages, in black ruled notebook (See Item 118) (7½ × 9¾), in ink.

73. THE DANCE OF THE SPROUTING CORN $100

   HOLOGRAPH MANUSCRIPT, 6 pages, ruled punched paper (8½ × 11), in ink.

74. INDIANS AND ENTERTAINMENT $150

   HOLOGRAPH MANUSCRIPT, 13 pages, ruled punched paper (8½ × 11), in ink.

75. A LITTLE MOONSHINE WITH LEMON $75

   HOLOGRAPH MANUSCRIPT, 6 pages, ruled paper (6½ × 8), in ink. Bound at the top in marbled boards. [*Jake Zeitlin's note*: "Gift by Frieda to young man (unknown)."]

76. MORNINGS IN MEXICO [*not priced separately*]

   Friday Morning (Corasmin and the Parrots)
   Saturday Morning (Market Day)
   Sunday Morning (Walk to Huayapa)
   Monday Morning (The Mozo)

   HOLOGRAPH MANUSCRIPT, 44 pages, in black notebook (7½ × 9¾), in ink. (See Item 118.) Also corrected typescripts of two of the pieces ["Corasmin and the Parrots" and "The Mozo"].

77. SEA AND SARDINIA (1921) Hanley $500

   CORRECTED TYPESCRIPT, 305 pages, with many corrections and revisions in Lawrence's hand, and the original title "Diary of a Trip to Sardinia." [Hanley: $450]

78. LETTER FROM GERMANY $100

   HOLOGRAPH MANUSCRIPT, 6 pages, ruled paper (6 × 8), in ink.

79. MERCURY $150
     HOLOGRAPH MANUSCRIPT, 9 pages, ruled paper (6½ × 8), in ink.

80. FIREWORKS $100
     HOLOGRAPH MANUSCRIPT, 8 pages, ruled paper (7 × 9), in ink.
     Published in *Phoenix* as "Fireworks in Florence."   [Hanley: $150]

81. SUMMER IN TUSCANY, or, GERMANS AND LATINS $75
     HOLOGRAPH MANUSCRIPT, 10 pages, ruled paper (6 × 9), in ink.
     [*Jake Zeitlin's note*: "Sent to Mrs. Dieterle at FL's request."]

82. DAVID $75
     CORRECTED TYPESCRIPT, 7 pages.

83. ETRUSCAN PLACES $350
     A.   CORRECTED TYPESCRIPT, 160 pages, with numerous corrections
     and revisions in Lawrence's hand.   [Hanley: $250]
     B.   PHOTOGRAPHS (8 × 10) of Etruscan places and relics, 44 in all,
     with titles and explanatory notes on the backs in Lawrence's hand.
     A selection from this comprehensive group was used to illustrate
     the published volume.

                         ASSORTED ARTICLES

84. ASSORTED ARTICLES $500
     A.   HOLOGRAPH MANUSCRIPT, totaling 180 pages, on paper of
     different sizes, mostly in ink.   [*Sold individually; see Appendix C.*]
     B.   SIXTEEN CORRECTED TYPESCRIPTS.   [Hanley: $550]
     The manuscripts include the following articles, ranging from
     four to sixteen pages each:

     The Risen Lord
     Ownership
     Cocksure Women and Hen-Sure Men
     Laura-Phillipine [*Jake Zeitlin's note*: "Ret. to Frieda for Mary
     Christine [Hughes]."]
     Individual vs. Social Consciousness
     The Jeune Fille Wants to Know
     Red Trousers
     Is England Still a Man's Country?
     Making Love to Music (together with an unpublished letter)
     Insouciance
     Men Must Rule

Enslaved by Civilization
The State of Funk
Oh These Women
Thinking about Oneself
Why I Don't Like Living in London
Do Women Change
Sex Appeal
Aristocracy
Women are so Cocksure
Books
All There
Men and Women
Matriarchy
Noah's Flood (dramatic in form)
Invocation to Fire, The Elephants of Dionysos, Notes for Apocalypse, on recto and verso of 10 sheets.

Fragments of four articles, in notebook with some Spanish songs in ms.

CRITICAL WRITINGS

85. FOUR ESSAYS ON THE NOVEL $250
     A. *Why the Novel Matters*
HOLOGRAPH MANUSCRIPT, 14 pages, ruled paper (6½ × 8½), in ink. [Hanley: $250]
     B. *The Modern Novel*
HOLOGRAPH MANUSCRIPT, 13 pages, ruled paper (6½ × 8½), in ink. An earlier and shorter version of the essay "The Novel" in *Reflections on the Death of a Porcupine*. [Hanley: $250]
     C. *The Novel and the Feelings*
HOLOGRAPH MANUSCRIPT, 12 pages, ruled paper (6½ × 8½), in ink. [Hanley: $100]
     D. *Morality and the Novel*
HOLOGRAPH MANUSCRIPT, 9 and 10 pages, ruled paper (7 × 9), in ink. Two versions of one essay, the first unpublished, the second collected in *Phoenix*. [Hanley: $100]

86. STUDY OF THOMAS HARDY $25
     TYPESCRIPT, 194 pages, uncorrected, forming ten chapters. [*Jake Zeitlin's note*: "Returned Frieda."]

87. A SCRUTINY OF THE WORK OF JOHN GALSWORTHY $100
     HOLOGRAPH MANUSCRIPT, 15 pages, ruled paper (7 × 9), in ink.

Lacks five final paragraphs of the published version. Bound at the top in marbled boards.   [Hanley: $100]

88.   STUDIES IN CLASSIC AMERICAN LITERATURE $250
      A.   *Nathaniel Hawthorne*
HOLOGRAPH MANUSCRIPT, 10 pages, and corrected typescript, 15 pages.
      B.   *The Scarlet Letter* and *The Blithedale Romance*
CORRECTED TYPESCRIPT, 12 pages.
      C.   *Herman Melville's "Typee" and "Omoo"*
TYPESCRIPT, 12 pages.
      D.   *Herman Melville's "Moby Dick"*
TYPESCRIPT, 19 pages.
      Early, unpublished versions of two essays on Melville which appeared in different form in the STUDIES.   [Hanley: $150]

89.   THE DUC DE LAUZUN $35
      HOLOGRAPH MANUSCRIPT, 9 and 8 pages, ruled paper (6¾ × 9¾), in ink.

90.   LAWRENCE'S INTRODUCTION TO THE BIBLIOGRAPHY OF HIS WRITINGS BY EDWARD D. McDONALD, PHILADELPHIA 1925
      HOLOGRAPH MANUSCRIPT, 4 pages, in black notebook (see Item 118), written at Kiowa Ranch, 1924.   [*Not priced separately.*]

91.   INTRODUCTION TO "THE MOTHER" BY GRAZIA DELEDDA, LONDON 1928 $50
      HOLOGRAPH MANUSCRIPT, 7 pages, ruled paper (6 × 8¼), in ink.

92.   "CHAOS IN POETRY": INTRODUCTION TO "CHARIOT OF THE SUN", POEMS BY HARRY CROSBY, PARIS 1931 $50
      CORRECTED TYPESCRIPT, 10 pages, with numerous corrections and revisions in Lawrence's hand.   [Hanley: $60]

93.   INTRODUCTION TO "BOTTOM DOGS" BY EDWARD DAHL-BERG, LONDON 1929, NEW YORK 1930 $150
      HOLOGRAPH MANUSCRIPT, 8 pages (8 × 10½), in ink.

94.   INTRODUCTION TO "THE GRAND INQUISITOR" BY DOSTOIEVSKY. TRANSLATED BY S. S. KOTELIANSKY, LONDON 1931 $100
      HOLOGRAPH MANUSCRIPT, 14 pages in *cahier* (7 × 9), the remaining pages blank, in ink.

95. INTRODUCTION TO "DRAGON OF THE APOCALYPSE" BY
    FREDERICK CARTER $100
    HOLOGRAPH MANUSCRIPT, 21 pages, ruled paper (7 × 9), in ink.

BOOK REVIEWS

96. REVIEW OF "THE ORIGINS OF PROHIBITION" BY J. A.
    KROUT $50
    HOLOGRAPH MANUSCRIPT, 8 pages, ruled paper (6¾ × 8¼), in
    pencil. Published in *N. Y. Herald-Tribune Books*, Jan. 31,
    1926. [Hanley: $60]

97. REVIEW OF "HEAT" BY ISA GLENN $35
    HOLOGRAPH MANUSCRIPT, 8 pages, ruled paper (7 × 9), in ink.

98. REVIEW OF "GIFTS OF FORTUNE" BY H. M. TOMLINSON $50
    HOLOGRAPH MANUSCRIPT, 8 pages, ruled paper (6 × 8), in ink.
    [Hanley: $50]

99. FOUR REVIEWS $50

    Carl Van Vechten's *Nigger Heaven*
    Walter White's *Flight*
    John dos Passos' *Manhattan Transfer*
    Ernest Hemingway's *In Our Time*

    HOLOGRAPH MANUSCRIPT, 10 pages, ruled paper (7 × 9), in ink.
    Bound at the top in marbled boards.

100. REVIEW OF "SOLITARIA" AND "THE APOCALYPSE OF OUR
     TIMES" BY V. V. ROZANOV, TRANSLATED BY S. S. KOTEL-
     IANSKY $35
     HOLOGRAPH MANUSCRIPT, 10 pages, ruled paper (6 × 8), in
     ink. [Hanley: $100]

101. REVIEW OF "THE PEEP SHOW" BY WALTER WILKINSON $25
     HOLOGRAPH MANUSCRIPT, 6 pages, incomplete (3–8 present),
     ruled paper (6 × 8), in ink.

102. REVIEW OF "THE SOCIAL BASIS OF CONSCIOUSNESS" BY
     DR. TRIGANT BURROW $125
     HOLOGRAPH MANUSCRIPT, 12 pages, ruled paper (7 × 9), in
     ink. [Hanley: $125]

103. FOUR REVIEWS   Hanley $135

    Robert Byron's *The Station*
    Clough Williams's *England and the Octopus*
    Maurice Baring's *Comfortless Memory*
    W. Somerset Maugham's *Ashenden or The British Agent*

    A. HOLOGRAPH MANUSCRIPT, 8 pages, ruled paper (6½ × 9), in ink. [Hanley: $150]
    B. An earlier, unpublished version. HOLOGRAPH MANUSCRIPT, 4 pages, ruled paper (6½ × 9), in ink. [Hanley: $150]

104. REVIEW OF "FALLEN LEAVES" BY V. V. ROZANOV, TRANS-
LATED BY S. S. KOTELIANSKY $35
    HOLOGRAPH MANUSCRIPT, 8 pages, ruled paper (7 × 9), in ink. [Hanley: $75]

105. REVIEW OF "ART NONSENSE & OTHER ESSAYS" BY ERIC
GILL $300
    HOLOGRAPH MANUSCRIPT, 7 pages, unfinished, in 100 page *cahier*, the rest blank (7 × 9), in ink. Written at Vence, February 1930.

TRANSLATIONS FROM THE ITALIAN

106. "MASTRO-DON GESUALDO" BY GIOVANNI VERGA, TRANS-
LATED BY D. H. LAWRENCE (1923)   Hanley $750
    HOLOGRAPH MANUSCRIPT, 550 pages in four separate notebooks (6 × 8), in ink. [Hanley: $750]
    Also a HOLOGRAPH MANUSCRIPT, 17 pages (6 × 8), in ink, of a second and longer Introductory Note, written in Ceylon and also different from the one published.

107. VERGA'S "LITTLE NOVELS OF SICILY" (NOVELLE RUSTI-
CANA) TRANSLATED BY D. H. LAWRENCE (1925)
                                      Hanley $350
    HOLOGRAPH MANUSCRIPT, 176 pages, ruled paper (6½ × 8, 8 × 10), in ink. [Hanley: $500] Includes the following *novelle*:

Black Bread (48 pp.)	So Much for the King (16 pp.)
The Gentry (13 pp.)	The Mystery Play (10 pp.)
Liberty (11 pp.)	Malaria (12 pp.)
Across the Sea (13 pp.)	The Orphans (10 pp.)
Don Licciu Papa (9 pp.)	Property (9 pp.)
His Reverence (16 pp.)	History of St. Joseph's Ass (18 pp.)

108. VERGA'S "CAVALLERIA RUSTICANA AND OTHER STORIES" TRANSLATED BY D. H. LAWRENCE (1928) $250
HOLOGRAPH MANUSCRIPT, 58 pages, in black notebook (7 × 9), in ink. Includes the following *novelle*:

Cavalleria Rusticana (9 pages)
The She-Wolf (7 pages)
Fantasticalities (10 pages)
Jeli the Shepherd (32 pages)

Also part of Introductory Note: HOLOGRAPH MANUSCRIPT, 11 pages (12–21), ruled paper (6½ × 8), in ink.
The notebook also contains a 7 page unfinished travel sketch called "Journey to the Southwest".

109. IL LASCA'S "THE STORY OF DOCTOR MANENTE", TRANSLATED BY D. H. LAWRENCE (1929) $150
HOLOGRAPH MANUSCRIPT, 69 pages, in notebook (6½ × 8½), in ink. (Together with "Introduction to Pictures", 17 pages.) [Hanley: *see No. 48.*]

ESSAYS ON RELIGION, EDUCATION, DEMOCRACY, ART, LOVE

110. APOCALYPSE $400
A. HOLOGRAPH MANUSCRIPT, 105 pages, ruled paper (6½ × 8¾), in ink.
B. Fragments of earlier versions. HOLOGRAPH MANUSCRIPTS, pages 33–42, in pink *cahier*, on the cover of which is written "Apocalypsis II, DHL." Holograph manuscript, pages 11–53, 23–58, 27–32, 43–56, 13–14, in green notebook (7 × 9), inscribed "For Uncle David with best wishes for a happy birthday from Harwood [Brewster Picard]. Sept. 11, 1929."
C. CORRECTED TYPESCRIPT, 116 pages, with many revisions in Lawrence's hand. [*Jake Zeitlin's note*: "not in Merrild lot."] [Hanley: $450]

111. EDUCATION OF THE PEOPLE $300
HOLOGRAPH MANUSCRIPT, 116 pages, ruled paper (8½ × 10½), in ink. [Hanley: $400]

112. DEMOCRACY $50
CORRECTED TYPESCRIPT, 29 pages, in four parts (8 × 10).

113. INTRODUCTION TO PAINTINGS Hanley Sold
HOLOGRAPH MANUSCRIPT, 37 pages (8 × 10½), in ink. Published

as the foreword to *The Paintings of D. H. Lawrence*, London, 1929. [Hanley: $250]

114. MAKING PICTURES $100
     HOLOGRAPH MANUSCRIPT, 6 pages (6 × 8), in ink on imprinted stationery of the Hotel de la Cité, Carcassonne. Also a 9 page corrected typescript. [Hanley: $100]

115. PICTURES ON THE WALL $100
     HOLOGRAPH MANUSCRIPT, 9 pages (8½ × 10½), in ink, and corrected typescript, 14 pages.

116. ART AND MORALITY $150
     HOLOGRAPH MANUSCRIPTS, 9 and 10 pages, ruled paper (7 × 9), in ink. Two versions (the first unpublished) of an essay collected in *Phoenix*.

117. THREE ESSAYS ON LOVE $300

     We Need One Another (11 pages)
     Nobody Loves Me (12 pages)
     The Real Thing (10 pages)

     HOLOGRAPH MANUSCRIPT, 33 pages, in *cahier* (7 × 9), in ink. [*Jake Zeitlin's note on* "We Need One Another": "Gift to J.Z."]

118. A SUPERB HOLOGRAPH NOTEBOOK $850
     BLACK NOTEBOOK, with the following written on fly-leaf in Lawrence's hand: "D. H. Lawrence, Kiowa Ranch, near Taos, N.M., 26 August 1924." Contains:

     Hopi Snake Dance (18 pp.) (See Item 72)
     Introduction to McDonald's Bibliography of D.H.L. (4 pp.) (Item 90).
     The Princess (53 pp.) (Item 16)
     Mornings in Mexico (44 pp.) (Item 76)
     Resurrection (4 pp.)
     See Mexico After (1 p.)   A Lawrence-corrected story by a young Mexican.
     Suggestions for Stories "Never Carried Out!" (2 pp.)
     Philosophical Fragment (3 pp.)
     Noah's Flood (10 pp.)
     Two Poems: Mediterranean in January and Beyond the Rockies (2 pp.)
     Preface to Black Swans by M. L. Skinner (4 pp.)   *Unpublished.*
     Climbing Down Pisgah (6 pp.)

     Totaling 161 pages entirely in Lawrence's hand.

Appendix C

Appraisal of Manuscripts, Corrected Typescripts, and Books of D. H. Lawrence in the Possession of Frieda Lawrence Ravagli

by Jake Zeitlin
10 October 1954

LIST I

D. H. LAWRENCE HOLOGRAPH MANUSCRIPTS

10 & 36.　THE TRESPASSER. 1912.
Holograph Manuscript, complete as published, 487 pp., ruled notebook paper (6½ × 8), in ink (pp. 477–84 missing). The first page reads: "The Trespasser, A Novel by D. H. Lawrence. 13, Queen's Square. Eastwood. Notts."

Holograph Manuscript, incomplete, first version, 225 pp., unstitched ruled booklets and loose sheets (6½ × 8), in ink.

Powell: 2.　　　　　　　　　　　　　　　　　　　$2750.00

11 & 72.　"MASTRO-DON GESUALDO" BY GIOVANNI VERGA, TRANSLATED BY D. H. LAWRENCE. 1923.
Holograph Manuscript, 550 pp. in four separate notebooks (6 × 8), in ink. A 6 page Introductory Note (differing from that published) at the end of the Fourth notebook is signed "Kandy, March 1922, D. H. Lawrence."

Also a Holograph Manuscript, 17 pp. (6 × 8), in ink, of a second and longer Introductory Note, written in Ceylon and also different from the one published.

Powell: 106.　　　　　　　　　　　　　　　　　　$750.00

Note: *Powell numbers shown indicate the item numbers in Lawrence Clark Powell's* The Manuscripts of D. H. Lawrence *(Los Angeles, 1937). (See Appendix B.)*

12. POEMS FROM "BIRDS, BEASTS AND FLOWERS" AND A DIARY. Tropic. Peace. Southern Night. Sicilian Cyclamens. Hibiscus and Salvia Flowers. Purple Anemones. The Ass. Eagle in New Mexico. The American Eagle.

    Holograph Manuscript, 22 pp. in bound ruled notebook (6½ × 8½), in ink. The final poem of the Sicilian group is dated Taormina, March 2, 1921; the two New Mexican poems are dated Taos, October 11, 1922. The first twelve pages at the opposite end of the notebook in which these poems are written are given over to notes in diary form, from February 7, 1920 to November 17, 1924. They cover all the details of Lawrence's busy life, receipts from his books, data concerning their publication, his journeys, callers, letters written, etc. The entries range from Sicily to Australia and finally New Mexico.

    Powell: 56. $650.00

19. THE ELEPHANTS OF DIONYSOS. Holograph Manuscript written on back of first part of fragment called *Fire* published in *Phoenix*, 1936. 2 pp. and notes for *Apocalypse*.

    Powell: 84. $100.00

20. OH, THESE WOMEN! Holograph Manuscript. Article, 6 pp., published in *Assorted Articles* as *Give Her a Pattern*.

    Powell: 84. $150.00

26. UNTITLED, UNFINISHED SHORT STORY. "There were, three years back, two schools in the mining village of High Park." Holograph Manuscript, unfinished, 7 un-numbered pages, ruled paper (6 × 8), in pencil. Probably written at Croydon, 1910–11.

    Powell: 51B. $150.00

27. UNTITLED, UNFINISHED SHORT STORY. "There was a man not long ago, who felt he was through with the world, so he decided to be a hermit." Holograph Manuscript, unfinished, 10 pp., ruled paper in black patent-leather notebook (6 × 8), in ink. Notes for his *Etruscan Studies* on the inside covers of the notebook place this fragment in Lawrence's late period.

    Powell: 51E. $200.00

29. ALTITUDE. Holograph Manuscript, unfinished, 28 pp., in notebook (7 × 8½), in pencil. The first two scenes of a humorous

satirical play centering around breakfast at Mabel Dodge Luhan's ranch at Taos. The characters' names are not fictitious, and include Mrs. Luhan, the late Mary Austin, etc. Written at Taos.

Powell: 68. $300.00

30. UNFINISHED NOVEL OR NOVELETTE. "There is a small cottage off the Addiscombe Road about a mile from East Croydon station." Holograph Manuscript, unfinished, 48 pp., in four unstitched ruled booklets (6½ × 8), in ink. Forms the first chapter and a half of a projected novel or novelette, written at Croydon, 1910–11.

Powell: 51C. $450.00

31. [NEWTHORPE IN 2927] Holograph Manuscript, 41 pp., in ruled notebook (6½ × 8), pages torn from covers but preserved intact, in ink. Unfinished.

Powell: 50. $450.00

32. REVIEW OF "THE PEEP SHOW" BY WALTER WILKINSON. Holograph Manuscript, 6 pp., incomplete (3–8 present), ruled paper (6 × 8), in ink. Quite different from the review published in *The Calendar* of July 1927 and in *Phoenix*.

Powell: 101. $100.00

33. UNTITLED, UNPUBLISHED SHORT STORY. "Then come into the Kitchen," said Mrs. Bircumshaw. Holograph Manuscript, incomplete, 11 pp. (9–19), ruled paper (6 × 8), in ink.

Powell: 51D. $200.00

34. THE DUC DE LAUZUN. Holograph Manuscripts, 9 and 8 pages, ruled paper (6¾ × 9¾), in ink. Two essays, published in *Phoenix* as *The Good Man* and the *Duc de Lauzun*, which grew out of Lawrence's reading of the *Memoirs of the Duc de Lauzun* – possibly in C. K. Moncrieff's translation (1928).

Powell: 89. $200.00

35. THE WHITE PEACOCK. 1911. Holograph Manuscript, incomplete, early version, probably second draft. Five separate unstitched notebooks (5 × 8) totaling 116 pp. Differs considerably from published version. Entirely unpublished.

Powell: 1A. $1000.00

39. THE RAINBOW. 1915. Holograph Manuscript, complete and un-expurgated as published in the original Methuen edition; 707 pp., ruled tablet paper (8 × 10, some 8 × 12½), in ink. Pp. 1–14 are Lawrence's own typescript, hand-corrected; pp. 548–614 corrected typescript. The first page has note in L[awrence]'s hand, "Pre-viously The Wedding Ring by D. H. Lawrence," while the final page is dated "Greatham. March 2nd 1915."

Powell: 4. $3500.00

40. NOTEBOOK – PHEASANT.
    a. Practice lessons in Spanish, by Frieda Lawrence.
    b. *See Mexico After*, by Luis (Quintanilla?). One page attempt at rewriting.

[Powell: 118.] $35.00

42. BLACK NOTEBOOK.
    a. *Cavalleria Rusticana* (9 pp.)
    b. *La Lupa* (The She-Wolf) (7 pp.)
    c. *Fantasticalities* (10 pp.)
    d. *Jeli the Shepherd* (32 pp.)
    e. Spanish Lesson – 2 practice pages
    f. *Fragment* – Journey to Southwest – unfinished (17 pp.)

Powell: 108. $650.00

43. DULL BLUE NOTEBOOK (L'Ancora–Firenze).
    a. NOAH'S FLOOD (dramatic in form). Holograph Manuscript, 10 pp. Published in *Phoenix*.
    b. List of letters written March 13, 1928 (32 letters in one day).

Powell: 84. $200.00

44. VERGA'S "LITTLE NOVELS OF SICILY" (NOVELLE RUSTI-CANA) TRANSLATED BY D. H. LAWRENCE. 1925. Holograph Manuscript, 167 pp., ruled paper (6½ × 8, 8 × 10), in ink. Includes the following novelle:

Black Bread (48 pp.)	So Much for the King (16 pp.)
The Gentry (13 pp.)	The Mystery Play (10 pp.)
Liberty (11 pp.)	Malaria (12 pp.)
Across the Sea (13 pp.)	The Orphans (10 pp.)
Don Licciu Papa (9 pp.)	Property (9 pp.)
His Reverence (16 pp.)	

Powell: 107. $500.00

45. ARTICLE. IS ENGLAND STILL A MAN'S COUNTRY? Holograph Manuscript, 6 pp., of article published in *Assorted Articles*.

Powell: 84. $150.00 [Hanley: $150]

46. ARTICLE. THE STATE OF FUNK. Holograph Manuscript, 6 pp. Article published in *Assorted Articles*.

Powell: 84. $150.00 [Hanley: $150]

47. ARTICLES. INSOUCIANCE. Holograph Manuscript, 4 pp. [and] MEN MUST RULE. Holograph Manuscript, 4 pp., published in *Assorted Articles* under title of *Master in His Own House*.

Powell: 84. $150.00 [Hanley: $150]

49. ARTICLE. WHY I DON'T LIKE LIVING IN LONDON. Holograph Manuscript, 4 pp. Article published as *Dull London* in *Assorted Articles*.

Powell: 84. $100.00 [Hanley: $100]

50. ARTICLE. THINKING ABOUT ONESELF. Holograph Manuscript, 4 pp. Published in *Phoenix*, 1936, for first time.

Powell: 84. $100.00 [Hanley: $100]

51. ARTICLE. MATRIARCHY. Holograph Manuscript, 6 pp. Published in *Assorted Articles*.

Powell: 84. $150.00 [Hanley: $150]

52. WHY THE NOVEL MATTERS. Holograph Manuscript, 14 pp., ruled paper (6½ × 8½), in ink. First published in *Phoenix*, 1936.

Powell: 85A. $250.00

53. ARTICLE. BOOKS. Holograph Manuscript, 8 pp. Published in *Phoenix*, 1936, for the first time, but written in 1924.

Powell: 84. $200.00

56. INDIANS AND ENTERTAINMENT. Holograph Manuscript, 13 pp., ruled punched paper (8½ × 11), in ink. The third of Lawrence's essays on the Indian ceremonial dances of Arizona and New Mexico. Published in *Mornings in Mexico*.

Powell: 74. $250.00

57. ARTICLE. OWNERSHIP. Holograph Manuscript, 4 pp. Article published in *Assorted Articles*.

    Powell: 84.　　　　　　　　　　　　　　　　　　　　$150.00

58. ARTICLE. THE RISEN LORD. Holograph Manuscript, 6 pp. Published in *Assorted Articles*.

    Powell: 84.　　　　　　　　　　　　　　　　　　　　$250.00

59. THE MODERN NOVEL. Holograph Manuscript, 13 pp., ruled paper (6½ × 8½), in ink. An earlier and shorter version of the essay *The Novel* in *Reflections on the Death of a Porcupine*.

    Powell: 85B.　　　　　　　　　　　　　　　　　　　$250.00

60. ARTICLE. ARISTOCRACY. Holograph Manuscript, 16 pp. Published in *Reflections on the Death of a Porcupine*.

    Powell: 84.　　　　　　　　　　　　　　　　　　　　$300.00

61. ARTICLE. COCKSURE WOMEN AND HEN-SURE MEN. Holograph Manuscript, 2½ pp. Published in *Assorted Articles*. With a Letter to Nancy Pearn, 28 August 1928.

    Powell: 84.　　　　　　　　　　　　　　　　　　　　$200.00

64. MERCURY. Holograph Manuscript, 9 pp., ruled paper (6½ × 8), in ink. First published in the *Atlantic Monthly*, collected in *Phoenix*. A descriptive sketch.

    Powell: 79.　　　　　　　　　　　　　　　　　　　　$250.00

65. ARTICLE. ALL THERE. Holograph Manuscript, 4 pp. Published in *Phoenix*, 1936.

    Powell: 84.　　　　　　　　　　　　　　　　　　　　$150.00

67. FIREWORKS. Holograph Manuscript, 8 pp., ruled paper (7 × 9), in ink. Published in *Phoenix* as *Fireworks in Florence*.

    [Powell: 80.]　　　　　　　　　　　　　　　　　　　$150.00

68. VERGA'S "CAVALLERIA RUSTICANA AND OTHER STORIES" TRANSLATED BY D. H. LAWRENCE. 1928. Part of Introductory Note: Holograph Manuscript, 11 pp. (12–21), ruled paper (6½ × 8), in ink.

    Powell: 108.　　　　　　　　　　　　　　　　　　　$150.00

69. INTRODUCTION TO "THE GRAND INQUISITOR" BY DOS-
TOIEVSKY. TRANSLATED BY S. S. KOTELIANSKY, LONDON,
1931. Holograph Manuscript, 14 pp. in cahier (7 × 9), the remaining pages blank, in ink. Published in *Phoenix*.

Powell: 94. $350.00

70. FOUR REVIEWS.

Robert Byron's *The Station*.
Clough Williams's *England and the Octopus*.
Maurice Baring's *Comfortless Memory*.
W. Somerset Maugham's *Ashenden, or the British Agent*.

A. Holograph Manuscript, 8 pp., ruled paper (6½ × 9), in ink.
Vogue (London) July 20, 1928.
B. An earlier unpublished version. Holograph Manuscript,
4 pp., ruled paper (6½ × 9), in ink.

Powell: 103. $150.00

73. INTRODUCTION TO "THE MOTHER" BY GRAZIA DELEDDA.
London, 1928. Holograph Manuscript, 7 pp., ruled paper (6 × 8¼),
in ink. Published in *Phoenix*.

Powell: 91. $100.00

74. INTRODUCTION TO "BOTTOM DOGS" BY EDWARD DAHL-
BERG. London, 1929; New York, 1930. Holograph Manuscript,
8 pp. (8 × 10½), in ink. Manuscript signed and dated Bandol, 1929.

Powell: 93. $250.00

75. INTRODUCTION TO "DRAGON OF THE APOCALYPSE" BY
FREDERICK CARTER. Holograph Manuscript, 21 pp., ruled paper
(7 × 9), in ink. First published in *London Mercury*, July 1930; also in
Phoenix.

Powell: 95. $350.00

76. REVIEW OF "HEAT" BY ISA GLENN. Holograph Manuscript,
8 pp., ruled paper (7 × 9), in ink. First published in *Phoenix*.

Powell: 97. $100.00

79. THE MARRIED MAN. Holograph Manuscript, 72 pp. (complete
except for the first 5 pp.), ruled paper (8 × 10), in ink. Produced in
England, summer 1936, from this manuscript. It is variously

known as *The Married Man, The Daughter-in-Law, The Mother-in-Law*.

Powell: 66. $500.00

81. THE MERRY-GO-ROUND. Holograph Manuscript, 148 pp., in 13 unstitched ruled booklets, in ink. Complete unpublished play written in Germany probably in 1912.

Powell: 65. $600.00

82. UNPUBLISHED STORY, UNFINISHED. Holograph Manuscript, unfinished, 9 pp., ruled notebook paper (6½ × 8½), in ink. An English girl tells of her conquest by an Italian lover. Written *c*.1924.

Powell: 51F. $250.00

83. DAVID. Holograph Manuscript of Frieda Lawrence, 104 pp. A translation of the play written at Lawrence's Kiowa Ranch in New Mexico in 1925 and translated by Frieda Lawrence. With extensive holograph corrections by D. H. Lawrence.

[Powell: 69.] $300.00

84. LAWRENCE'S HOLOGRAPH LETTERS TO FRIEDA AND TO FRIEDA'S MOTHER. 44 Holograph Letters consisting of 126 pp. Also 2 Holograph Letters unfinished and unsigned and 2 Autograph Signed Postcards. Mostly written in German.

                                                              $750.00

85. LADY CHATTERLEY'S LOVER. THREE VERSIONS.[1]

   a. THE FIRST LADY CHATTERLEY. Holograph Manuscript. One volume bound in plain boards, 420 pp., ruled paper, in ink. Entitled "Lady Chatterley's Lover by D. H. Lawrence."
   b. SECOND LADY CHATTERLEY'S LOVER. Holograph Manuscript. Two volumes ruled paper, in ink. First volume bound in floral design boards and marbleized flyleafs, pages numbered 1 to 265. Second volume bound in star design boards and marbleized flyleaf, pages numbered 265 (sic) to 570. Flyleaf of each volume bears signature "D. H. Lawrence, Villa Mirenda, Scandicci (Firenze)." Entitled "Lady Chatterley's Lover by D. H. Lawrence."

1. This entry, dated 11 August 1956 (the day Frieda Lawrence died), is titled "D. H. Lawrence Holograph Manuscripts, concluded".

c.   MY LADY'S KEEPER. Holograph Manuscript. Two booklets (6 ×
8), unstitched ruled paper in black notebook covers, in ink.
First volume pages numbered 1 to 408. Second volume pages
numbered 409 to 707. Both volumes signed on flyleaf "D. H.
Lawrence, Villa Mirenda, Scandicci (Firenze)." The first
volume flyleaf is dated 3rd Dec. 1927. Entitled "My Lady's
Keeper by D. H. Lawrence."

LIST II
D. H. LAWRENCE CORRECTED TYPESCRIPTS

4.   CORASMIN AND THE PARROTS. Corrected typescript, 9 pp.

Powell: 76. $15.00   [Hanley: $15]

5.   THE MOZO. Corrected typescript, 14 pp.

Powell: 76. $15.00   [Hanley: $15]

6.   DAVID. Corrected typescript, 7 pp. A wonderfully suggestive
reaction to Michelangelo's statue of David. Collected in *Phoenix*.

Powell: 82. $15.00

7.   DEMOCRACY. Corrected typescript, 29 pp., in four parts (8 × 10).
Written *c.* 1923 and first published in *Phoenix*.

Powell: 112. $75.00

8.   IS ENGLAND STILL A MAN'S COUNTRY? Corrected typescript,
4 pp.

[Powell: 84.] $15.00

10. COLLECTED POEMS. VOL. I "RHYMING POEMS". Corrected
typescript, 178 pp.

Powell: 57. $75.00

12. MR. NOON. Corrected typescript, 142 pp., with numerous revisions in Lawrence's hand. Written at Taormina in 1921, this
humorous story was published posthumously in *A Modern Lover*.

Powell: 13. $250.00

14. ETRUSCAN PLACES. Corrected typescript, 160 pp., with numerous corrections and revisions in Lawrence's hand. Duplicate copies of Chapters IV and V.

   Powell: 83A. $250.00

15. HIM WITH HIS TAIL IN HIS MOUTH. Corrected typescript, 6 pp. Published.

                                                                    $75.00

17. EQUILIBRIUM (?). Corrected typescript, pp. 7–11.

                                                                    $50.00

18. LOVE WAS ONCE A LITTLE BOY. Corrected typescript, 21 pp.

                                                                    $75.00

19. LOVE. Corrected typescript, 7 pp.

                                                                    $15.00

20. From THE PLUMED SERPENT. Corrected typescript of Chapter VI, pp. 119–136; Chapter VII, pp. 137–142.

                                                                    $75.00

21. PEDRO DE VALDIVIA – CONQUEROR OF CHILE, BY R. B. CUNNINGHAME GRAHAM. A Review. Corrected typescript, 6 pp. Published in *Calendar*.

                                                                    $10.00

23. ON COMING HOME. LIFE. Corrected typescripts, 11 and 5 pp., respectively.

                                                                     $5.00

25. ARTICLE ON MAN'S RELATION TO THE UNIVERSE. Corrected typescript, pp. 4–12.

                                                                    $10.00

26. INTRODUCTION TO "DRAGON OF THE APOCALYPSE" BY FREDERICK CARTER. Corrected typescript, 12 pp.

                                                                    $15.00

27. RAWDON'S ROOF. Corrected typescript, 20 pp., with a few corrections and revisions in Lawrence's hand.

Powell: 44B. $150.00

LIST III

FIRST AND SPECIAL EDITIONS OF D. H. LAWRENCE'S BOOKS

BLUE PAPER EDITIONS

1. LADY CHATTERLEY'S LOVER. Florence, Tipografia Giuntina, 1928. Privately printed. One of only two copies, printed on blue paper, inscribed by Lawrence: "Only two copies. One for the master, one for the dame. None for the little boy that lives down the lane." Uncut pages.

$500.00

2. LAST POEMS. Florence, Tipografia Giuntina. Edited by Richard Aldington and Giuseppe Orioli. The Lungarno Series No. 10. One of only two copies printed on blue paper. Inscribed to Frieda Lawrence. Uncut pages.

$200.00

3. THE VIRGIN AND THE GYPSY. Florence, Tipografia Giuntina. The Lungarno Series No. 4. One of only two copies printed on blue paper; one for Frieda, one for Pino Orioli.

$150.00

4. THE STORY OF DOCTOR MANENTE. Florence, Tipografia Giuntina. The Lungarno Series. One of only two copies printed on blue paper. Signed by D. H. L. Uncut pages.

$75.00

SPECIAL ALBATROSS EDITIONS

5. APOCALYPSE. Albatross Modern Continental Library, 1932. Special Edition. One of only twelve copies printed on handmade

paper and bound in half leather. This copy was printed for Frieda Lawrence.

$20.00

6. THE RAINBOW. Special Albatross Edition, 1934. One of twelve copies printed on handmade paper and bound in half leather. This copy was printed for Frieda Lawrence.

$20.00

7. THE PLUMED SERPENT. Special Albatross Edition, 1933.

$20.00

8. THE WHITE PEACOCK. Special Albatross Edition, 1932.

$20.00

9. THE TRESPASSER. Special Albatross Edition, 1934. Printed for Frieda Lawrence.

$20.00

10. AARON'S ROD. Special Albatross Edition, 1937. Printed for Frieda Lawrence.

$20.00

11. THE LOVELY LADY. Special Albatross Edition, 1934. Printed for Frieda Lawrence.

$20.00

12. KANGAROO. Special Albatross Edition, 1938. Printed for Frieda Lawrence.

$20.00

13. THE LOST GIRL. Special Albatross Edition, 1936. Printed for Frieda Lawrence.

$20.00

ALBERT AND CHARLES BONI UNIFORM EDITIONS

14. THE CAPTAIN'S DOLL. New York, Albert & Charles Boni, 1930.

$2.50

15. THE BOY IN THE BUSH. New York, Albert & Charles Boni, 1930.

$2.50

16. THE LOST GIRL. New York, Albert & Charles Boni, 1930.

$2.50

17. SEA AND SARDINIA. New York, Albert & Charles Boni, 1930.

$2.50

18. WOMEN IN LOVE. New York, Albert & Charles Boni, 1930.

$2.50

SPECIAL EDITIONS – MISCELLANEOUS

19. THE WIDOWING OF MRS. HOLROYD. New York, Mitchell Kennerly, 1914. Autographed by Frieda Lawrence.

$15.00

20. A PRELUDE. Surrey, The Merle Press, 1949. Lawrence's First and Previously Unrecorded Work. Copy No. 77 of 160 copies printed.

$15.00

21. LOVE AMONG THE HAYSTACKS. London, Nonesuch Press, [n.d.] Limited Edition printed on handmade paper. This copy is out of series.

$7.00

22. SONS AND LOVERS. London, William Heinemann Ltd., 1935. Leather bound edition.

$2.50

23. THE ESCAPED COCK. Paris, Black Sun Press, 1929. First Edition, with water-color decorations by the author. Edition limited to 500 copies.

$25.00

24. PANSIES. London, privately printed. Copy No. 13 of 500 copies. Signed by D. H. L.

$25.00

25. REFLECTIONS ON THE DEATH OF A PORCUPINE AND OTHER ESSAYS. Philadelphia, Centaur Press, 1925.

$10.00

27. MOVEMENTS IN EUROPEAN HISTORY. London, Oxford University Press, 1925.

$12.50

——. Another copy corrected and censored in blue pencil by the Irish Catholic Church.

$25.00

28. TOUCH AND GO. A Play in Three Acts. New York, Thomas Seltzer, 1920.

2 copies   Each $5.00

29. THE RAINBOW. London, Methuen & Co., Ltd., 1928. Signed by D. H. L.

$50.00

——. Another copy signed in pencil, no date.

$35.00

30–31A. THE LETTERS OF D. H. LAWRENCE, 1909–1930. Albatross Collected Edition. 3 vols. Paper-bound.

$7.50

32. THE LETTERS OF D. H. LAWRENCE, 1909–1930. London, William Heinemann, Ltd. Copy No. 509 of the limited edition of 525 copies.

$25.00

33. D. H. LAWRENCE'S LETTERS TO BERTRAND RUSSELL. New York, Gotham Book Mart, 1948.

3 copies   Each $3.00

34. DER HENGST ST. MAWR. Leipzig, Insel-Verlag, 1931.

$2.50

35. A PROPOS OF "LADY CHATTERLEY". Vienna, E. P. Tal & Co., 1931. In German.

$5.00

SECKER AND OTHER EDITIONS

36. BIRDS, BEASTS, AND FLOWERS. London, Martin Secker, Ltd., 1923. Lawrence's own copy autographed and with autograph printer's instructions.

$75.00

37. A MODERN LOVER. London, Martin Secker, Ltd., 1934.

$5.00

38. A COLLIER'S FRIDAY NIGHT. London, Martin Secker, 1934. Lawrence's first play.

$5.00

39. LADY CHATTERLEY'S LOVER. London, Martin Secker, Ltd., 1933.

$1.00

40. STUDIES IN CLASSIC AMERICAN LITERATURE. London, Martin Secker, Ltd., 1924.

$12.50

41. THE PRUSSIAN OFFICER AND OTHER STORIES. London, Martin Secker, Ltd., 1932. Pocket Edition.

$1.00

42. FANTASIA OF THE UNCONSCIOUS. London, Martin Secker, Ltd., 1923.

$5.00

43. THE MAN WHO DIED. London, Martin Secker, Ltd., 1931.

$2.50

44. THE BOY IN THE BUSH. By D. H. Lawrence and M. L. Skinner. London, Martin Secker, Ltd., 1924.

$5.00

45. LOVE AMONG THE HAYSTACKS. London, Martin Secker, Ltd., 1933.

$1.00

46. AARON'S ROD. New York, Thomas Seltzer, 1922.

$4.50

47. THE PLUMED SERPENT. New York, Alfred A. Knopf, 1926.

$7.50

———. Another copy. Condition poor.

$1.00

48. MEMOIRS OF THE FOREIGN LEGION BY M. M. With an Introduction by D. H. Lawrence. With a typed transcript of a letter to
Lawrence from [Walter] Salomonee concerning Magnus.

$5.00

49. "NOT I, BUT THE WIND . . .". Memoirs of her husband by Frieda
Lawrence.
     Copy 1. London, William Heinemann Ltd., 1935.

$5.00

     Copy 2. Santa Fe, New Mexico, The Rydal Press, 1934. Privately
printed.

$10.00

50. THE FIRST LADY CHATTERLEY. New York, Dial Press, 1944.

$2.75

51. SELECTED POEMS. New York, New Directions, 1947.

$1.50

52. PSYCHOANALYSIS AND THE UNCONSCIOUS. London, William Heinemann Ltd., 1923.

$1.50

53. THE MOTHER (La Madre) by Grazia Deledda. With an Introduction by D. H. Lawrence. London, Jonathan Cape, 1928. Proof copy
with MS. corrections. Wrappers.

$7.50

54. I RISE IN FLAME, CRIED THE PHOENIX. A Play about D. H.
Lawrence by Tennessee Williams. With a Note by Frieda Lawrence.

New York, New Directions, 1951. One of a limited edition of 310 copies. Presentation copy inscribed to Frieda Lawrence by Tennessee Williams.

$25.00

55. SELECTED POEMS. London, William Heinemann Ltd., 1951.

$1.50

56. MY SKIRMISH WITH JOLLY ROGER. New York, Random House, 1929.

$5.00

57. PORNOGRAPHY AND OBSCENITY. London, Faber & Faber, Ltd., 1929. Criterion Miscellany No. 5. Paper-bound pamphlet.

$5.00

58. GLAD GHOSTS. London, Ernest Benn Ltd., 1926. Limited First Edition of 500 copies.

$5.00

59. ENGLAND, MY ENGLAND AND OTHER STORIES. Tokyo, Nan'Un-Do [n.d.].

$1.50

60. THE FRIEDA LAWRENCE COLLECTION OF D. H. LAWRENCE MANUSCRIPTS, A DESCRIPTIVE BIBLIOGRAPHY, by E. W. Tedlock, Jr. Albuquerque, University of New Mexico Press, 1948. Special copy bound in full morocco.

$25.00

61. D. H. LAWRENCE, by Edward D. McDonald. Philadelphia, The Centaur Book Shop, 1925.

$5.00

62. BAY – A BOOK OF POEMS. Westminster, Beaumont Press. Copy No. 176 of 200 copies. [*Angelo Ravagli's note in his copy of the appraisal*: "Gave it to Witter Bynner for his 75 Birthday."]

$25.00

63. THE SHIP OF DEATH AND OTHER POEMS. London, Faber & Faber, 1941.

$1.50

64. THE HOUSE BY THE MEDLAR TREE, by Giovanni Verga. Translated by Mary A. Craig. New York, Harper & Brothers, 1890. With D. H. Lawrence's signature.

$10.00

65. I MALAVOGLIA, per Giovanni Verga. Tipografia Treves, 1920. Used by D. H. Lawrence for his translation. With marginal notes in pencil.

$35.00

66. NOVELLE RUSTICANE, per Giovanni Verga. Casa Editrice Madella, 1918. Used by D. H. Lawrence for his translation. With many marginal notes in ink.

$35.00

67. A STUDY OF THE LITERATURE AND ART OF GIOVANNI VERGA, by Luigi Russo. Naples, Riccardo Ricciardi, 1920. In Italian.

$2.50

68. OXFORD DICTIONARY. London, Oxford Press, 1912. With D. H. Lawrence's signature. With a note in Latin: "Fata volentem ducunt, nolentem traluent."

$10.00

69. EARLY GREEK PHILOSOPHY, by John Burnet. London, A. & C. Black, 1920. Signed by D. H. and Frieda Lawrence.

$10.00

70. THE MANUSCRIPTS OF D. H. LAWRENCE. A Descriptive Catalogue compiled by Lawrence Clark Powell. Los Angeles, Ward Ritchie Press, 1937. With a Foreword by Aldous Huxley.

$3.50

71. LA CONQUISTA DE NUEVA ESPAÑA, by Bernal Diaz del Castillo.

Published by Louis Michaud. 4 vols. Signature of Lawrence in Vol. I only.

$10.00

72. APPLETON'S SPANISH–ENGLISH AND ENGLISH–SPANISH DICTIONARY. Signed on flyleaf by D. H. Lawrence.

$5.00

73. THE VIRGIN AND THE GYPSY AND OTHER SHORT STORIES. New York, Alfred A. Knopf, Inc., 1944. First printing, January, 1944.

$3.00

74. ENGLAND, MY ENGLAND AND OTHER STORIES. New York, Thomas Seltzer, Inc. [*c.* 1922].

$5.00

75. THE LADYBIRD AND OTHER STORIES. London, William Heinemann Ltd., 1933.

$1.50

Index

Note: The works of D. H. Lawrence listed in Appendixes A, B and C are not indexed.